"Although there are many textbooks designed to teach counseling theories and techniques, most fail to apply these theories and techniques specifically to addiction treatment and recovery. When counselors understand how to correctly apply counseling theories and techniques to addiction treatment and recovery, they become extremely valuable tools in assisting individuals to develop and maintain effective recovery solutions. *A Comprehensive Guide to Addiction Theory and Counseling Techniques* was specifically designed and written by two of our nation's most outstanding addiction counselor educators. They understand how to teach future addiction professionals and how to apply counseling theories and techniques to addiction treatment and recovery. *A Comprehensive Guide to Addiction Theory and Counseling Techniques* is an extremely valuable tool for both addiction counseling students and professionals. I highly recommend it."

Kirk Bowden, PhD, Chair of the Rio Salado College Addiction and Substance Use Disorder Program; Professor-in-Charge of the Ottawa University Addiction Counseling Program; Past president of NAADAC, The Association of Addiction Professionals; Past president of the International Coalition for Addiction Studies Education

"*A Comprehensive Guide to Addiction Theory and Counseling Techniques* provides a much-needed overview of major theoretical approaches in the counseling field and, specifically, how these theories may be applied practically to the field of addiction studies. Written in an engaging and accessible way, the book offers both Bachelor's and Master's level students a foundation from which to develop skills and critical thinking as they work through various examples and case studies. I would also consider this book for the Associate's level educator as an appropriate additional resource for students."

Joan E. Standora, PhD, Lic. Clinical & Drug Cnslr. (NJ); Lic. Alcohol & Drug Cnslr. (CT); CASAC-Adv. (NY); CADC (PA); MAC

"The authors have written a comprehensive review of addiction theories and provided case conceptualization examples and student activity suggestions to facilitate better earning and understanding of the application of the theories. The case conceptualizations and activities are valuable in assisting students in gaining an understanding of the different theoretical perspectives and their impact on practitioners' approaches to assessment and treatment of clients."

Vicki Michels, PhD, Minot State University

A Comprehensive Guide to Addiction Theory and Counseling Techniques

A blend of theory and counseling techniques, this comprehensive text provides readers with an overview of several major counseling theories and their application to substance use disorders and addiction counseling, along with related techniques and interventions.

Chapters incorporate cutting-edge evidenced-based research on neuroscience, psychological and sociocultural theories explaining the biopsychosocial influences of substance use disorders, and examine how substance use disorder risk factors can be utilized when assessing someone who may have a substance use disorder. The text additionally helps apply theory to practice, offering intervention techniques and using accessible case studies. Throughout the text, highlighted learning opportunities and key terms further help students to practice and apply the theories, interventions and techniques that the book discusses.

Mental health professionals, undergraduate and graduate students alike will benefit from this deft mix of prominent theory, innovative research and accessible case studies.

Alan A. Cavaiola, PhD, LPC, LCADC, is a full professor in the department of professional counseling at Monmouth University and currently serves as the director of the addiction studies program. He is the former clinical director of addiction treatment programs at Monmouth Medical Center.

Margaret Smith, EdD, MLADC, is a full professor in public health/addiction and pre-professional mental health at Keene State College. Her clinical experience includes alcohol and other drug counseling specializing in co-occurring disorders, elderly, women and LGBT populations. She also worked as the coordinator of alcohol and other drug education at Dartmouth College.

A Comprehensive Guide to Addiction Theory and Counseling Techniques

Alan A. Cavaiola
Margaret Smith

Routledge
Taylor & Francis Group

NEW YORK AND LONDON

First published 2020
by Routledge
52 Vanderbilt Avenue, New York, NY 10017

and by Routledge
2 Park Square, Milton Park, Abingdon, Oxon, OX14 4RN

Routledge is an imprint of the Taylor & Francis Group, an informa business

© 2020 Taylor & Francis

Library of Congress Cataloging-in-Publication Data
Names: Cavaiola, Alan A., author. | Smith, Margaret
(Professor in public health/addiction), author.
Title: A comprehensive guide to addiction theory and counseling
techniques / Alan A. Cavaiola, Margaret Smith.
Description: New York, NY : Routledge, 2020. |
Includes bibliographical references and index.
Identifiers: LCCN 2020000903 (print) | LCCN 2020000904 (ebook) |
ISBN 9780367245665 (hardback) | ISBN 9780367252724 (paperback) |
ISBN 9780429286933 (ebook)
Subjects: MESH: Substance-Related Disorders–therapy |
Behavior, Addictive–therapy | Psychotherapy–methods |
Psychological Theory Classification: LCC RC564 (print) |
LCC RC564 (ebook) | NLM WM 270 | DDC 362.29–dc23
LC record available at https://lccn.loc.gov/2020000903
LC ebook record available at https://lccn.loc.gov/2020000904

ISBN: 978-0-367-24566-5 (hbk)
ISBN: 978-0-367-25272-4 (pbk)
ISBN: 978-0-429-28693-3 (ebk)

Typeset in Bembo
by Newgen Publishing UK

We dedicate this book to all of our clients and students for sharing their strength, hopes and experiences with us over the many years of our teaching and counseling practice. We also dedicate this book to those who have died as a result of America's opioid epidemic and as a result of other substance use disorders, as well as those who are still suffering, including their families, loved ones and significant others. Also to those who fight on the front lines of our nation's addiction epidemic, to all the addiction treatment professionals and members of the recovering community.

Contents

Acknowledgements

I am very appreciative for my family's support throughout this entire process. Thank you Carolann, Jay and Taylor, Chris and Morgan! I am also very appreciative of the hard work and help provided by my colleagues at Monmouth University's Guggenheim Memorial Library. AAC

I thank my partner, Paula McLaughlin, and my siblings, Kerrie, Marian, Amy and Matt! Additional thanks to Jeff Salvador, Angela Poirier, Lorraine Russell & Angela Graziano, Anne Martin, Mona McLaughlin Booe, and Drs. Rebecca Dunn and John Finneran. MAS

1 Introduction to Addiction Theory

Alan A. Cavaiola

Welcome! We appreciate your selecting our book, but even more so, we appreciate your interest in wanting to help and treat people who are impacted by substance use disorders (SUD) and related process addictions (e.g. gambling). As we are writing this book, the United States finds itself in the grips of an opioid epidemic which has killed approximately 72,000 Americans in 2017 and 60,000 in 2016 (Centers for Disease Control, 2018). Furthermore, in spite of increased treatment services, Narcan trainings and the like, there are few indications that the opioid epidemic will lessen anytime soon. And yet while federal budgets allocated to treat other diseases like cancer or AIDS have increased, the same has not held true for substance use disorders. For example, in 2016 the National Institutes of Health allocated $5.6 billion to research treatments for cancer and $3 billion in research funds to fight AIDS, while substance use disorders received only $1.6 billion in spite of the fact that more people suffer and die from addiction than from all other cancers combined (Hilgers, 2017). As authors, substance abuse counselors and addiction educators, who have both worked in the substance use disorder treatment field for over 25 years, we can attest to the fact that the United States has not witnessed an epidemic such as this in its history. It is estimated that 1 in 6 Americans know someone who has overdosed whether it's a loved one, a friend or the sons and daughters of neighbors, co-workers and friends. So, you may be saying, "Why another book on substance abuse treatment or counseling?" Here's why we wrote this book.

For years we would receive at our university campus offices, sample copies of textbooks to assign to our SUD counseling classes. We hate to sound negative or critical but you've probably have heard the old adage, "If you've seen one, you've seen them all." Such was the case with many of the addiction counseling textbooks in that, they all contained chapters on ethics, assessment, individual counseling, group counseling, couples and family counseling, relapse prevention, and usually there was a chapter or two on working with people from diverse backgrounds, race/ethnicities or cultures. Some texts would even include an obligatory chapter on etiology of addictions but, other than summarizing a few etiological or causal models of addiction (e.g. genetic models), there was not much information offered about why these models were important or how they connected to assessment or treatment of substance use disorders. Our goal in writing this book is to provide addiction studies students with practical information regarding addiction theories that would be relevant to any future counseling you may do with clients experiencing substance use disorders and process addictions. For example, nearly all addictions counselors are trained to do biopsychosocial assessments. Some structured interviews like the Addiction Severity Index (ASI) (McLellan, Kushner, Metzger, Peters, Grissom, & Argeriou, 1992) even have quite elaborate scoring systems, in which counselors are asked to count the number of items endorsed and also to rate their subjective confidence in the information he or she is hearing from the client as they progress through the biopsychosocial interview. We've often heard our students remark, "Why bother gathering all this information when the client is just going to deny everything or will just minimize or rationalize how their drinking or drug use has not been a problem that in any way impacts their lives?" Okay, that's a valid criticism, but let's take that a step further. It is common for clients to minimize when asked direct questions about their alcohol or drug use. So, while screening instruments such as the Michigan Assessment & Screening Test for Alcohol/Drugs (MAST-AD) (Westermeyer, Yargic, & Thuras, 2004); or Alcohol Use Disorders Identification Test (AUDIT) (Babor, de la Fuente, Saunders, & Grant (1992) or the Simple Screening Instrument for Alcohol and Other Drugs (SSI-AOD) (CSAT, 2004) (see Figure 1.1) are valuable in asking direct questions about alcohol and/or drug use, for someone who subjectively feels that their drinking or drug use is non-problematic, it's pretty easy to figure out the nature of these direct questions and to "fake good" in order to avoid falling into the scoring range for being classified as someone who may have an alcohol or substance use disorder. This is where addiction theory comes in. Let's take an example. One of the theories we'll be presenting later in this text are genetic models of addiction. Most people accept that, like other diseases, SUDs tend to run in families, and that there may be a genetic link as evidenced by research that suggests that people who do not grow up with their biological parent who has an alcohol use disorder can still develop problems related to alcohol use in their teen or young adult years. Similarly, it is very common for people with SUDs to have experienced trauma. Trauma also becomes a risk factor for developing a substance use disorder. Therefore, when you're asked to do a biopsychosocial assessment with a client, you're essentially looking for *risk factors* that may place individuals at higher risk for developing SUDs. So, although clients who may be ambivalent or even resistant to being mandated to treatment will not be willing to tell us how their drinking or substance use has impacted their lives, they may be more willing to tell us about those factors that place them at risk for developing a substance use disorder. Here's a quick example of where risk factors may help in screening individuals with substance use disorders. For several years, I (AAC) had done screenings of individuals who had DUI (Driving Under the Influence) offenses. The purpose of the screening was to determine those first offenders who were in need of further counseling beyond the usual educational programs mandated to first offenders. A 12-year follow-up study (Cavaiola, Strohmetz, & Abreo, 2007) we conducted found that while screening tests such as the Minnesota Multiphasic Personality Inventory (MMPI & MMPI-2) and the MAST were not found to be especially predictive of those who would go on to commit a second offense, one

Simple Screening Instrument for Alcohol and Other Drugs (SSI-AOD)
Screening Instrument
Screening Date:_____

I'm going to ask you a few questions about your use of alcohol and other drugs during the past 6 months. During the **past 6 months** …

1. Have you used alcohol or other drugs? (such as wine, beer, hard liquor, pot, coke, heroin or other opiates, uppers, downers, hallucinogens, or inhalants).
YES _____ NO _____
2. Have you felt that you use too much alcohol or other drugs? YES _____ NO _____
3. Have you tried to cut down or quit drinking or using drugs? YES _____ NO _____
4. Have you gone to anyone for help because of your drinking or drug use?
YES___ NO _____
5. Have you had any health problems? For example, have you:
___ had blackouts or other periods of memory loss?
___ injured your head after drinking or using drugs?
___ had convulsions, delirium tremens (DTs)?
___ had hepatitis or other liver problems?
___ felt sick, shaky, or depressed when you stopped?
___ felt "coke bugs" or a crawling feeling under the skin after you stopped using drugs?
___ been injured after drinking or using?
___ used needles to shoot drugs?

Give a "YES" answer if at least one of the 8 presented items is marked
YES _____ NO _____
1. Has drinking or other drug use caused problems between you and family or friends?
YES _____ NO _____
2. Has your drinking or other drug use caused problems at school or work?
YES _____ NO _____
3. Have you been arrested or had other legal problems? (such as bouncing bad checks, driving while intoxicated, theft, or drug possession)?
YES _____ NO _____
4. Have you lost your temper or gotten into arguments or fights while drinking or using other drugs?
YES _____ NO _____

5. Are you needing to drink or use drugs more and more to get the effect you want?
YES _____ NO _____
6. Do you spend a lot of time thinking about or trying to get alcohol or other drugs?
YES _____ NO _____
7. When drinking or using drugs, are you more likely to do something you wouldn't normally do, such as break rules, break the law, sell things that are important to you, or have unprotected sex with someone?
YES _____ NO _____
8. Do you feel bad or guilty about your drinking or drug use?
YES _____ NO _____

The next questions are about your lifetime experiences.
1. Have you **ever** had a drinking or other drug problem? YES _____ NO _____
2. Have any of your family members **ever** had a drinking or drug problem?
YES _____ NO _____
3. Do you feel that you have a drinking or drug problem **now**? YES _____ NO _____

SCORING
SCORE: (Questions 1 and 15 are not scored)
Number of "Yes" Answers _____
        Screened positive = a score of 4 or greater.

Figure 1.1 Simple Screening Instrument for Alcohol and Other Drugs (SSI-AOD)

of the risk factors we found to be significant was having a poor driving record (i.e. multiple moving violations for offenses other than DUI). So, although most DUI offenders were unwilling to admit to experiencing any alcohol problems on a direct measure such as the MAST, their poor driving records became a way to predict who would be likely to commit a second DUI offense.

A few things to keep in mind, however, as we explain various addiction theories or models. First, not all models are etiological or causal models. Genetic theories or models mentioned above are good examples of etiology models in that they claim that SUD can be predicted based upon having blood relatives who experienced alcohol or substance use disorders at some point in their lives. Yet, other theories or models we will be presenting are not about etiology or causes but rather are helpful in describing what maintains or sustains the addiction. Such would be the case with behavioral models, whereby the reinforcing or rewarding properties of alcohol or substances become "the fuel" that keeps the addiction going. You may be thinking, though, if alcohol or substances are reinforcing or rewarding why wouldn't this be considered an etiological model or explanation for addictions? The problem is that since alcohol or drugs are inherently reinforcing or rewarding for most people, then why doesn't everyone who has ever taken a drink or drug become addicted? For example, the Monitoring the Future survey (Johnston, O'Malley, Miech, Bachmann, & Schulenberg, 2014), which is a large epidemiological survey of high school students in 8th, 10th and 12th grade, indicates that 46.4% of those students surveyed had consumed alcohol at some point during their high school career. But the question remains, if nearly half of these students reported consuming alcohol, then why didn't all of them become alcoholic? For this reason, we have divided the models or theories presented in this textbook to include *etiological theories, sustaining theories, theories of change* and *relapse theories.* Etiological theories include those theories or models that assert what factors will predict who will develop a substance use disorder (e.g. having a family history of alcoholism or having a personal history of trauma). Sustaining theories are those models that describe how substance use disorders are maintained over time (e.g. behavior theory claims that substances are rewarding or reinforcing or help to relieve tension, or, in the instance of negative reinforcement, a person may continue to drink or use drugs to avoid going into withdrawal). Theories of change examine the process by which individuals go from total denial of having problems related to substance use to a point where he or she is willing to seek help. Relapse theory examines the process by which people go from being abstinent or sober to where he or she resumes substance use (e.g. a relapse progression chain). If the models or theories we allude to here are unfamiliar to you, try not to become frustrated, as we will come back to these different types of models in the last chapter of this text. For the time being, just keep in mind that some models do a better job at describing what caused the SUD, others do a better job in describing what sustains or maintains the SUD over time, while the change models describe how one might transition from being an active SUD person to a recovering person.

This brings us to how to conceptualize what makes for a good or practical addiction theory. Bickel, Mueller and Jarmolowicz (2013), Edwards and Lader (1990) and Peele, (1985) have proposed several different explanations for what essential components make for a good and useful addiction theory. Accordingly, a sound or practical addiction theory should be able to explain: (1) why some substances are addictive and others are not; (2) why individuals with addiction, despite recognizing that their addiction is problematic and self-handicapping, continue to use and are unable to stop, cut down or remain abstinent from the addictive commodity or event; (3) the developmental sequence of addiction wherein addictive consumption most often begins in adolescence and, in some individuals, may end as they grow older (referred to as "maturing out"), or they get into recovery; (4) why addiction is highly comorbid with a wide variety of unhealthy behaviors and mental health disorders; and (5) how the theoretical view can directly inform effective therapeutic approaches (Bickel et al., 2013, p. 4). Similarly Kuhn (1962) describes five criteria that account for a theory's effectiveness: (1) accuracy – the theory should be in agreement with existing observations and experiments; (2) consistency – a theory should be internally consistent as well as broadly consistent with other accepted theories in terms of compatibility; (3) broad scope – a theory's consequences and implications should extend beyond the initial observations that led to its formation; (4) simplicity – the theory should bring order to observations that would otherwise be considered isolated, or collectively confusing (e.g. the theory of natural selection); (5) fruitful – a theory should lead to new and innovative research questions and experiments that enhance understanding of novel relationships between phenomena and/or uncover previously unknown phenomena.

We'd like you to conduct an informal survey with your family and friends. First, ask them if they've ever had a tooth pulled or some other major dental procedure like a root canal and if so, were they prescribed pain medication (e.g. Vicodin, Percoset, Tylenol with Codeine) to help manage their pain after the procedure? Now here's the next important questions, ask if they experienced any difficulty with that medication either in terms of their reactions when taking it *and* did they have trouble when stopping the medication after taking it for a few days? These may seem like odd questions but, as you will see from reading this book, they're not such unusual questions. Also keep in mind that the majority of today's opioid epidemic originated with medical and/or dental patients being prescribed opioid pain analgesics. Here's what you may have discovered in doing this brief informal survey. Generally, the vast majority of dental patients who are prescribed pain analgesics or pain medication after having a tooth removed or a root canal, do not become addicted or dependent on those medications. Most will say that that they stopped taking the pain medication as soon as the pain subsided, or that they switched to an over-the-counter pain reliever like Tylenol, Motrin or Aleve. Some might even tell you that they felt nauseous when they took the prescription pain analgesic. However, there may be those who took the pain medication beyond the prescribed dose or beyond the time period for which it was prescribed. There will be those who may have had trouble stopping the medication or who may report having become addicted or dependent on that medication, as evidenced by continued use, begging their oral surgeon or dentist for another refill. There may also be those who sought another pain medication prescription from another doctor or who may become involved in "doctor shopping" (i.e. making multiple visits to doctors in order to find one who will write a prescription). As most of you are aware, the current opioid crisis was fueled by three important factors: (1) doctors were told that pain medications had a very low (almost non-existent) potential to cause addiction; (2) pharmaceutical companies began heavily marketing strong opioid-based pain analgesics as a means of alleviating all types of pain (and thereby making huge profits); and (3) once prescribed opioid-based pain analgesics became too expensive (either through prescription or through illegal street dealers, people who had become addicted to pain meds found that heroin was a cheaper (albeit also illegal) alternative (Quinones, 2016). Now let's go back to the informal survey you were asked to do earlier. Were you able to predict who had trouble with the medication and who did not? Were you able to predict the outcome your family member or friend experienced as a result of taking the pain medication? Were you surprised by any of your findings? What does your survey tell you about addiction theory? As you're going through the various models or theories described in this textbook, are any of those theories able to predict and explain who had trouble stopping painkilling medication and who did not? The role of a good theory is that it will both predict and explain behavior. That's another reason why we wrote this book.

Let's look at this from a different perspective by examining some of the more recent epidemiological studies that are done in the United States pertaining to mental health and substance use disorders. According to the Monitoring the Future Survey (Johnston et al., 2014), which is a large epidemiological survey which examines alcohol and drug use among 8th, 10th and 12th grade students as well as college-age students, approximately 96% of 12th graders report that they drink alcohol while another 62% report that they smoke cannabis or marijuana. According to the Epidemiological Catchment Area Survey (ECA) approximately 24% of Americans experience a substance use disorder at some point in his or her lifetime. That's nearly one in four Americans. Another large, national epidemiological study called the National Co-Morbidity Survey (NCS) also estimates that approximately 25% of Americans will experience a substance use disorder while another 26% will experience a mental health disorder at some point in his or her lifetime. Yet if we look at the rates of substance use disorders from the ECA and NCS surveys, it's easy to see that not everyone who uses alcohol or marijuana as a teenager, will necessarily develop a full-blown substance use disorder as an adult. So, the question that has plagued researchers for decades is why do some people become addicted, while others do not? Why did over 60,000 Americans die of drug overdoses (primarily due to opioid use)? What was it about those individuals who became addicted to opioids that was different from all those people who were prescribed analgesic opioids (like Vicodin or Percoset) who did not become addicted?

Disease Model vs Moral Model of Addiction

We decided not to devote full chapters to presenting the disease model and the moral model of addiction because these particular models are considered to be overarching models that encompass a lot of information and are derived from various theories. For example, the disease model posits that substance use disorders are like other medical and mental health disorders which have a bio-logical (e.g. neurological) basis. Indeed, substance use disorders are often described as "biologically-based brain diseases" or as "biologically based, chronic, relapsing diseases." So, similar to how pancreatic cancer, Alzheimer's or diabetes would be considered a biologically based disease, so too, can substance use disorders be viewed through the lens of this same biological perspective. In Chapter 5 we will explore some of the biological or medical explanations of addiction including gen-etic influences, the role of hormones and neurotransmitter anomalies or abnor-malities. It's also important to take into account that when the disease model came into popularity (some say as early as the 1930s) it coincided with the advent of Alcoholics Anonymous (AA). However, the founders of AA (Bill W and Dr. Bob) were very wary of using the word "disease" to describe alcoholism because they were concerned that it would discount the important role of recovery by way of working the 12 Steps of AA, which were designed to promote personal growth, honesty and humility (Kurtz, 1979). The origins of the disease model of alcoholism can be traced back even earlier, to around 1924 when Dr. William Silkworth, the Medical Director of Charles B. Towns Hospital in New York City had treated Bill W. several times for acute intoxication. From his years of treating alcoholics, Silkworth had concluded "alcoholism is not just a vice or habit. This is a com-pulsion, this is pathological craving, this is a *disease*" (Silkworth, 1939a p. xxvii). Silkworth (1937) had likened alcoholism to having an allergy to alcohol and had written extensively regarding his contention that alcoholism was a disease and therefore not the result of a flawed personality or moral failing. Jellinek (1946) also advocated for alcoholism being viewed from a disease model perspective by addressing the physical dimensions and progression of alcoholism. Jellinek felt that physiological craving for alcohol was key feature that could distinguish alcohol-dependent individuals from heavy drinkers. Under pressure from several factions, including a number of Hollywood celebrities, politicians and other notables in the arts and sciences, the American Medical Association issued a formal statement in the 1950s that concluded alcoholism was indeed a disease.

As brain-imaging technologies had become more advanced towards the end of the 20th century and at the onset of the 21st century, there appeared to be even greater emphasis on the disease model; more specifically, however, tech-nology now shifted the emphasis to addiction as being essentially a "brain disease." In a landmark article in *Science*, Alan Leshner, then director of NIDA (National Institute on Drug Abuse), wrote "That addiction is tied to changes in brain struc-ture and function is what makes it, fundamentally, a brain disease" (Leshner, 1997). This same mantra was taken up by Nora Volkow (a neuroscientist who took over as director of NIDA in 2003). According to Volkow, "I've never come across a single person who was addicted who wanted to be addicted" (Volkow, 2008). The

Boxed Item 1.1 Do New Year's Resolutions Hold a Key to Achieving Lasting Sobriety?

David Destino's December 31, 2017 *New York Times* article entitled "How to keep your resolutions" holds some rather interesting keys not only to keeping New Year's resolutions but also to providing some salient recommendations for those who are attempting to achieve long-term recovery. Destino points out that the problem with resolutions is "the problems of life itself," referring to human nature as being shortsighted when it comes to setting and achieving goals. As human beings we tend to value immediate pleasures rather than the potential satisfaction of the future. Destino references psychologist Dr. Walter Mischel's classic marshmallow experiments, in which children who could resist the temptation of immediately being allowed to eat one marshmallow would be awarded a second marshmallow by waiting 15 minutes. What was noteworthy in his study is that those children who had better "self-control" were also found to have better academic and professional success upon follow-up years later. It appears that those who can tough it out and persevere in the face of immediate temptation seem to do better in several areas, such as personal finances, healthy eating, exercise and job performance. Destino takes issue with the self-help publications that encourage us to use willpower to ignore our cravings and temptations for immediate pleasures. But, as Destino points out, after decades of self-help recommendations to resist the impulse purchase and save for retirement or to forgo the Twinkie in favor of fresh fruit, it seems to be part of human nature want to light up our limbic pathways with immediate pleasures (remember just about all drugs, along with chocolate, sex and impulse spending, can flood our brain with dopamine and serotonin, the "feel-good" neurotransmitters in our brains). Destino points out that exercising willpower, self-control and muscling through can be stressful and can have a negative effect on our health. Destino has developed an interesting line of research in which social emotions (such as gratitude, compassion, humility, pride in achievements not hubris) seem to counteract the negative health consequences of using willpower alone. These social emotions seem to bring us around more gently to becoming more patient and less egocentric. By putting the needs of others ahead of your own or working hard to make sure you're shouldering your end of the bargain, or simply by behaving morally in our interactions with others leads to strengthening our social bonds and, according to Destino, helps us to behave in ways that show more self-control by putting the needs of others before our own. Interestingly, AA happened upon this same conclusion when the founders came upon the conclusion that the best way to stay sober was to "give the program away" or give to others, and that by working the 12 Steps, one is essentially living a moral, honest life (Alcoholics Anonymous, 1939).

advent of the 21st century also brought a number of pharmacological therapies for substance use disorders, including medications that help alleviate craving (e.g. Topiramate, Naltrexone, Acamprosate for alcohol craving; Naltrexone for opioid craving) as well as medication-assisted opioid replacement therapies for opioid use disorders in the form of methadone and, more recently, buprenorphine (trade name: suboxone or subutex (Koob, Lloyd, & Mason, 2009).

Yet the disease model is not without its controversies and detractors who feel that this model is very much a double-edged sword. On the one hand, it helps bring addictions out from under the stigma that brands those with SUDs as being weak and morally flawed into the realm of other medical diseases or disorders. However, there are those who see the disease model as exonerating the person with SUDs from personal responsibility. For example, from a legal standpoint would a driver who is under the influence of alcohol and/or drugs be exonerated from responsibility for killing a pedestrian crossing the street? Most states would consider this to be vehicular manslaughter, which would result in prison time. Does this differ from a person with severe mental illness who kills someone in a paranoid rage? Here the courts would most likely deem this individual "not guilty by reason of insanity." Many feel that that the disease model puts too much stock in addiction as a brain disease at the expense of the behavioral, personal, sociocultural aspects of addiction. For example, Satel and Lilienfeld (2013) felt that much of the neuroscientific explanations of addictions were not as convincing as they were initially proposed to be, and that they tended to discount important personal and sociocultural factors that influence substance use disorders. Also, inherent aspects of the disease model include concepts such as "loss of control" and "craving." Loss of control is described as a phenomenon that occurs after a period of abstinence whereby, if a person with SUD takes a drink or engages in substance use, he or she automatically lapses into addiction. Craving refers to the overwhelming desire or obsession that people with substance use disorders experience during periods of abstinence or withdrawal. In both instances (according to the disease model), the person who manifests a SUD is seen as a passive onlooker and therefore has neither choice nor control with regard to substance use (Skog, 2000).

Inherent also in the disease model is the notion of chronicity (expressed in the old saying "Once an alcoholic/addict, always an alcoholic/addict") and progression. SUDs are considered to be chronic and progressive diseases. Essentially, the term "chronic" refers to SUDs as being lifelong diseases – there is no "cure" but the disease can be arrested or stopped in tracks most assuredly with abstinence and a combination of both 12-Step program involvement and treatment. This is one of the reasons you'll more likely to hear people in SUD recovery refer to themselves as "recovering alcoholics or addicts" instead of "recovered alcoholics or addicts." Recovery is a lifelong process. Progression is also a basic concept within the disease model. Since SUDs are considered to be progressive disorders or diseases, this means that they get worse over time, which is usually accompanied by increased substance use, both in frequency and amount of use.

Essentially, the moral model claims that substance use disorders come about as a result of moral failing or willful, sinful behavior on the part of substance users. Similar to how people suffering with severe mental health disorders were considered to be possessed by the devil during colonial times in America, the moral model suggests that substance users are willful sinners who should be punished. Then Benjamin Rush came along and began to advocate for more humane treatment of people with mental illness and substance use disorders. Benjamin Rush was a physician in colonial Philadelphia and was a signer of the Declaration of Independence who founded one of the first treatment programs for individuals with alcohol use disorders, which was called the Home for Inebriates. However, the moral model dictated that people with mental illness and substance use disorders be punished, hence many "public inebriates" were thrown in jail or prisons.

This trend continued through the early 19th century which was around the time the Women's Christian Temperance Union (WCTU) was formed. Although not prohibitionists at first, the WCTU advocated for "blue laws" that would close taverns on Sundays so that men would go to church rather than to the local taverns which were the center of political and community life at the time. Just prior to the Civil War, however, there was a growing trend towards prohibition. This was said to have begun in Maine, when the Mayor of Portland, Maine passed a city ban on alcohol. This ban resulted in decreased rates of crime, domestic violence and public intoxication. The mayor eventually became Governor of Maine. After the Civil War, a prohibitionist candidate ran against Ulysses S. Grant for president but lost. It was not until 1920, however, that the Volstead Act (the 19th Amendment) was passed, which was the beginning of Prohibition. Interestingly, this seemed to have come about because of a rising prohibitionist movement among many religious groups, as well as anti-German sentiment following World War I. Prohibition essentially put the entire German brewing industry out of business (e.g. German brewers such as Anhauser-Busch, Miller, Schlitz, Schaeffer, Blatz, etc.). Depending on what you read, Prohibition can either be viewed as a huge success (in terms of curbing medical and social ills resulting from alcoholism) or a dismal failure (in terms of creating tremendous black market demand for alcohol). The recent HBO series, *Boardwalk Empire*, provides a glimpse into the black market racketeers who dominated the underworld during Prohibition. When Prohibition was repealed in 1933 (with the passage of the 21st Amendment to the Constitution, during the Franklin D. Roosevelt administration), it was done in part to put Americans back to work during the Great Depression. Prohibition brought about many challenges for the federal government in terms of enforcement and control. Directing the Prohibition efforts for the federal government was a young bureaucrat by the name of Harry J. Anslinger. As Anslinger was beginning to "see the writing on the wall," that Prohibition would soon be repealed, being an adept government bureaucrat, he began to take up another cause, drugs, most notably, marijuana, cocaine and morphine/heroin. Anslinger was appointed to be the director of the Federal Bureau of Narcotics. This set the stage for decades of draconian laws that would target mostly people of color. Anslinger refrained from going after European Americans and instead focused his reign of terror on Chinese-Americans in the opium dens of San Francisco, Mexican-Americans who brought cannabis to America when they arrived in the southwestern states in search of work and a better quality of life, and African-Americans from port cities like New Orleans who would be given cocaine to help increase their work productivity, and jazz musicians in cities like Chicago, New York and St. Louis. Anslinger's answer to the ever-growing number of men and women who were being incarcerated throughout the United States was to create the Lexington Narcotic Farm in Lexington, Kentucky. Lexington was essentially a prison for those convicted of drug-related offenses, who were sent there for often indeterminate amounts of time, although some therapeutic activities were offered. Famous jazz musicians such as Billie Holiday, Sonny Rollins, Chet Baker and Elvin Jones all spent time in Lexington. Here was a 20th-century example of the moral model in action.

Learning Opportunity 1.1

See what you can find out about the Lexington Narcotic Farm and discuss your reactions to what you learned with your classmates either as an in-class discussion or in a chatroom. What are your opinions about this approach to addressing substance use disorders back in the 1930s?

We wish we could tell you that the moral model no longer influences public policy and legal sanctions in 21st-century America but to do so would be false and misleading. Indeed, the moral model is being played out every day in the United States as we witness ever-burgeoning number of individuals with substance use disorders who are being incarcerated in our jails and prisons. Also, when we look at the disproportionate percentages of racial and ethnic minorities who are being incarcerated, it's very clear that racial bias is built into American drug laws which hark back to Anslinger's racially motivated discrimination against people of color in the 1930s. The question is whether the United States will continue to build more prisons to manage the current opioid epidemic or whether a more humane, public health approach will be taken and instead of constructing more prisons, more treatment centers will be built.

Brief Remarks Regarding the Use of Pejorative Language Pertaining to Substance Use Disorders

There are many terms used to describe what we know today as substance use disorders, a term that is used in the *Diagnostic and statistical manual of mental disorders* (American Psychiatric Association, 2014, 5th edn). However, American culture has many colloquial or popular terms used to describe SUDs. Terms such as "addicts," "alcoholics," "junkies," "drunks," "dope fiends" have permeated our everyday, popular language over the course of decades and still persist to this day (Broyles, Binswanger et al., 2014; Heit & Gourlay, 2009; Warren, 2007). For example, the term "junkie" came about during the Great Depression of the 1920s when Americans who were using heroin would go around finding junk metal to exchange for cash in order to purchase heroin. Many of these aforementioned terms are pejorative or negative and sustain the stigma that, we as Americans attach to substance use disorders. This stigma also stems from the perception that many individuals hold, that substance use disorders are not a disease but rather the result of character flaws or moral failings.

Throughout this book we have attempted to use non-pejorative language. There are instances however, when we have used these terms, especially when from quoting older research studies using pejorative language (e.g. "alcoholic" or "addict"). It is important, that we, as professionals who treat SUDs are aware of the language we use when describing these disorders.

Summary: The Three Blind Men and the Elephant

There's an ancient parable which is often referred to as "the three blind men and the elephant" (Blind Men and an Elephant, 2018). In this parable, three blind men learn that a strange animal called an elephant has been brought to the town where they live and having never experienced such a creature, the three men venture down to the town square to inspect the animal by touch. The first blind man hand lands on the elephant's trunk and declares that "an elephant is like a thick snake." The second blind man's hand feels the elephant's leg and determines that "an elephant is like a thick tree trunk." While the third blind man feels the elephant's ear and decides that "an elephant is like a large fan." This parable is often used to describe how a partial truth can be true and yet at the same time may be limited or even false by limiting an account of other truths or perceptions. The parable is also prescriptive in that it advocates the need to take other perspectives into account as well as the need for communication between "experts," as each blind man could claim expertise based upon the particular part of the elephant he happened to touch. Such is the case with addiction theory. As we describe each theory, you'll see how each has its own merits and limitations. You may also think about people in your life who have struggled with addiction and how or why he or she may have developed a substance use disorder. We also know that timing is important, as some people may develop addictive behaviors early in life, only to "mature out" of those behaviors as they take on new responsibilities and endeavors (such as a family and/or career). Yet, we also know of many individuals who developed addictions later in life, in retirement for example, or after the death of a spouse.

In order to be good addiction counselors, we must always keep an open mind to various perspectives and we must keenly listen to the stories of each of our clients, as each will be unique. When people go to AA or Narcotics Anonymous (NA) they are often encouraged to "identify don't compare." In other words, look for similarities between your substance use and that of others in the room because if you just focus on differences you bound to come up with the conclusion "I'm different! I'm unique and therefore I can't be an alcoholic or addict!" Also from the perspective of AA and NA, the etiology or causes of addiction are generally not considered to be important. For example, in Father Martin's well-known video "Chalk Talk on Alcoholism," he cautions "if you have a toothache, do you want to know why it aches or do you want to have it pulled?" Yet, in counseling we, as addiction counselors are concerned with causes as it will help to guide effective treatment and also assists in identifying those issues that clients may need to address in counseling.

References

Alcoholics Anonymous (1939). *Alcoholics Anonymous (Big Book)*. New York: Alcoholics Anonymous World Services.

Babor, T. F., de la Fuente, J. R., Saunders, J. B., & Grant, M. (1989). AUDIT – The Alcohol Use Disorders Identification Test: Guidelines for use in primary care. Geneva: World Health Organization.

Bickel, W.K., Mueller, E.T., & Jarmolowicz, D.P. (2013). What is addiction? In B. McCrady & E. Epstein (Eds). *Addictions: A comprehensive guidebook*. Oxford: Oxford University Press (pp 3–16).

Blind Men and an Elephant (2018). Parable. *Wikipedia*. Retrieved from https://en.wikipedia.org/wiki/Blind_men_and_an_elephant

Broyles, L.M., Binswanger, I.A., Jenkins, J.A., Finnell, D.S., Faseru, B., Cavaiola, A., Pugatch, M., & Gordon, A.J. (2014). Confronting inadvertent stigma and pejorative language in addiction scholarship: A recognition and response. *Substance Abuse, 35(3),* 217–221.

Cavaiola, A.A., Strohmetz, D.B., & Abreo, S. (2007). Characteristics of DUI recidivists: A 12-year follow-up study of first time DUI offenders. *Addictive Behaviors, 32(4),* 855–861.

Centers for Disease Control (2018). Drug overdose death data. Washington, DC: Centers for Disease Control. Retrieved from www.cdc.gov/drugoverdose/data/statedeaths.html

CSAT (Center for Substance Abuse Treatment) (2004). *Simple screening instruments for outreach for alcohol and other drug abuse and infectious diseases.* Treatment Improvement Protocol (TIP) Series 11. DHHS Publication No. (SMA) 94–2094. Rockville, MD: Substance Abuse and Mental Health Services Administration.

Destino, D. (2017, December 31). How to keep your resolutions. *New York Times, Sunday Review,* pp. 1, 4.

Edwards, G., & Lader, M. (Eds). (1990). *The nature of drug dependence*. Oxford: Oxford University Press.

Heit, H.A., & Gourlay, D.L. (2009). DSM-V and the definitions: Time to get it right. *American Academy of Pain Medicine, 10(5),* 784–786.

Hilgers, L. (2017, November 5). Let's open up about addiction and recovery. *New York Times,* Sunday Review, p. 3.

Jellinek, E.M. (1946). Phases in the drinking history of alcoholics. *Quarterly Journal of Studies on Alcohol, 7,* 1–18.

Johnston, L.D., O'Malley, P.M., Miech, R.A., Bachman, J.G., & Schulenberg, J.D. (2014) *Monitoring the Future: 2014 overview of key findings on adolescent drug use.* Ann Arbor: Institute for Social Research, University of Michigan.

Koob, G.F., Lloyd, G.K., & Mason, B.J. (2009). The development of pharmacotherapies for drug addiction: A Rosetta Stone approach. *Nature Reviews Drug Discovery, 8(6),* 500–515.

Kuhn, T.S. (1962). *The structure of scientific revolutions*. Chicago, IL: Chicago University Press.

Kurtz, E. (1979). *Not God: A history of Alcoholics Anonymous*. Center City, MN: Hazelden.

Leshner, A.J. (1997). Addiction is a brain disease and it matters. *Science, 278,* 45–47.

McLellan, A. T., Kushner, H., Metzger, D., Peters, R. I., Grissom, G., & Argeriou, M. (1992). The 5th edition of the Addiction Severity Index. *Journal of Substance Abuse Treatment, 9(3)*, 199–213.

Monitoring the Future (2016, December 13). Teen use of any illicit drug other than marijuana at new low, same true for alcohol. *Michigan News*. Ann Arbor: Institute for Social Research, The University of Michigan. Retrieved from http://monitoringthefuture.org//pressreleases/16drugpr_complete.pdf

Peele, S. (1985). *The meaning of addiction: An unconventional view*. San Francisco, CA: Jossey Bass.

Quinones, S. (2016). *Dreamland: The true tale of America's opiate epidemic*. New York: Bloomsbury Press.

Satel, S., & Lilienfeld, S.O. (2013). *Brainwashed: The seductive appeal of mindless neuroscience*. New York: Basic Books.

Silkworth, W.D. (1937). Alcoholism as a manifestation of allergy. *Medical Records (New York), 145*, 249–251

Silkworth, W.D. (1939). The doctor's opinion. In Alcoholics Anonymous, *Alcoholics Anonymous (Big Book)* (pp. xi–xiv). New York: Alcoholics Anonymous World Services.

Skog, O.J. (2000). Addicts' choice. *Addiction, 95(9)*, 1309–1314.

Volkow, N.D. (2008, October 24). It's time for addiction science to supersede stigma. *Science News*.

Warren, J.F. (2007). Those damned substance abusers! *PsycCritiques, 52(45)*, 1–2.

Westermeyer, J., Yargic, I., & Thuras, P. (2004). Michigan Assessment-Screening Test for Alcohol and Drugs (MAST/AD): Evaluation in a clinical sample. *American Journal on Addictions, 13(2)*, 151–162.

2 Psychoanalytic Theory

Alan A. Cavaiola

Introduction

According to classical psychoanalytic theory, the key to determining psycho-pathology (whether it be anxiety or neurosis, depression, interpersonal relationship issues or substance use disorders) lies in the past. Therefore, psychoanalysis seeks not only to uncover these past traumas, conflicts and so on but to do so in such a way that the client develops insight. Insight can be viewed as a deep understanding of both the unconscious and conscious understanding of the origins of one's disorders. This is often a very emotional (or cathartic) and often an anxiety-provoking process, which is why psychoanalysis is often considered an inappropriate treatment for substance use disorders, especially for those who are in early recovery. Yet, psychoanalytic theory provides counselors with an understanding of how trauma impacts on people's lives, often for years after the traumatizing incident. Psychoanalytic theory also provides counselors with an understanding of defense mechanisms such as denial, rationalization and sublimation, which often fuel the addiction by distorting the painful reality of the impact that alcohol and/or drug use has on his or her life. There's an old Alcoholics Anonymous (AA) saying that addresses these distortions, "alcoholism is a disease that tells you, you don't have a disease" and it's the defense mechanisms that account for these distortions. And yet, everyone employs defense mechanisms in their daily life, not just those with substance use disorders (SUDs).

Another reason that psychoanalysis and psychoanalytic theory are not viewed as acceptable or effective in substance use disorders is due, in part, to the fact that psychoanalytic theory is often viewed as antiquated or outdated. Also, traditional or classical analysis is done over the course of months and often years, with clients attending therapy sessions sometimes three or four times a week. This makes psychoanalysis not only time-consuming, but also very costly and, in many instances, not very practical. Addiction counseling, especially in the early phases of treatment, tends to be very practical and focuses more on the here-and-now (Washton & Zweben, 2006). As many of us who have worked with individuals with substance use disorders know, insight alone doesn't necessarily translate into behavioral change when it comes to achieving sobriety.

Yet, psychoanalytic theory has made, often indirectly, many contributions to the addictions treatment field. For example, we will talk about Attachment Theory (a theory which grew out of psychoanalytic theory), which examines how disturbed relationships with significant others can often be a precursor to addictions later in life. In addition, Attachment Theory suggests that one's ability to form healthy connections with others can often become the foundation of sobriety, whether those connections be in 12-Step programs or in counseling. For now, however, let's go back to the beginnings of psychoanalytic theory with its founder, Sigmund Freud.

Sigmund Freud was born in Moravia on May 6, 1856, although he lived in worked in Vienna, Austria for nearly 80 years. Freud was interested in becoming a scientist, so he entered Medical School at the University of Vienna in 1873. Freud never intended to practice medicine, however, given the lack of rewards for scientific research and few faculty positions for Jewish scholars in Austria and Germany, he began a private practice specializing in neurology. It was as a result of his private practice work that Freud, developed the psychoanalytic approach to treating neuroses (i.e. a type of mental disorder), in the latter part of the 19th century. Freud was originally trained as a neurologist but the psychological origins of the symptoms of many of his patients piqued his interest in studying how emotional trauma would transform into complaints of various neurological ailments (Hall & Lindzey, 1970). Freud had treated many patients who manifested neurological symptoms such as paralysis, blindness and numbness for which he could find no medical/neurological explanations. (Freud later labeled these pseudo-neurological symptoms as "conversion disorders" because he concluded that psychological or emotionally painful experiences had "converted" into physical symptoms.) These types of symptoms initially led Freud into studying hypnosis, which he employed as a means of helping to uncover the psychological or emotional trauma that had caused these various conversion reactions in his patients. Freud later discovered that hypnosis was limited in allowing his patients to experience catharsis (or an outpouring of emotions), which is when he began to use free association, a therapeutic technique in which patients were encouraged to say whatever came to mind in the session. Free association, dream interpretation, and analysis of resistance and transference became the hallmarks of psychoanalysis and psychoanalytically oriented psychotherapy.

Learning Opportunity 2.1

Can you recall something that took place in your childhood (prior to age 8) that may have had an impact on the person you've become today? If you're working on this in class, break into groups of three and share what you've written with the two other people in your triad.

Key Terms

abreaction: the process by which patients experience extreme emotional catharsis as they re-live a traumatic episode or event.

catharsis: similar to abreaction — the patient experiences an outpouring of emotions in response to a traumatic or stressful event or episode that is recollected in therapy.

ego: a part of one's personality structure which is responsible for making executive daily decisions based upon current realities; the ego's major role is to act as a mediator between the id and superego.

id: a part of one's personality structure that is often part of one's unconscious (or outside of one's awareness). The id operates on the "pleasure principle," (i.e. if it feels good, do it) without concern for reality. The id would contain sexual urges and impulses and any other behaviors that produce pleasure for the individual (including alcohol and mood-altering substances).

superego: a part of one's personality structure from which one's sense of conscience or morals are derived. The superego exists in opposition to the id.

defense mechanism: often referred to as ego, defense mechanisms are distortions which serve to protect the ego from harsh or traumatic realities. For example, repression protects the ego by pushing traumatic memories out of conscious awareness. Anna Freud had conceptualized most of the defense mechanism described in Table 2.1.

dream interpretation: a technique used in psychoanalysis and psychoanalytically oriented therapy. Dreams are thought to hold valuable repressed or unconscious information.

free association: a psychoanalytic technique in which a client is asked to speak about whatever thoughts, feelings or images come into their mind without censoring.

unconscious: that part of the mind that is outside of one's everyday awareness. Unconscious urges may include one's sexual or aggressive impulses or urges that are considered to be unacceptable (especially to the superego).

transference: refers to the relationship the patient has with his or her therapist. Here the patient is thought to unconsciously *transfer* feelings, attitudes, attributes or motives towards a significant person in his or her life towards the therapist. One of the key roles of the therapist is to interpret this transference as part of the therapeutic relationship.

countertransference: just as the patient harbors unconscious feelings towards the therapist, so too does the therapist *transfer* feelings, attributes, motives towards the patient of someone significant in their life or from their past.

resistance: Sigmund Freud warned that resistance is very much part of the therapeutic process and may be encountered during every aspect of therapy. Just as there's a part of the patient who wants to get well and improve, there's another part that wants to maintain the status quo or that part of the personality which opposes change.

Classical Psychoanalytic Approach to Substance Use Disorders

Very interestingly, although Freud did not specifically speak of addictions or substance use disorders, he was no stranger to addiction in his personal life. Given that most drugs which are considered illegal by today's standards could be prescribed or obtained over-the-counter in the late 1800s, Freud thought he had discovered a cure for depression and fatigue when he began using and prescribing cocaine for his patients. He chronicled his findings in the well-known monograph he had written aptly named, *The cocaine papers* (Freud, 1974 [1884]). Over time, it became clear to his family and colleagues that Freud was himself addicted to cocaine, in spite of his being an advocate for the drug. Freud also concluded that cocaine could be used as a "cure" for morphine addiction. It was not until the death of his friend and colleague, Ernst von Fleishel-Markow, whom Freud had attempted to detox using cocaine, that he began to change his opinion of cocaine. Apparently, von Fleishel-Markow had become addicted to morphine after suffering an infection sustained while doing an autopsy and was subsequently prescribed morphine to lessen excruciating nerve pain. Freud eventually concluded that cocaine was a dangerous drug with highly addictive qualities. It was also well known from biographical accounts (Jones, 1957) that Freud smoked upwards of ten cigars a day. He eventually developed cancer of the jaw/mouth which resulted in his death on September 23, 1939. When Freud left Vienna, partially in response to Kristallnacht on November 8– 9, 1938 (in which the Nazis destroyed all Jewish prayer houses, synagogues and Jewish-owned shops/businesses) and partially in response to the urgings of his followers, he secured safe passage to live in London, England. In addition to obtaining passage for his family, Freud was also able to secure passage for his personal physician, who was prescribing pain medication that allowed Freud to function on a daily basis (Jones, 1953, 1955, 1957).

If we go back to the earliest formulation of psychoanalytic theory, we can find some description of how addictions may develop from the Freudian perspective. In Freud's theory of psychosexual development, he outlined the various stages that children go through from birth to around age 12 (you may recall these as the oral stage, anal stage, phallic, latency stage). Each stage carries a primary source of "gratification" although it's important to remember that Freud defined sexual gratification in a very broad sense. For example, the oral stage which takes place from birth to around 2 years old, is marked by oral gratification being the primary source of gratification. Therefore, the sucking reflex and the pleasure derived from sucking and food intake is considered to be the primary source of "sexual gratification." However, if the infant is either under-stimulated or frustrated in the feeding process or if they are over-stimulated, then something Freud referred to as *fixation* could result. If one were to become orally fixated, he or she could go on to develop addictions to food, smoking, drinking (alcoholically), as a means of continued attempts for oral gratification. Although this theory has some intuitive appeal, it's very difficult to determine what would be considered under-stimulation versus over-stimulation, or who would become fixated versus those who would not.

Later, Freudian theory evoked another, albeit, lesser known theory of substance use disorders, in which addictions were derived from death instincts or a form of slow suicide (Khantzian, 1980). Indeed, substance use disorders were described by the famous psychiatrist, Karl Menninger (1938) as "suicide on the installment plan" (borrowing from the title of a book by Ferdinand Céline in 1938) because of the progressive physical, psychological, emotional and spiritual deterioration that many individuals with substance use disorders often experience. Just as the id is thought to strive for pleasure and operates according to the "pleasure principle" or "eros," Freud hypothesized that an opposite drive referred to as the death instinct which operate according to "Thanatos," which is an expression of the death wish or death instinct.

Contemporary Psychoanalytic Models of Addiction

Morgenstern and Leeds (1993) describe four contemporary theorists who have contributed to the present-day psychoanalytic conceptualization of addiction. For example, Wurmser (1985) hypothesizes that people with substance use disorders suffer from destructive and overly harsh superegos which plague the person with fear, rage and overwhelming guilt. This overly harsh superego is thought to begin in the aftermath of childhood sexual abuse, sexual seduction or parental abandonment. As a result of these traumatic experiences, the individual reacts by rejecting authority; over time, however, an internalized harsh authority persona (superego) develops which then drives the person to drink or use drugs in an effort to "sedate" or quiet this overly harsh superego. Unfortunately, not only are feelings of fear, rage and guilt numbed or anesthetized but other superego functions as well (such as conscience, and moral decision-making).

For Khantzian (1985, 2014) substance use arises not as a result of a harsh superego, but rather from ego deficits, which result in feelings of low self-esteem and low self-worth. Many people who experience substance use disorders report feeling as if "there's a hole inside" him or her which miraculously disappears with the onset of alcohol or substance use. Khantzian refers to this as the "self-medication" hypothesis (SMH) in which substance abusers are seeking to alleviate feelings of low self-esteem or self-worth, depression or anxiety. Khantzian is the only psychodynamic theorist who pays attention to one's drug of preference. According to SMH, addiction is a "self-regulation disorder," that is, an attempt to manage painful emotions, an attempt to "self-repair." Painful emotions often pre-date SUD (e.g. childhood trauma, abandonment, loss) but addictions often *cause* painful emotions, (as would be the case when a person with a SUD is served with divorce papers because of alcohol- or drug-related infidelities). Khantzian provides examples of the emotional self-regulation and self-medication function of specific substances. He proposes that those individuals who use opioids are seeking to manage feelings of aggression or rage. Those with cocaine use disorders are thought to seek relief from depression, boredom and symptoms of ADHD (not surprisingly most medications for ADHD are stimulants) or bipolar disorder. Although common sense would suggest that people suffering from bipolar disorder would be likely to self-medicate the depressive cycle of bipolar with cocaine or other stimulant drugs, it's actually the opposite. People with bipolar disorder are more likely to use cocaine as a means to sustain the burst of energy that one experiences during the manic phase. Alcohol and cannabis are often attractive to those suffering from post-traumatic stress disorders (PTSD) who experience difficulty sleeping because of an inability to "shut off" intrusive thoughts related to the trauma.

In addition, several research studies found that substance use was perceived as being helpful in reducing distressing symptoms among individuals with bipolar disorder (e.g. Mayfield & Coleman, 1968; Dunner, Hensel, & Fieve, 1979; Bernardt & Murray, 1986; Kessler, 2004; Weiss, Kolodziej, Griffin, Najavits, Jacobson, & Greenfield, 2004.)

Krystal proposed two theories to explain substance use disorders. The first is based on an object relations approach to addiction which looks at the impact of early maternal relationships as influencing whether one will develop satisfying intimate, romantic relationships in adulthood. When someone is unable to connect with others or form satisfying intimate adult relationships, then (according to Krystal), one is more likely to turn to alcohol or drugs to fill that void. This first theory of addiction laid the groundwork for Attachment Theory's perspective on the origin of addictions, which we will discuss later in this chapter. The second theory of addiction that Krystal puts forth is based on the condition known as "alexithymia" or the inability to correctly identify and label emotions. Therefore, individuals with substance use disorders often have difficulty identifying feelings of anger, happiness, joy, dysthymia or depression, sadness. According to Krystal, alexithymia makes for difficulty in being able to use emotions as a guide towards accurate self-understanding. This lack of self-understanding results in a predisposition towards using alcohol or other substances to alleviate feelings of frustration. Imagine being devoid of emotions and how that might impact on you.

The fourth theorist, McDougall, hypothesizes that substance use disorders are merely one of a variety of compulsive behaviors which also include eating disorders, sexual addictions, gambling disorders and addictive relationships or co-dependent relationships, which, she concluded, are all examples of "psychosomatic disorders." Here, McDougall uses the term "psychosomatic" to describe instances whereby emotional symptoms (fear, loneliness, anxiety) are converted into behavioral manifestations (i.e. compulsive behaviors). McDougall contends that although everyone uses strategies such as compulsive behaviors to manage painful emotions, people with SUD do so habitually. Addictive behaviors therefore become a way to avoid feelings of deadness or emptiness, which is somewhat similar to Khantzian's self-medication theory of addiction discussed earlier. There are three other contemporary psychoanalytic theories which deserve out attention: Attachment theory, Self-Psychology and Trauma theory.

Addiction as an Attachment Disorder

Freudian theory provided the basis for many other theoretical approaches which are sometimes referred to as neo-Freudian theories. One of those theories is Attachment Theory. Based on the early work of British psychoanalyst, John Bowlby, it was hypothesized that, from the beginning of life, infants have a basic need to establish a bond with a caregiving adult (or parent). According to Bowlby, attachment is a primary drive like the need for food or sex. Mary Ainsworth, an American psychologist, developed what was called the Strange Situation Test, whereby she studied infants' reactions when separated from their primary caregiver and placed in the presence of a stranger. Ainsworth found that children/ infants would respond in one of three attachment styles, depending on the type of relationship that had been established with the primary caregiver. Securely attached infants/children responded by continuing to explore their environment, undisturbed by the presence of a stranger. Insecurely attached infants/children responded to the stranger by crying, screaming or showing other manifestations of fear or apprehension. Ambivalent infants/children showed no reactions whatsoever but would not explore their environment. These attachment styles are hypothesized to be pervasive and would therefore continue into adulthood. Attachment style is also associated with both the recognition and expression of emotion as well as emotional regulation. Furthermore, it's thought that the inability to form secure adult attachments or relationships is predictive of those who develop substance use disorders or process addictions. From an Attachment Theory perspective, those who are unable to attach securely to others are more prone to "attaching" to alcohol and other mood-altering substances. Recent research also finds that the ability to effectively regulate moods (especially negative mood states) is vital in resisting relapse triggers (Fowler, Groat, & Ulanday, 2013). Also, being able to form a secure attachment with one's counselor is predictive of success in opioid maintenance treatment (Cavaiola, Fulmer, & Stout, 2015). The very process of the counseling relationship (especially when there's a positive transference in the counseling relationship) that can be viewed as a healing experience which can sometimes repair the early damage caused by early loss, abandonment or inconsistent parenting that may have caused insecure attachments.

Flores (2004) outlines several basic tenets of Attachment Theory that have important implications for addiction treatment. First, is that *attachment is a primary motivation and is not secondary to some other drive.* Second, *actual real-world events are more significant and more important to the individual than unconscious fantasies or internal drives.* Traditional psychoanalytic theory believes somewhat the opposite, that is, that unconscious fantasies and internal drives (like sexual drives) play a more important role. Third, *affect regulation (i.e. the ability to regulate one's emotions) is determined by one's early attachment experiences.* In other words, those who experienced secure attachments to parents or caretakers during infancy and childhood, are often better able to regulate or modulate their emotions. Fourth, *the need for attachment is a lifelong process and not just something that occurs during infancy or childhood.* Flores concluded that healthy adults seek attachments throughout the lifespan.

Boxed Item 2.1 Attachment Style

There are several measures that are used to assess one's attachment style. One of these is available online and can be accessed at www.web-research-design. net/cgi-bin/crq/crq/pl; it is called the Experiences in Close Relationships – Revised assessment (ECR-R). The directions for administering and scoring the ECR-R are included. Pair off with another student in the class and each of you should then fill out the ECR-R and score it. The score will provide you with an assessment of your attachment style (i.e. secure, insecure, ambivalent attachment). Discuss whether you feel the score you received is accurate with the person you've paired off with. If you feel the score is accurate or inaccurate describe why.

Kohut's Self-Psychology Approach to Addictions

Heinz Kohut's Self-Psychology theory of addiction (1977) has similarities to Khantzian's self-medication hypothesis described earlier in this chapter. For Kohut, the singular motive or goal behind any addictive behavior is that the addiction represents a misguided attempt at affect or emotional regulation. The other goal or motive for addictive behaviors is that they represent attempts to make up for deficits in one's personality or what Kohut refers to as "psychic structure." It's not uncommon for many individuals with substance use disorders to explain their experience the first time they used a particular mood-altering drug to be one of "feeling whole" or feeling that a "void within me had just been filled." This is similar to what Kohut (and Khantzian describe as "ego deficits." In the early phases of a substance use disorder, individuals report that they feel great, they feel whole, they may feel euphoric or even confident. Yet we know how this erodes (for some more quickly than for others) over time, to the point where substance use begins to interfere with life functioning rather than enhancing it. Kohut sums this up best:

> The explanatory power of the new psychology of the self is nowhere as evident as with regard to these four types of psychological disturbance: 1) narcissistic personality disorders 2) the perversions 3) the delinquencies and 4) the addictions. Why can these seemingly disparate conditions be examined so fruitfully with the aid of the same conceptual framework? ... What do they have in common [?] ... in all these disorders the afflicted individual suffers from a central weakness, from a weakness in the core of his personality. He suffers from the consequences of a defect in the self.
>
> (Kohut, 1977, p. vii)

Kohut views addiction as a failed attempt of the part of the person suffering from an SUD to remedy or repair that defect in personality or character. Essentially, because one's sense of self is fragile, he or she then becomes vulnerable to addiction as an

---

Boxed Item 2.2 Shame vs. Guilt

It's very common for people to confuse feelings of shame and guilt. Many people use these labels synonymously or interchangeably. However, there is a saying which aptly describes the distinction. "Guilt is about what we do … shame is about who we are." Guilt therefore refers to behavioral transgressions in which we end up feeling bad (guilty) for things we may have said or done to others. So, if I were to tell a lie or steal something that belongs to someone else, I would (hopefully), feel guilty over these behaviors. However, if I were to label myself as a "cruel or heartless person" or label myself as a thief, then, these labels or self-definitions are reflective of shame.

---

attempt at self-cure. According to Kohut, these self-deficits may be experienced as feelings of depression, inadequacy, low self-worth or low self-esteem, and shame. (see Boxed Item 2.2: Shame vs Guilt). *Pathological narcissism* may develop as a means of coping with or overcoming these feelings of inadequacy. What is pathological narcissism? Pathological narcissism can best be viewed through the lens of a type of defense mechanism (in some ways similar to Anna Freud's defense mechanism of *reaction formation*, whereby one defends against unacceptable impulses by taking on the opposite persona or values). However, according to Kohut, narcissism is considered to be a normal part of development which, as a result of addiction, becomes a pathological character trait. Alcoholics Anonymous seems to have been aware of the type of pathological narcissism that Kohut describes before they had a label for it. A common saying in AA is "alcoholics are egomaniacs with inferiority complexes," is the embodiment of Kohut's description of pathological narcissism as a defense against feelings of inferiority or inadequacy. Also, AA uses the concept of "King Baby" (Cunningham, 1986) to describe the alcoholic who must have everything his or her way, with no consideration of the needs of others.

Trauma Theory

Of the contemporary psychodynamic theories described above, the theories proposed by Wurmser (1978, 1985) and Khantzian (1985) lends support to the role of trauma in the etiology of addictions. It should come as no surprise that victims of sexual assault, child and adolescent physical and sexual abuse (Cavaiola & Schiff, 1988; Wilsnack, Vogeltanz, Klassen, & Harris, 1997; Briere & Elliot, 2003; Spatz-Widom, Marmorstein, & Raskin-White, 2006; Lee, Lyvers, & Edwards, 2008; Asberg & Renk, 2013; Tonmyr & Shields, 2017;) combat trauma (Brady, 2001) and perhaps to a lesser extent, those victimized by natural disasters (e.g. floods, earthquakes, hurricanes) are all more likely to experience co-occurring substance use disorders along with PTSD. In keeping with the self-medication hypothesis, many individuals describe how alcohol or other substances will help them to cope with PTSD symptoms (e.g. anxiety, apprehensions, depression and difficulty turning off intrusive thoughts that makes it hard to fall asleep). It is important for addictions counselors to keep in mind that clients may not disclose traumatic experiences in the early stages of counseling. It is imperative that a trusting therapeutic bond be established in order for a client to feel confident that he or she can make such disclosures. Counselors also need to consider that often traumatic memories may be repressed and may not surface for months or years following the traumatic event. That brings us to the role of defense mechanisms.

Learning Opportunity 2.2 – The Power of the Unconscious

Pair off with someone in the class. Now each of you take a sheet of paper and at the top write the words, "alcoholic" and "addict." Now under those words list any and all words that come to mind in response to those words. What you're doing is a psychoanalytic technique called "free association." Now exchange your list with your partner. Do you notice any negative or pejorative words that might reflect an unconscious bias towards individuals with substance use disorders? Read the article referenced below which will give you an idea of how negative or pejorative labels often creep into our vocabulary when we're discussing substance use disorders:

  Broyles, L.M, Binswanger, I.A., Jenkins, J.A., Finnell, D.S., Faseru, B., Cavaiola, A., Pugatch, M., & Gordon, A.J. (2014). Confronting inadvertent stigma and pejorative language in addiction scholarship: A recognition and response. *Substance Abuse, 35(3)*, 217–221.

Defense Mechanisms and Addiction Theory

Try to recall a particularly embarrassing or humiliating experience. Most people find that it's difficult to recall these memories and there's a tendency to want to push that memory out of our conscious awareness and think of something more pleasant. According to Anna Freud, the daughter of Sigmund Freud, this would be known as a *suppression*, and it's one of the many ego defense mechanisms that Anna described in her renowned text entitled *The ego and mechanisms of defense* first published in 1936. As described earlier, defense mechanisms are ways for the ego to cope with difficult or painful emotions. For example, while the defense mechanism, *suppression* is thought to describe when we try to consciously push a painful memory out of awareness, there's another defense mechanism, *repression*, which occurs unconsciously or outside of one's awareness. This may occur following a particularly traumatic event, like a car accident or sexual assault, in which the person is unable to recall particular memories of the event. A client of mine (AAC) once described having been in a horrible car accident as a child, however, all he could to recollect of the accident was being med-evac'd by helicopter to the nearest hospital trauma center. In this example, the car accident itself had been totally *repressed*, leaving my client with no memories of the car accident.

Table 2.1 Defense Mechanisms

Defense Mechanism	Definition	Example
Repression	Excluding disturbing thoughts, or experiences from conscious awareness (unconscious process)	"I can't remember anything about the night I was attacked"
Sublimation	Taking unacceptable thoughts, desires or impulses and turning them into socially acceptable thoughts or interests	"I really hate homeless people, but instead, I'll donate my time to helping them."
Regression	When faced with conflict or stress reverting to childish behavior	"I'm really angry with you but instead of expressing I'm going to pout instead"
Denial	Refusing to acknowledge the reality of a situation or a conflict, that may be well known or apparent to others	"It's not my drinking that's the problem … drinking helps me to cope"
Projection	Attributing unacceptable traits or feelings to another person rather than oneself	"I don't have a problem, it's you that has the problem. I think you're out to get me"
Reaction Formation	Taking an unacceptable feeling or impulse and turning it into the exact opposite in order to make it acceptable	"When I drink or use drugs, I have urges to molest children … Instead I'll become a coach or scout leader"
Intellectualization/ Rationalization	Providing a rational or intellectual explanation for irrational or unacceptable behavior	"I'm under so much stress at work, who wouldn't want a drink or to get high at the end of a long day?"

Table 2.1 provides a list of defense mechanisms and how they may be experienced. As indicated earlier, everyone uses defense mechanisms at one time or another; when someone is over-reliant on defense mechanisms, however, or when they distort reality, defense mechanisms become problematic or patho-logical. Such would be the case when a person with an SUD over-relies on *denial* in order to convince him or herself that their heroin use is not really a problem and, if anything, helps them to cope with life.

Another common defense mechanism counselors often find expressed by people with SUDs is *rationalization*. Here someone basically distorts reality and comes up with an alternative, rational explanation for why a particular event or behavior has occurred. For example, if a person were to get fired from their job for coming into work under the influence, they may rationalize that they were unjustly accused or that they were one of the top employees in their department.

Or they may conclude "I really didn't like that job anyway" or "I was really over-qualified for the job" as a means of avoiding the harsh reality that he or she was just fired from their job.

Interestingly, when Vernon Johnson had created the Intervention technique by which people with SUD could be confronted in a loving way, he concluded that there were specific reasons why Interventions could be helpful in getting someone to accept treatment. In the traditional intervention procedure, family members and significant others are encouraged to come up with two or three instances whereby their loved one's alcohol or drug use had caused them worry or concern. Johnson felt this was important because often people with SUD were unable to recall these instances or, if remembered, he or she would recall the event in a distorted way. Vernon Johnson said these, often horrific incidents, were not recalled because of (1) blackouts (similar to amnesia, not to be confused with passing out), (2) repression (see definition of this defense mechanism in Table 2.1) and (3) euphoric recall (i.e. the tendency to recall only the pleasurable parts of the drinking or substance use incident). What Johnson is describing are memory distortions created by ego defense mechanisms. No one likes to recall painful memories, so they are either distorted, suppressed or totally repressed from memory.

Advantages and Limitations of Psychoanalytic Theory and Contemporary Analytic Theories

The advantages of the psychoanalytic theories described in this chapter are clearly found in their truly etiological or causal explanations of substance use disorders. Psychoanalytic theories are very specific and forthright in describing how addictions come about as a direct result of life events like trauma, parental aban-donment, ego deficits, self-medication and insecure attachments or the inability to form securely attached adult relationships. Anna Freud's conceptualizations of defense mechanisms are probably better described as *sustaining* models, in that the defense mechanisms provide cognitive distortions (e.g. rationalizations, denial, reaction formation), that may allow the alcoholic or addicted individual to con-vince themselves that their substance use helps them to deal with life rather than interfering with life functioning. There's a saying in AA which probably best sums this up, "Alcoholism is a disease that tells you, you don't have a disease." It's not uncommon to hear people with SUDs to say things like, "I'd be okay if my wife/husband/partner, boss, friends would just get off my back about my drinking." In essence they are saying, "It's not my drinking or drug use that's the problem, it's my significant others' complaining about my drinking or drug use that's the problem." That is a rationalization.

Psychoanalytic theory is limited as a treatment approach for substance use disorders. If you think of classical psychoanalysis as intensive therapy four or five times a week which occurs over the course of months or years, this is not a prac-tical approach for someone in the throes of a substance use disorder. Generally, addiction counseling is considered more pragmatic, directive and action oriented when it comes to trying to help people take steps towards sobriety and recovery (Washton & Zweben, 2006). Also, one of the primary goals of psychoanalytic therapy is that the client will gain *insight* into their drives, motivations and behavior. For example, analysis of dreams is a central technique used in psychoanalysis. Freud once said that "dreams were the royal road to the unconscious" (Freud, 1905). As stated earlier, however, insight alone does not always translate into behavioral change and when it comes to SUDs, behavioral change is necessary if the person is going to progress beyond their SUD. Imagine a client who shows up intoxicated or stoned for every session? It would not take long for the counselor to conclude that the client is probably not deriving much benefit from counseling without the prerequisite behavioral change of abstinence. We've both counseled clients who have fairly good insight into the origins of their SUD, however they've not been able to translate this insight into lasting behavior change (see Table 2.2).

Yet this doesn't mean that psychoanalytically oriented approaches have no place or value in the counseling process with SUD clients. Keller (2003) provides an excellent illustration whereby interpretation of behaviors can have real value in relapse prevention. For example, Keller describes a client who is in early recovery and is considering attending an annual family reunion fishing trip. Every year, since this family gathering was instituted, an uncle of the client would bring cases

Table 2.2 Advantages and Limitations of Psychoanalytic Theory

Advantages

- Psychoanalytic theories are truly causal etiological theories. For example, the self-medication hypothesis claims that people use alcohol or drugs to help control emotional pain. This theory also emphasizes the role of traumatic experiences, parental abandonment and other types of disrupted attachments in how and why people develop SUDs.
- Psychoanalytic theory was the first to provide counselors with descriptions of the various defense mechanisms which help to explain why people may deny or rationalize the serious harm caused by alcohol or substance use.
- Psychoanalytic theory recommends a variety of treatment strategies that can help to avoid re-traumatizing clients.
- Attachment Theory helps to explain the importance of having emotional connections with others as a way to help support one's sobriety.
- Attachment Theory helps clients to gain insight into how understanding one's past, especially past relationships with important caregivers, can explain present-day relationships and behavior.

Limitations

- Psychoanalytic theory places too much emphasis on the past and not here-and-now problems.
- Some feel psychoanalytic counseling places too much emphasis on developing insight and therefore is not as pragmatic as traditional addiction counseling.
- Psychoanalytic theory claims that developing insight will result in behaviour change, which may not always be the case.
- Not all clients will respond to psychoanalytically oriented therapy or they may not be able to benefit from developing insight.
- Psychoanalytic therapy involves uncovering and exposing past hurts which for some clients may be too stressful or anxiety-provoking and may result in relapse.

of beer and heavy drinking both during and after fishing had become part of this annual family ritual. Hearing the client weigh out whether or not he would attend the fishing trip, his counselor commented that the client's wanting to go on the trip was similar to a "craving." The following week, the client decided that it was best that he not go on the trip. Keller's example provides an effective illustration of how unconscious motivations can often be influential in relapses. Although we will be discussing relapse prevention in greater depth in a subsequent chapter, it's important for counselors to keep in mind that relapses often occur weeks or months before a person actually picks up a drink or drug. This refers to the unconscious processes that often occur outside the conscious awareness of the client. For example, a client who is thinking about contacting an old college friend she used to get high with would be an example of unconscious influences. Or the newly recovering cocaine-addicted person who has not deleted his cocaine dealer's phone number from his or her cell phone, may also be unconsciously setting him or herself up for relapse.

Case Example: Psychoanalytic Theory – Katie

Katie is a 27-year-old mother of three children (ages 2, 4 and 6) who is currently unemployed due to her smoking crystal meth (methamphetamine) several times daily. During the past three years Katie has also been taking OxyContin on a near daily basis. Her children are currently in the custody of her older sister, but Katie's goal is to regain custody of her children once she is clean and sober. Katie has a 14-year history of substance use which began on her 13th birthday (when she started stealing Vicodin from her parent's medicine cabinet and began smoking marijuana). Also significant in Katie's history is that when she was 12 years old her parents had separated and Katie's mother began dating a younger man who would sleep over at their home many nights per week. Katie disclosed that her mother's boyfriend had violently raped her on several occasions when he would sleep at the mother's home. Katie was afraid of telling her mother about the rape incidents out of fear that her mother and boyfriend would blame her or not believe her.

Following the parents' separation and subsequent divorce, Katie's father did not have much contact with her and eventually any visitation stopped altogether when her father moved to Arizona to take a new job. At that point, she would only hear from her father by phone, on her birthday and holidays.

Case Conceptualization

Katie provides an example where trauma occurs prior to the initiation of substance use. Similar to the self-medication hypothesis, substances become a way of avoiding the psychological and emotional pain (and PTSD symptoms) associated with the trauma. It also appears that Katie felt very isolated during the time of the sexual assaults and seemed to have no one she could turn to, especially her parents or her older sister, Janine. Often children who are sexually abused, feel guilty about the abuse or they feel that they will be blamed. However, it is also common that sexual predators will threaten to harm their victims or their families as a means of gaining coercive control over the children they abuse. Katie may be experiencing the trauma of abandonment due to her parents' divorce. Not only did her parents get divorced, but, more significant in understanding the etiology of Katie's SUD, her father had little contact with her after he moved to Arizona.

Learning Opportunity 2.3

After reviewing the different types of defense mechanisms described in Table 2.1, make a list of ways in which someone with a SUD might use these defense mechanisms to convince him or herself, as well as others, that their alcohol or drug use is not a problem.

Case Example: Attachment Theory – David

David is 36 years old and has been abusing alcohol and drinking hand sanitizer for several years. Although most hard alcohol (vodka, gin, whiskey) has about a 40% alcohol content, hand sanitizer contains approximately 90% alcohol. David is a college graduate who majored in Communications. Upon graduating, he went to work as a salesman for a pharmaceutical company. David is currently separated from his wife, Tracy, who had been married previously and has a daughter from her first marriage. When David and Tracy met, he was 18 years old and Tracey was 34 years old. At first, Tracy was hesitant about getting involved with a younger man; they continued to date, however, and fell in love.

In terms of background information relevant to Attachment Theory, when David was 5 years old, his mother left him because of constant fighting with David's father. His mother went back to Florida to live with her parents while David remained with his father and stepmother in Connecticut. David indicated that he and his father did not get along. His father had been in the military and was very strict with David. Also, David was artistic and liked music which his father wasn't interested in therefore David felt alone and isolated. He tried to cope with his despair by eating and by the time he was in high school he was 75 lb overweight. Unfortunately, David's mother died from pancreatic cancer two years after moving to Florida to live with her parents.

Case Conceptualization

From an Attachment Theory perspective, we can see David was probably deeply impacted by his mother's abandoning him when he was 5 years old and then her subsequent death. Even though David was adequately cared for by his father and stepmother, he seemed to yearn for the times when he could be reunited with his mother. He even planned to attend college in Florida so that he could live close to his mother. One could also hypothesize that David's having fallen in love with a much older woman (Tracy) had been his attempt to find a woman who was maternal and nurturing, as a means of filling the void left by his mother's absence.

David's case history also provides a great deal of information that supports the self-medication hypothesis. As a result of his extreme weight gain, David had developed several medical problems including Type 2 diabetes and severe back pain, which required surgery. Following his back surgery, David reports that he was prescribed a variety of opioid painkillers (e.g. OxyContin, Vicodin and Fentanyl) and he was using huge doses of these pills. When his supplies ran out, he turned to pills he would buy on the street; this was also around the time that he began drinking heavily when opioids were unavailable. He later found that hand sanitizer had a high alcohol content and was inexpensive. As a result of his extreme alcohol intake, David has been hospitalized several times for alcohol withdrawal seizures and alcohol overdose.

Learning Opportunity 2.4

Make a list of different types of trauma that may lead to PTSD symptoms. Then look up symptoms of post-traumatic stress disorder and consider how alcohol or other mood-altering substances might help to self-medicate these symptoms.

Learning Opportunity 2.5

Discuss how Katie's traumatic episodes may have influenced her substance use. In addition to the rape incidents, what other factors may have influenced Katie's drug use?

Case Example: Addiction and Trauma Theory – Kim

Kim joined the Army shortly after graduating from high school. Having come from a family with a long and distinguished military background, Kim felt proud of her decision to join the Army as a way to serve her country. After going through rigorous boot camp, Kim trained to become a helicopter pilot. It was her responsibility to make certain that soldiers could be safely dispatched to combat zones. Being the only woman helicopter pilot in her unit posed many challenges as Kim felt that she was under a great deal of stress from having to prove herself a vital and reliable member of her platoon, which she certainly succeeded in doing. Upon graduating from helicopter pilot school, Kim was dispatched to Afghanistan and was immediately assigned to fly some very dangerous combat missions. Kim was constantly afraid that her helicopter would be struck by an RPG (rocket propelled grenade) which could take out her and her entire crew. Kim describes incidents when her helicopter would be flying over Afghan villages and civilians would wave to her. It was always difficult to discern if these civilians were friendly or enemy combatants or whether a flash of light was merely a reflection or an RPG. When Kim returned to the US after serving her first tour, she found it difficult to fall asleep, as she would have intrusive thoughts about being back in combat and nightmares about her helicopter exploding. Although Kim was not interested in drinking when she was in high school, she found that having a few glasses of wine would help to settle her down and allow her to sleep. Kim also describes many other symptoms of PTSD, such as hypervigilance (where loud noises would immediately result in her having a panic attack). Kim also found it difficult to adjust to being back in the US and was constantly worried about the new pilots who replaced her when she returned home and whether they were safe. Kim found day-to-day life back home to be mundane and boring. She tried going back to college but found herself feeling out of place among students younger than her. Kim also felt that they couldn't relate to the horrors of combat she witnessed during the time she was in Afghanistan. Fortunately, Kim did have family support from her parents and her older brother, who also served in the military in Iraq, but Kim felt isolated from her high school friends and she didn't know many other women helicopter pilots who would be able to relate to what she had been through during Operation Enduring Freedom.

Case Conceptualization

Kim is experiencing common symptoms of PTSD (e.g. hypervigilance, nightmares, intrusive thoughts, inability to focus) which she has tried to self-medicate by drinking. By drinking herself to sleep at night she hoped to stop the horrible, repeated nightmares she would experience in which her helicopter was hit by a RPG. This has been a common pattern among many combat veterans and, unfortunately, since drinking interferes with normal REM (rapid eye movement) and deep sleep patterns, it often exacerbates vivid dream states and nightmares.

Psychoanalytic Applications to Addiction Counseling: Assessment, Techniques and Interventions – Clinical Implications for Counselors

Although psychoanalytic theory provides some useful explanations as to how to understand the etiology of substance use disorders, there seem to be few formal applications of psychoanalytic techniques that are used to treat SUDs. Addictions counselors generally tend to focus on "here and now" problems or issues with their clients and assist them in developing effective coping strategies. Therefore, traditional addiction counseling is less likely to focus on the past or childhood events. However, once the client has achieved confidence in their sobriety and is well-stabilized, then it may be helpful to explore these issues from the past, or even past trauma. This depends, however, on whether the client wishes to address these issues.

Assessment Considerations

From a psychoanalytic perspective, it's important for counselors to explore early childhood history as well as any possible traumatic events the client may have experienced throughout their lifetime, including instances of disruption in parent–child relationships (such as abandonment or neglect).Traditionally, a more in-depth assessment would explore other childhood experiences, such as early school/educational events, social/ peer relationships and family dynamics. There are some helpful assessment tools that can be utilized as part of the assessment process that helps counselors to gather background information. For example, the Life Events Inventory – Revised (see Appendix 2.1; see also Van Houten & Golembiewski, 1978); the Adverse Childhood Experiences Scales (ACES) (Centers for Disease Control, 2018) the Life History Calendar (Freedman,Thornton, Camburn Alwin, &Young-DeMarco, 1988) and the Things I've Seen and Heard Interview (Richters & Martinez, 1990) all provide a structured way of helping a client to disclose traumatic and stressful experiences he or she may have experienced during childhood and adolescent years. As mentioned earlier, clients may not readily disclose traumatic or adverse life events, especially in the early stages of treatment, however, the aforementioned assessment tools provide a means of informing clients that it will be important to disclose these issues later in the treatment process once trust in the counselor has been established.

Also, in assessing the possible self-medication hypothesis motivations for using mood-altering substances, it would be helpful to explore ways in which alcohol or other substance use is perceived by the client as helping him or her to cope with everyday stress. There are a few questionnaires that can assist counselors and clients in this exploration. For example, the Brief Symptom Inventory (BSI) (Derogatis, 1993) and the SCL-90-R (Derogatis, 1994) are both effective at providing counselors with an idea of what types of symptoms or problems the client is currently experiencing, and to what degree or level of intensity. In addition, there are a couple of assessment measures which examine ways in which clients cope with these everyday stressors. For example the Ways of Coping Checklist (WOC) (Folkman & Lazarus, 1980) and the Coping Response Inventory (CRI) (Moos, 1997) are both effective in providing information on the client's coping styles.

Learning Opportunity 2.6

Given David's struggles with alcohol, hand sanitizer and prescription opioids, discuss or list ways in his substance use was influenced by disruptions in significant attachments in his life.

In the glossary at the beginning of this chapter we provided a definition for a psychoanalytic technique known as "free association," which we defined as "a psychoanalytic technique in which a client is asked to speak about whatever thoughts, feelings or images come into their mind without censoring."Whenever, a counselor is meeting with a client and asks "Tell me how your week went?" or "Tell me how you reacted when your boyfriend made that comment?" we are essentially asking our clients to free associate or say what they feel are the most important or salient features to talk about.

Counseling Techniques

Given the prevalence of individuals who suffer with both SUDs and PTSD as a result of trauma, counselors really need to be able to address trauma-related issues. Therefore, counselors look to other therapeutic techniques that are useful in treating trauma. Two techniques, that have been found helpful for PTSD are clinical hypnosis (Kluft, 2016; Platoni, 2013; Poon, 2009) and Eye Movement Desensitization Response (EMDR) (Shapiro, 1989a, 1989b, 1995; Harford, 2010) have been used extensively to help individuals contain the impact of their traumatic symptoms. Clinical hypnosis has been employed in the treatment of various types of trauma for quite some time. Unfortunately, both clinical hypnosis and EMDR require extensive specialized training; however, many SUD counselors can be more easily trained in utilizing techniques such as diaphragmatic breathing, guided imagery and progressive muscle relaxation, which can be mastered more quickly. Eye Movement Desensitization Response (EMDR) treatment, has been found to be an effective technique when used to treat traumatized clients. Also, EMDR has no contraindications for those experiencing SUD. Similarly, clinical hypnosis can also be utilized to treat traumatized individuals. EMDR and clinical hypnosis do not entirely rid a person of traumatic recollections but both approaches do allow the client to gain control over these often debilitating symptoms (Harford, 2010).

In addition, there is a therapeutic approach to managing trauma or what SAMHSA (Substance Abuse & Mental Health Services Administration, 2015) refers to as a *trauma-informed approach*. A program, organization or treatment is considered to be "trauma-informed" when it addresses the following (often referred to as the "4 Rs"):

(1) *realizes* the widespread impact of trauma and understands the potential paths for recovery
(2) *recognizes* the signs and symptoms of trauma in clients, families, staff and others involved with the system
(3) *responds* by fully integrating knowledge about trauma into policies, procedures, and practices … *and*
(4) seeks to actively resist *re-traumatization* of the client

It's important to explain what's meant by "actively resisting re-traumatization of the client." Here, counselors need to take their lead from where the client is and not force the client to re-live traumatic memories at times when he or she is not prepared to or willing to do so. An example would be instances where combat veterans were essentially forced to re-experience traumatic combat experiences in order to do extinction training (this is a behavioral technique derived from classical conditioning models, in which a client is asked to "re-live" a traumatic memory either by having them describe the traumatic incident in great detail or watching videos that would simulate the traumatic memory). When the client is not prepared or willing to re-live these traumatic memories it can be re-traumatizing. As counselors, it's important to work collaboratively with our clients to bring about change and not force them to re-live traumatic experiences when he or she feels unprepared to do so (see Boxed Item 2.3).

There are also six key principles to the trauma-informed therapeutic approach.

(1) safety
(2) trustworthiness and transparency
(3) peer support
(4) collaboration and mutuality
(5) empowerment, voice and choice
(6) cultural, historical and gender issues

Safety refers to the notion that trauma-informed counseling always provides a safe atmosphere for the client and his or her family. Counseling sessions become a safe place for the client and/or family to share their fears, concerns, difficulties and any other areas they wish to explore. Trustworthiness and transparency are essential in any counseling relationship. Counselors must be conscientious in explaining the counseling process to clients and to be faithful in keeping commitments. Trust is built upon consistency. There's an old saying, "People we trust are those who say what they do and they do what they say," such that actions and words are consistent. In terms of transparency it's important that counselors let clients know well in advance when they may be taking time off or may be unable to meet with their client. It's also important for counselors to be transparent about their own reactions and feelings and to provide clients with regular feedback. There are many support groups for people who have experienced trauma. Peer support groups are often an essential component of trauma-recovery just as 12-Step and other addiction support groups (e.g. SMART recovery) are essential to SUD recovery. But here's the key thing. In referring someone to a support group it's best when the group is composed of individuals who have experienced similar trauma. For example, it's helpful to have a group made up of combat veterans; though generally it's not helpful to mix Viet Nam veterans with Operation Iraqi Freedom veterans, just as it's not as helpful to mix Operation Desert Storm veterans with Operation Enduring Freedom (Afghanistan) veterans. Similarly, we would not mix sexual assault survivors with incest survivors.

The SAMHSA website (2015) also provides links to trauma-informed care treatment models such as ATRIUM (Addiction & Trauma Recovery & Integration Model), Seeking Safety and TAMAR (Trauma, Addiction and Mental Health Recovery), which are helpful models that provide counselors with ways to address both substance use disorder and trauma.

In addition, "collaboration and mutuality" refer to the need to work collaboratively when addressing trauma-related issues, while "empowerment, voice and choice" addresses the need for trauma survivors to be able to tell their story and to begin to express to trusted others what they have gone through in an effort to gain better understanding and support. Finally, it is important for counselors and others working with trauma survivors to take culture, history and gender issues into account when working with trauma survivors. For example, gender issues are of the utmost importance in the description of Kim's trauma and the responsibility she felt as the only female Marine in her unit and as part of her helicopter crew.

Summary

Psychoanalytic theory has a lot to offer addictions counselors when it comes to gaining an understanding of the etiology of substance use disorders for some clients. This is especially true from the perspective of the more contemporary psychoanalytic models (e.g. the self-medication hypothesis and Attachment Theory), which provide ways in which to conceptualize substance use disorder risk based upon a prior history of trauma or insecure attachments to others. While psychoanalytically oriented therapists such as Keller (2003) find that unconscious processes often play a role in relapse, generally, psychoanalytic-oriented therapy, which helps clients gain insight into their motivations and behavior, may not be as useful to clients in the early stages of recovery. Anna Freud's contributions in describing defense mechanisms are as relevant today as they were back in 1936 in describing ways in which people with substance use disorders may avoid the harsh realities of the pain caused by substance abuse by means of rationalization, repression and denial. Given the high incidence of trauma within the population of people with SUDs it's imperative for counselors to be aware of ways to provide trauma-informed care to their clients.

Boxed Item 2.3 Avoiding Re-traumatization

As described in this section, it's important that we avoid re-traumatizing clients by allowing them to work at their own pace. This is true especially when working with combat veterans, who often have been taught through their military training to focus on the mission and to make sure that everyone in the platoon or group comes back alive. Veterans are often hesitant or fearful to talk with non-combat veterans about their experiences overseas, so it's important to establish trust and a working therapeutic alliance. Veterans will share traumatic experiences when they're ready and when they feel they can trust you. An example of this was with a veteran who served in the US Army during the worst fighting in the Viet Nam War. One day, after several weeks of having this veteran in counseling for alcohol and prescription opioid use disorders, he called and asked if I was near a fax machine. I said and I was, and gave him the fax number. He proceeded to fax me a 20-page handwritten account of an incident which occurred during his time in Viet Nam in which a fellow soldier had stepped on a landmine within a few yards of where he was standing. He recounted the sound of the mine exploding, the soldier's cry, the smoke, the blood, the smell of the smoke as well as his own feelings of horror, and survivor guilt, all in great detail. We met the next day to talk about the traumatic experience but what was most important was that by faxing this information first, it was his way of wanting to make sure I was not going to judge him.

Appendix 2.1

Adolescent Life Events Inventory – Revised (Van Houten & Golembiewski, 1978)
(Revision Cavaiola, 1985)

Instructions

On the following pages are a list of events which may have happened to you.

Circle the "Yes" after the event if it ever happened to you, then in the last column write in how old you were at the time that event occurred.

If the event did NOT happen to you, circle the "No" and move on to the next item.

Examples:

	Answer		*Your age at the time*
I changed schools	**Yes**	No	8
My brother or sister was hospitalized	**Yes**	No	15
My father was hospitalized	Yes	**No**	
I was taken to court	Yes	**No**	

Start here	*Answer*		*Your age at the time*
I got poor grades in school	Yes	No	
I got into trouble for cutting classes	Yes	No	
My father was laid off	Yes	No	
My father was fired from his job	Yes	No	
My mother was fired from her job	Yes	No	
My parents asked me to leave home	Yes	No	
My parents seemed worried about money	Yes	No	
I got into trouble with a teacher or principal	Yes	No	
I got into trouble for fighting in school	Yes	No	
My father said he didn't want me	Yes	No	
My mother died	Yes	No	
My father died	Yes	No	
My brother or sister died	Yes	No	
One of my grandparents died	Yes	No	
Another relative died	Yes	No	
I moved to another house	Yes	No	
I was accused of something I didn't do	Yes	No	
My mother was sick or hurt	Yes	No	
My father was sick or hurt	Yes	No	
My brother or sister was sick or hurt	Yes	No	
A good friend of mine was sick or hurt	Yes	No	

Adolescent Life Events Inventory (cont'd)

	Answer		*Your age at the time*
I was hospitalized	Yes	No	
My mother was hospitalized	Yes	No	
My father was hospitalized	Yes	No	

	Answer		Your age at the time
My brother or sister was hospitalized	Yes	No	_____
My friend found out my mother was an alcoholic	Yes	No	_____
My friend found out my father was an alcoholic	Yes	No	_____
My friend found out my brother or sister was an alcoholic	Yes	No	_____
I was picked up by the police	Yes	No	_____
I had to appear in court	Yes	No	_____
I realized my mother was an alcoholic or addict	Yes	No	_____
I realized my father was an alcoholic or addict	Yes	No	_____
I realized my brother or sister was an alcoholic or addict	Yes	No	_____
I was put on Probation	Yes	No	_____
A relative asked me to leave his/her home	Yes	No	_____
I was sick or hurt	Yes	No	_____
I got someone pregnant or I got pregnant	Yes	No	_____
I got a sexually transmitted infection	Yes	No	_____
My boyfriend or girlfriend broke up with me	Yes	No	_____
I lost a good friend	Yes	No	_____
I was robbed	Yes	No	_____
I was beaten up	Yes	No	_____
My mother said she did not want me	Yes	No	_____
My father was put in a mental hospital	Yes	No	_____
My mother was put in a mental hospital	Yes	No	_____
I was put in a mental hospital	Yes	No	_____
I was raped	Yes	No	_____
I was put in jail, a detention center	Yes	No	_____
My parents got divorced	Yes	No	_____
I had to choose which parent to live with	Yes	No	_____
My brother or sister ran away from home	Yes	No	_____
My brother or sister had trouble with my parents	Yes	No	_____
I got into trouble for doing drugs at school	Yes	No	_____
My parents were fighting more than usual	Yes	No	_____
My parents threatened to leave one another	Yes	No	_____
My parents separated	Yes	No	_____
A member of my family was treated for drug or alcohol abuse	Yes	No	_____
I was evaluated by the Child Study Team at school	Yes	No	_____
I was classified or diagnosed with a Learning Disorder	Yes	No	_____

Adolescent Life Events Inventory (cont'd)

	Answer		Your age at the time
I was sent to see a psychiatrist, psychologist	Yes	No	_____
I was forced to participate in sexual activity with a relative or member of my family	Yes	No	_____
I was forced to participate in sexual activity for which I later felt guilty	Yes	No	_____

	Answer		Your age at the time
A member of my family or relative committed suicide	Yes	No	_____
I was depressed	Yes	No	_____
I felt suicidal	Yes	No	_____
I attempted suicide	Yes	No	_____
I avoided groups of people because of feeling different from others	Yes	No	_____
I was made fun of by my peers	Yes	No	_____
I was bullied	Yes	No	_____

Recommended Reading and Resources

Freud, A. (1936). *The ego and mechanisms of defense*. New York: International Universities Press, 1966.

Flores, P.J. (2004). *Addiction as an attachment disorder*. New York: Jason Aronson.

Gill, R. (2014). *Addiction from an attachment perspective: Do broken bonds and early trauma lead to addictive behaviors?* London: Karnac Books.

Khantzian, E.J. (2014). The self-medication hypothesis and Attachment Theory: Pathways to understanding and ameliorating addictive suffering. In. R. Gill (Ed.). *Addiction from an attachment perspective: Do broken bonds and early trauma lead to addictive behaviors?* London: Karnac Books.

Kluft, R.P. (2016). The wounded self in trauma treatment. *American Journal of Clinical Hypnosis, 59(1),* 69–87.

Washton, A.M., & Zweben, J.E. (2006). *Treating alcohol and drug problems in psychotherapy practice: Doing what works.* New York: Guilford.

Resources

William Alanson White Institute: A world-renowned psychoanalytic institute based in New York City which provides information, education and training, as well as clinical services. www.wawhite.org/

New York Psychoanalytic Society & Institute: Provides information, education and training. Website contains a lot of useful information. https://nypsi.org/training-programs/

What is psychoanalytic theory? by Dr. Todd Grande (YouTube video): www.youtube.com/watch?v=XZQA6JVNZAo

Jordan Peterson explains psychoanalytic theory (YouTube video): Video provides an explanation of psychoanalytic theory and neo-Freudian theories. www.youtube.com/watch?v=PC8FNfMIIhg

What is psychoanalysis? Toronto Psychoanalytic Society (YouTube video): www.youtube.com/watch?v=UwMsBrNCT64

References

Asberg, K., & Renk, K. (2013). Comparing incarcerated and college student women with histories of childhood sexual abuse: The roles of abuse severity, support, and substance use. *Psychological Trauma: Theory, Research, Practice and Policy, 5(2),* 167–175.

Brady, K.T. (2001). Comorbid posttraumatic stress disorder and substance use disorders. *Psychiatric Annals, 31(5)*, 313–319.

Briere, J., & Elliot, D.M. (2003). Prevalence and psychological sequalae of self-reported child-hood physical and sexual abuse in a general population sample of men and women. *Child Abuse & Neglect, 27,* 1205–1222. doi:10.1016/j.chiabu.2003.09.008

Bernardt, M.W., & Murray, R.M. (1986). Psychiatric disorder, drinking and alcoholism: What are the links? *British Journal of Psychiatry, 148,* 393–400.

Broyles, L.M, Binswanger, I.A., Jenkins, J.A., Finnell, D.S., Faseru, B., Cavaiola, A., Pugatch, M. et al. (2014). Confronting inadvertent stigma and pejorative language in addiction scholarship: A recognition and response. *Substance Abuse, 35(3),* 217–221.

Cavaiola, A.A. (1985). Life stress, personality correlates and the effect of treatment on adolescent chemical dependency. *Dissertation Abstracts International.*

Cavaiola, A.A., & Schiff, M. (1988). Behavioral sequelae of physical and/or sexual abuse in adolescents. *Child Abuse & Neglect, 12,* 181–188.

Cavaiola, A.A., Fulmer, B.A., & Stout, D. (2015). The impact of social support and attachment style on quality of life and readiness to change in a sample of individuals receiving medication-assisted treatment for opioid dependence. *Substance Abuse, 36,* 183–191.

Centers for Disease Control (2018). Adverse childhood experiences and related research. Retrieved from www.cdc.gov/violenceprevention/acestudy/ace_brfss.html

Cunningham, T. (1986). *King Baby.* Center City, MN: Hazelden Publications.

Derogatis, L.R. (1993). *Brief Symptom Inventory: Administration, scoring and procedures manual.* Bloomington, MN: Psych Corp/Pearson Assessments.

Derogatis, L.R. (1994). *The Symptom Checklist – 90-Revised (SCL-90-R) manual.* Bloomington, MN: Psych Corp/Pearson Assessments.

Dunner, D.L., Hensel, B.M., & Fieve, R.R. (1979). Bipolar illness: Factors in drinking behavior. *American Journal of Psychiatry, 136,* 583–585.

Céline, F.L. (1938). *Death on the installment plan.* New York: Little, Brown & Co.

Flores, P.J. (2004). *Addiction as an attachment disorder.* New York: Jason Aronson.

Folkman, S., & Lazarus, R.S. (1980). An analysis of coping in a middle-aged community sample. *Journal of Health & Social Behavior, 21(3),* 219–239.

Fowler, J.C., Groat, M., & Ulanday, M. (2013). Attachment style and treatment completion among psychiatric inpatients with substance use disorders. *American Journal on Addictions, 22(1),* 14–17.

Freedman, D., Thornton, A., Camburn, D., Alwin, D., & Young-DeMarco, I. (1988). The Life History Calendar: A technique for collecting retrospective data. *Sociological Methodology, 18,* 37–68.

Freud, A. (1936). *The ego and mechanisms of defense.* New York: International Universities Press, 1966.

Freud, S. (1974 [1884]). *Cocaine papers.* Edited by R. Byck. New York: Stonehill Publishers.

Freud, S. (1905). *The interpretation of dreams.* (Translated by G. Strachey, 1955). New York: Basic Books.

Hall, C.S., & Lindzey, G. (1970). *Theories of personality* (2nd edn). New York: Wiley & Sons.

Harford, P.M. (2010). The integrative use of EMDR and clinical hypnosis in the treatment of adults abused as children. *Journal of EMDR Practice and Research, 4(2),* 60–75.

Jones, E. (1953). *Sigmund Freud: Life and work. Vol. 1: The young Freud 1856–1900.* London: Hogarth Press.

Jones, E. (1955). *Sigmund Freud: Life and work. Vol. 2: The years of maturity 1901–1919.* London: Hogarth Press.

Jones, E. (1957). *Sigmund Freud: Life and work. Vol. 3: The last phase 1919–1939*. London: Hogarth Press.

Keller, D. (2003). Exploration in the service of relapse prevention: A psychoanalytic contribution to substance abuse treatment. In F. Rotgers, J. Morgenstern, & S.T. Walters (Eds). *Treating substance abuse: Theory and technique* (pp. 82–111). New York: Guilford.

Kessler, R.C. (2004). Impact of substance abuse on the diagnosis, course, and treatment of mood disorders: The epidemiology of dual disorders. *Biological Psychiatry, 56(10)*, 730–732.

Khantzian, E.J. (1980). The alcoholic patient: An overview and perspective. *American Journal of Psychotherapy, 34(1)*, 4–19.

Khantzian, E.J. (1985). The self-medication hypothesis of addictive disorders: Focus on heroin and cocaine addiction. *American Journal of Psychiatry, 142(11)*, 1259–1264.

Khantzian, E.J. (2014). The self-medication hypothesis and Attachment Theory: Pathways to understanding and ameliorating addictive suffering. In. R. Gill (Ed.). *Addiction from an attachment perspective: Do broken bonds and early trauma lead to addictive behaviors?* London: Karnac Books.

Kluft, R.P. (2016). The wounded self in trauma treatment. *American Journal of Clinical Hypnosis, 59(1)*, 69–87.

Kohut, H. (1977). *The restoration of the self*. Chicago, IL: University of Chicago Press.

Lee, S., Lyvers, M., & Edwards, M.S. (2008). Childhood sexual abuse and substance abuse in relation to depression and coping. *Journal of Substance Use, 13(5)*, 346–360.

Mayfield, D.G., & Coleman, L.L. (1968). Alcohol use and affective disorders. *Diseases of the Nervous System, 29*, 467–474.

Menninger, K. (1938). *Man against himself*. New York: Free Press.

Moos, R.H. (1997). Coping Response Inventory: A measure of approach and avoidance coping skills. In C.P. Zalaquett & R.J. Wood (Ed.). *Evaluating stress: A book of resources*. Lanham, MD: Scarecrow Education. pp 474–492.

Morgenstern, J., & Leeds, J. (1993). Contemporary psychoanalytic theories of substance abuse: A disorder in search of a paradigm. *Psychotherapy: Theory, Research, Practice, Training, 30(2)*, 194–206.

Platoni, K.T. (2013). Hypnotherapy in the wartime theater: OIF, OEF, and beyond. In R.M. Scurfield & K.T. Platoni (Eds). *Healing wartime trauma: A handbook of creative approaches* (pp. 159–171). New York: Routledge/Taylor & Francis.

Poon, M.W. (2009). Hypnosis for complex trauma survivors: Four case studies. *American Journal of Clinical Hypnosis, 51(3)*, 263–271.

Richters, J.E., & Martinez, P. (1990). *Things I've Seen and Heard: An interview for young children about exposure to violence*. Rockville, MD: Child & Adolescent Disorders Research Branch, Division of Clinical Research, National Institute of Mental Health.

Shapiro, F. (1989a). Efficacy of the eye movement desensitization procedure in the treatment of traumatic memories. *Journal of Traumatic Stress, 2*, 199–223.

Shapiro, F. (1989b). Eye movement desensitization: A new treatment for post-traumatic stress disorder. *Journal of Behavior Therapy & Experimental Psychiatry, 20*, 211–217.

Shapiro, F. (1995). *Eye movement desensitization and reprocessing (EMDR): Basic principles, protocols, and procedures*. New York: Guilford Press.

Spatz-Widom, C., Marmorstein, N.R., & Raskin-White, H. (2006). Childhood victimization and illicit drug use in middle adulthood. *Psychology of Addictive Behaviors, 20(4)*, 394–403.

Substance Abuse & Mental Health Services Administration (2015, August 14). Trauma-Informed Care. Retrieved from www.samhsa.gov/nctic/trauma-interventions

Tonmyr, L., & Shields, M. (2017). Childhood sexual abuse and substance abuse: A gender paradox. *Child Abuse & Neglect, 63,* 284–294.

Van Houten, T., & Golembiewski, G. (1978). *Adolescent life stress as a predictor of alcohol abuse and/or runaway behavior.* Washington, DC: National Youth Alternatives Project.

Washton, A.M., & Zweben, J.E. (2006). *Treating alcohol and drug problems in psychotherapy practice: Doing what works.* New York: Guilford.

Weiss, R.D., Kolodziej, M., Griffin, M.L., Najavits, L.M., Jacobson, L.M., & Greenfield, S.F. (2004). Substance use and perceived symptom improvement among patients with bipolar disorder and substance dependence. *Journal of Affective Disorders, 79,* 279–283.

Wilsnack, S.C., Vogeltanz, N.D., Klassen, A.D., & Harris, T.R. (1997). Childhood sexual abuse and women's substance abuse: National survey findings. *Journal of Studies on Alcohol and Drugs, 58(3),* 264–271.

Wurmser, L. (1978). *The hidden dimension.* New York: Jason Aronson.

Wursmer, L. (1985). Denial and split identity: Timely issues in the psychoanalytic psycho-therapy of compulsive drug users. *Journal of Substance Abuse Treatment, 2,* 89–96.

3 Behavioral and Learning Theory Model

Margaret Smith

Introduction

According to behavioral theory, substance use disorders are maladaptive behaviors that are *learned*. Think about how someone might "learn" an addiction. Do you learn from using a drug and associating it with a positive experience? Do you learn from being rewarded (a positive feeling) so you are likely to do it again? Do you learn from watching someone else drink or use and you copy him/her?

In counseling someone with an addiction, then, identifying the learning process can help in unlearning it or learning new behaviors. For example, does a person need to disassociate from the initial good experience with the drug? For prevention, should we decrease the visibility of drug use so that we don't watch and learn drug use from others? How can we look at how someone thinks in terms of his/her drug use and change self-defeating thoughts and behaviors that lead to use?

The first part of this chapter will focus on learning concepts of classical and operant conditioning. Later in this chapter we will discuss observational learning (also known as social learning) and the cognitive approach. Near the end of the chapter, we will talk about how to incorporate these conditioning, learning and cognitive concepts into your work as a substance use disorder counselor.

Learning Opportunity 3.1

Before reading this chapter either divide into groups of three or four, or participate in an online discussion, about people's reasons for using alcohol or other drugs. Your instructor will go over this list with you, identifying some terms you will become familiar with from reading this chapter.

Overview of Behavioral Theory

Unlike psychoanalytic theory, which examines unconscious motivations for substance use, behavioral theory focuses on the observable and/or measurable. There are no terms for such personality structures as the "id," "ego" and "superego," instead behavior theory utilizes concepts such as "positive reinforcement," "punishment" and "classical" and "operant conditioning." In this theory, maladaptive behaviors, such as addiction, can be learned through classical conditioning, operant conditioning, observational and cognitive learning.

Key Terms

discrimination: involves the ability to distinguish between one stimulus and similar stimuli.

environmental cue: is an aspect of an experience that triggers a reactive response (Steg, Van Den Berg, & De Groot, 2012).

generalization: is the probability that a response to one stimulus will be generalized to another if the conditions of the first stimulus are similar to the second one (Miltenberger, 2012).

neutral stimulus: is a stimulus which initially produces no specific response other than focusing attention. In classical conditioning, when used together with an unconditioned stimulus, the neutral stimulus becomes a conditioned stimulus.

positive reinforcement: following a behavior, there is a reinforcing stimulus or a reward which makes it more likely that the behavior will occur again in the future. When a favorable outcome, event, or reward occurs after an action, that particular response or behavior will be strengthened.

negative reinforcement: following a behavior, there is the removal of an aversive stimulus which makes it more likely that the behavior will occur again in the future. When a favorable outcome, event, or reward occurs after an action, that behavior will be strengthened.

punishment: refers to any change that occurs after a behavior that reduces the likelihood that that behavior will occur again in the future.

reinforcer: increases the likelihood that a specific behavior or response will occur.

unconditioned stimulus: is one that unconditionally, naturally, and automatically triggers a response.

unconditioned response: is an unlearned response that occurs naturally in reaction to the unconditioned stimulus.

Classical Conditioning

Understood as Pavlovian conditioning (Lamb, Schindler, & Pinkston, 2016) or respondent conditioning (Thombs & Osborn, 2013), classical conditioning is learning that occurs when two stimuli are repeatedly paired and a response that is at first elicited by one stimulus is eventually elicited by the second stimulus alone (CSAT, 1999). This type of learning was recognized by a Russian physiologist, Pavlov, who studied dogs and salivation. In his studies, Pavlov first presented food (unconditioned stimulus) to his dogs. At the presentation of the food the dogs would salivate (unconditioned response). During the learning process, Pavlov would then present the food with the sound of a tone (neutral stimulus). Then Pavlov would ring the tone (conditioned stimulus), *without* the presentation and food, and the dogs would salivate (conditioned response). The dogs have learned to *associate* the tone with the food.

Let's try this with drug use and addiction. A person uses alcohol for the first time (unconditioned stimulus) and feels euphoria or positive feelings (this is known as an unconditioned response). The person starts drinking at the local bar in town (neutral stimulus). Eventually, planning or going to the bar, alone (conditioned stimulus), will lead to euphoric or happy feelings (conditioned response). The bar itself, along with the aroma of alcohol, dimmed lighting, loud music or even the sound of ice cubes swirling around in a glass, becomes *associated* with alcohol and they produce the feelings of happiness.

Learning Opportunity 3.2

Use the following terms pertaining to classical conditioning and apply them to cocaine use. For example, use the terms unconditioned stimulus, unconditioned response, neutral stimulus, conditioned stimulus, conditioned response.

This process might help us understand, in particular, relapse. For example, we all may know someone who became sober (stopped all use of alcohol). But let's say this person's favorite place to drink was the local bar in town. This person would probably experience this environmental "cue" (the bar) with the original stimulus (alcohol) and the subsequent feelings of happiness. The bar, in and of itself, may lead someone to crave, then drink (again) when in the presence of the "cue." This process is why you may hear some people in recovery stating that "If you keep on going to the barber, eventually you will get a haircut" (i.e. if you continue going to a bar, you will eventually drink).

Operant Conditioning

Recognized by Thorndike and Skinner, operant conditioning is more voluntary in that it is not in response to an environmental cue or other specific stimulus. It is a behavior that is followed by a reinforcer, which increases the probability of its occurrence again. There is positive reinforcement, which involves an increase in the probability of a behavior recurring when a behavior is followed by a reinforcer (CSAT, 1999). In the case of drug use and addiction, the person smokes a marijuana and feels high, therefore the smoking behavior is followed by a reinforcer (i.e. the feeling of euphoria or being high). The person is likely to do this again due to the positive reinforcement he or she feels after smoking cannabis.

Negative reinforcement, often confused with punishment, is the removal of aversive stimulus (negative) to increase the likelihood that the behavior will happen again. With drug use and addiction, this would be the person who drinks alcohol to remove the tremors and agitation associated with withdrawal. Due to removal of something negative (e.g. no more withdrawal symptoms), the person is likely to do this behavior (e.g. drink) again. Another example of negative reinforcement is someone who is prescribed Vicodin after having a tooth pulled. Taking this opioid analgesic is meant to remove the aversive feeling of pain and therefore reinforces taking the medication to alleviate pain. The key thing to remember is that *both* positive and negative reinforcement increase a particular behavior.

Punishment, on the other hand, refers to any change that occurs after a behavior that reduces the likelihood that that behavior will occur again in the future (Miltenberger, 2012). An example in relation to drug use and addiction might be a person who drives drunk (behavior) and gets a Driving Under the Influence (DUI) charge (punishment) and no longer drives drunk (decrease in behavior). Basically, punishment is meant to suppress, reduce or terminate particular behaviors.

It's common for people to confuse negative reinforcement with punishment. However, here's the key thing to remember in order to make the distinction: negative reinforcement results in an increase in the behavior while punishment is meant to decrease or suppress the behavior. For example, if a person smokes cannabis because he or she feels cannabis helps them to be more creative, then that person is saying that they find pot reinforcing because it increases creative thinking or behavior. Whereas, if a person who has been using heroin for the past five years says they are shooting up in order to avoid going into withdrawal, they are describing negative reinforcement: because he or she is using heroin, not for the high, but to avoid withdrawal (the removal of an aversive stimulus is negative reinforcement).

Learning Opportunity 3.3

In groups of three or four or in an online discussion, try using methamphetamine as an example, applying such terms as "positive reinforcement," "negative reinforcement" and "punishment."

Generalization and Discrimination Learning

Two other terms that apply to here are "generalization" and "discrimination." Generalization is the probability that a response to one stimulus will be generalized to another if the conditions of the first stimulus are similar to the second one (Miltenberger, 2012). For example, a person uses cocaine. She decides to become "clean" and stops her use. Then one day when she is making coffee she runs out of sugar. She pours sugar into the sugar bowl and misses some of the bowl. The sugar makes a little mound near the sugar bowl. It is similar to the look of cocaine when she has used it. This mound produces cravings because of its similarity. This woman has generalized the cocaine to the sugar (because of how it looks).

An example of "discrimination" is if this woman had some experience in treatment or recovery, she may learn to discriminate between the two substances. In this case she would recognize the differences (discriminate) between the cocaine and the sugar.

Learning Opportunity 3.4

Provide an example of generalization and discrimination in relation to marijuana use.

Observational Learning

While Pavlov and Skinner focused on observable behavior, Albert Bandura believed that learning could occur beyond classical and operant conditioning and involve observational learning (Engler, 2014). Sometimes referred to as modeling, observational learning is observing (watching) another and imitating that behavior. While the subject doesn't receive direct reinforcement, it can learn "vicarious reinforcement" through observing.

Bandura's work on observational learning is based on modeling experiments and the famous Bobo doll experiment. A Bobo doll is a large inflated plastic clownlike doll that is about 4 feet tall. In the experiment, some young pre-school children watched adults aggressively playing with the doll, seeing them kick it, punch it and yell at it. Another set of children did not see these adults aggressively playing with the Bobo doll. Later, when the two groups of students were each introduced to the Bobo doll, the group that watched the adults play aggressively with the doll were twice as aggressive as the group that did not watch adults play aggressively with the doll (Engler, 2014).

This observational learning might explain why some children and adolescents start using alcohol or other drugs. They may observe parents, older siblings, or TV/music stars using these substances. In their observation of these substance using behaviors, they copy them.

The key thing about observational learning is that we're likely to imitate role models whom we perceive as being attractive or powerful. This might explain why street gang members will imitate the drug use or violent behaviors of older gang members or gang leaders whom they perceive as being powerful.

Learning Opportunity 3.5

Divide into groups of three or four, or participate in an online discussion, about how you may have observed others using alcohol and other drugs and how that influenced your own behavior.

Cognitive Approach

The cognitive approach explains addiction in terms of how it occurs through internal processing of information (thinking). It involves thoughts in terms of how they influence emotions and behaviors, and, in turn, how behavior and emotions influence thoughts. Addiction, then, would be the result of faulty thinking processes (CSAT, 1999). For example one might say, "I think I need cocaine to have fun, so therefore I use cocaine." Research indicates that expectancies, for example, of positive effects of alcohol or another drug, contributes to use, relapse, and poorer substance use disorder outcomes (CSAT, 1999, p. 74).

You may hear people in addictions refer to "stinkin' thinkin'," which is an example of cognitive processes. I think negatively, therefore I feel or act negatively. Consequently, I need to change my "stinkin' thinkin'" so that I have better behaviors.

Aaron Beck, who founded one of the schools of cognitive theory, examined how thoughts influence emotions and behavior. In order to change negative emotions and behaviors, a person would need to change my thinking (cognitions). Aaron Beck and later, David Burns, recognized "cognitive errors" or "distortions" which people make that impact their behaviors (see Table 3.1). Identifying these cognitive errors helps in changing them.

Learning Opportunity 3.6

Fill in these boxes with at least two negative thoughts you had had over the past two weeks. Then look at the cognitive distortion list and identify what types of cognitive distortions the negative thoughts are and, finally, give a rebuttal to the negative thought.

Negative thought	Cognitive distortion (state the cognition distortion associated with the negative thought)	Rebuttal to the negative thought

---

Extinction and Counterconditioning

As we stated at the beginning of the chapter, learning addiction means to "fix it," then we need to unlearn it. The terminology used to refer to unlearning, with regard to classical conditioning, is "extinction and counterconditioning" (CSAT, 1999). Extinction occurs when a behavior either diminishes or disappears. For classical conditioning, extinction happens when the conditioned stimulus appears repeatedly without the unconditioned stimulus. In classical conditioning, for example, the person (or animal) is re-exposed to the conditioned cue in the absence of the unconditioned stimulus. As the person or animal learns that the cue no longer predicts the coming of the unconditioned stimulus, conditioned responding gradually decreases, or extinguishes. In the example of Pavlov's dogs, who were classically conditioned to salivate to the sound of the bell, if the bell were to be rung over and over again but it is no longer being paired with the meat, then extinction would occur and the dog would eventually stop salivating. This process is also referred to as "cue extinction."

In operant conditioning, behaviors can also be "extinguished." Extinction occurs when positive reinforcement is withheld. Such would be the case when a rat is rewarded with a food pellet on an intermittent basis for bar-pressing. However, once the bar-pressing is no longer rewarded with a food pellet, eventually the rat stops bar-pressing. It's important to remember that after a response has been extinguished, it can be quickly re-established through a process known as spontaneous recovery. Spontaneous recovery refers to the sudden reappearance of a previously extinct response. We see this among substance use disorder (SUD) clients who take a drink or use a drug after weeks, months or years of abstinence and relapse back to active use, often at the rate they left off at, at the height of their drinking or drug use.

Counterconditioning is used to change behavior by making those behaviors associated with positive outcomes less "attractive" by associating them with negative consequences (CSAT, 1999).

For operant conditioning, a counselor could use contingency management and coping skills training to help "extinguish" the learned behaviors from positive and negative reinforcement. We will discuss these treatment approaches in more depth.

Opponent Process Theory

Opponent process theory can best be conceptualized as a behavioral theory, in that, it focuses primarily on observable behavior and self-reported affective responses. However, when it was initially introduced in the 1970s by psychologist Richard Solomon, it was put forth as a theory that would describe "acquired motivations" (Solomon, 1980; Solomon & Corbit, 1974). Acquired motives include such things as love and social attachments, food and taste cravings, thrill-seeking behaviors (e.g. bungee jumping, parachute jumping), as well as the motivated behaviors such as achievement and power. What Solomon found was that many of these acquired motives operated according to the same empirical principles as addictions. What he discovered, however, was that there were two unique and opposite processes that describe how addictive behaviors come about. The "a-process" is aroused by a stimulus which can be either pleasurable or aversive. An opponent loop or "b-process" occurs, which is directly opposite to the "a-process," therefore if the "a-process" after drinking alcohol is a pleasurable "buzz," then the "b-process" might include the discomfort of experiencing a hangover. It's important to take into account what happens with these two processes over time. Generally, the opponent process created by substance use becomes stronger over time and is only weakened by abstinence or disuse. Solomon (1980) claims "in every case of acquired motivation *affective or hedonic* processes are involved," referring to either emotional (affective) or pleasurable (hedonic) experiences that are derived from the behavior or substance use. He then goes on to state, "in every case I have found, describe or measure [there are] three affective or hedonic phenomena ... a) affective or hedonic *contrast* (between a-process and b-process), b) affective or hedonic *habituation* (tolerance) and c) affective or hedonic *withdrawal* (abstinence) *syndromes*" (1980, p. 692).

Therefore, just as one experiences a high or euphoria upon first taking a substance, that is then contrasted with the after-effect or withdrawal, and these emotional responses change over time as a result of habituation. As we know with opiate use disorders, over time the b-process or withdrawal becomes stronger such that continued opiate use is primarily to alleviate withdrawal symptoms such as cramping, aches and pains, nausea, diarrhea, etc.

There appear to be neurological changes as well, which may help to explain how and why opponent processes occur. For example, when one ingests a substance that causes an activation of dopamine in the mesolimbic center of the brain, which then projects onto the nucleus accumbens and amygdala, creating a feeling of positive reinforcement (a-process). The b-process then involves the down-regulation or shutting down of the mesolimbic dopamine system (Koob et al., 1997). The flood of dopamine in the mesolimbic system accounts for the subjective feeling of reward and hence is considered positively reinforcing. Keep in mind that this flood of dopamine can be activated by nearly all the drugs of abuse but also by particular foods, pleasurable sexual encounters, gambling and other process addictions.

Applications to Addiction Counseling

As stated in the outset of this chapter, one can learn addiction through classical and operant conditioning. The observational approach indicates how modeling can lead to maladaptive behavior. The cognitive approach shows how thinking influences behaviors and emotions. Once one learns "addiction," one must unlearn it (extinction). So how does all this information translate into clinical practice?

In working with clients, it can be helpful for the counselor to know about classical and operant conditioning so that you can teach the client about the conditions and responses that reinforce their behavior. While you might not go into depth with the terminology with a client, you can teach them about the conditions and contexts that help them maintain their drug-taking behaviors (e.g. reinforcers, conditions and contexts). For example, a client tends to gamble when he is with his friends at a casino. The two conditions, with his friends and at a casino, trigger his gambling. To extinguish this learning, he must not associate friends and casino with gambling. Therefore, he may want to remove himself from the context of casinos and stay away from friends with whom he gambles.

With operant conditioning, a counselor can work with a client on finding new reinforcers (e.g. exercise over stimulants) to change what is rewarding to him/her. One prominent approach is to use contingency management to work with clients (CSAT, 1999). Contingency management involves rewarding clients for

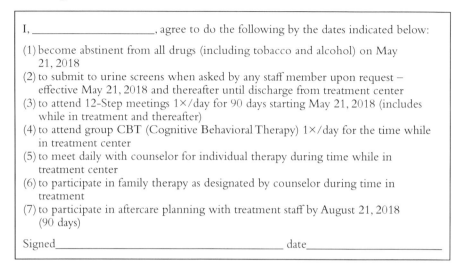

I, _____, agree to do the following by the dates indicated below:

(1) become abstinent from all drugs (including tobacco and alcohol) on May 21, 2018
(2) to submit to urine screens when asked by any staff member upon request – effective May 21, 2018 and thereafter until discharge from treatment center
(3) to attend 12-Step meetings 1×/day for 90 days starting May 21, 2018 (includes while in treatment and thereafter)
(4) to attend group CBT (Cognitive Behavioral Therapy) 1×/day for the time while in treatment center
(5) to meet daily with counselor for individual therapy during time while in treatment center
(6) to participate in family therapy as designated by counselor during time in treatment
(7) to participate in aftercare planning with treatment staff by August 21, 2018 (90 days)

Signed_____ date_____

Figure 3.1 Behavioral Contract Example

positive behaviors, such as abstinence (NIDA, 2012, p. 45). This involves targeting a behavior, analyzing the environmental cues that control the behavior, modifying the environmental events, and measuring the behavior change (Thombs & Osborn, 2013).

Similar to contingency management are behavioral contracts. A behavioral contract could include the targeted behavior to change, the rewards or reinforcements for incremental changes, and dates (see Figure 3.1). Behavioral contracts are often used with criminal justice clients (NIDA, 2014).

In the 1990s, there was research that used voucher-based treatment for cocaine dependence. Clients who were abstinent from cocaine earned vouchers which they could use for retail (with the counselor's approval) (Thombs & Osborn, 2013). The results indicated that those who participated showed better program retention than those who did not participate in such a program. With better retention there are better outcomes (Thombs & Osborn, 2013).

Another approach based on operant conditioning is the community reinforcement approach (CRA) (CSAT, 1999). CRA weakens "the influence of the reinforcement received by substance abuse and its related activities by increasing the availability and frequency of reinforcement derived from alternative activities, particularly those vocational, family, social and recreational activities that are incompatible with substance abuse" (Higgens et al., 1998 in CSAT, 1999, pp. 57–8). The combination of community reinforcement and vouchers has been shown to be effective (NIDA, 2018).

With observational learning a counselor may suggest that a client attend at 12 Step or other group meeting to "observe" and learn from those who are in recovery from gambling or stimulant abuse. Another form of observational learning in this context, is the role of a sponsor. The client can learn from observing his/her sponsor.

Table 3.1 Cognitive Distortions

(1)	filtering – taking negative details and magnifying them, while filtering out all positive aspects of a situation
(2)	polarized thinking – thinking of things as black or white, good or bad, perfect or failures, with no middle ground
(3)	overgeneralization – jumping to a general conclusion based on a single incident or piece of evidence; expecting something bad to happen over and over again if one bad thing occurs
(4)	mind reading – thinking that you know, without any external proof, what people are feeling and why they act the way they do; believing yourself able to discern how people are feeling about you
(5)	catastrophizing – expecting disaster; hearing about a problem and then automatically considering the possible negative consequences (e.g. "What if tragedy strikes?" "What if it happens to me?")
(6)	personalization – thinking that everything people do or say is some kind of reaction to you; comparing yourself to others, trying to determine who's smarter or better looking
(7)	vontrol fallacies – feeling externally controlled as helpless or a victim of fate or feeling internally controlled, responsible for the pain and happiness of everyone around
(8)	fallacy of fairness – feeling resentful because you think you know what is fair, even though other people do not agree
(9)	blaming – holding other people responsible for your pain or blaming yourself for every problem
(10)	"shoulds" – having a list of ironclad rules about how you and other people "should" act; becoming angry at people who break the rules and feeling guilty if you violate the rules
(11)	emotional reasoning – believing that what you feel must be true, automatically (e.g. if you feel stupid and boring, then you must be stupid and boring)
(12)	fallacy of change – expecting that other people will change to suit you if you pressure them enough; having to change people because your hopes for happiness seem to depend on them
(13)	global labeling – generalizing one or two qualities into a negative global judgment
(14)	being right – proving that your opinions and actions are correct on a continual basis; thinking that being wrong is unthinkable; going to any lengths to prove that you are correct (Beck, 1976 as cited in CSAT, 1999, p. 630)

With the cognitive approach, a counselor may help the client identify cognitive distortions and help the client change them to healthier thoughts. The counselor can develop a worksheet that has a column for "My thought" (e.g. "If I don't drink I will never have fun"), "the cognitive distortion" (e.g. overgeneralization) and the "healthier response" (e.g. "When I didn't drink I did have fun, I just have to find fun things to do again").

One of the more effective counseling approaches for addiction is cognitive behavioral therapy (CBT) (McHugh, Hearon, & Otto, 2010). Using principles of cognitive and behavioral approaches, CBT focuses on distorted cognitions and maladaptive behaviors. In this type of therapy, a counselor would help the client identify irrational, distorted thoughts or beliefs that lead to unhealthy behaviors. Additionally, with the cognitive distortion list (Table 3.1), the therapist and client can identify what type of distortion the client experiences and find healthier thoughts to replace such distortions. This in turn, impacts behavior. I think better, therefore, I behave better. The Substance Abuse and Mental Health Services Administration (SAMHSA) offers a resource for counselors that describes CBT among other brief therapies in the TIP (Treatment Improvement Protocol) 34: *Brief interventions and brief therapies for substance abuse* (CSAT, 1999).

Another approach is RET (Rational Emotive Therapy). "RET concentrates on people's current beliefs and attitudes and self statements contributing [to] or 'causing' and maintaining their emotional and behavioral disturbances" (Ellis, McInerney, DiGiuseppe, & Yeager, 1988, pp. 1–2). Ellis and colleagues would say that we do experience negative life events but these are not what leads to negativity in our lives. It is how we think about the event that leads to negativity. In order to help clients, RET therapists help them identify the ABCs. That is, the counselor helps the client identify the *Activating* (or adverse) event, the irrational *Belief*, and the *Consequences*. In identifying the activating event, the counselor and the client examine the situation which led to the irrational belief. The irrational belief tends to be rigid or extreme; inconsistent with reality; illogical or nonsensical; and lead to negative consequences (Dryden & Neenan, 2004). In addiction, the activating event could be preparing for an exam or test. The irrational belief might be "I can't cope with this stress. I have to have a cigarette to relax." The consequence could be smoking a cigarette. A counselor and client would then substitute the irrational belief with a rational one, such as "Yes, this is stressful but I have done well on exams before. I can do some deep breathing exercises," which would lead to a healthier response to the activating event.

Another approach used to help with alcohol and other drug problems in relation to negative thinking and maladaptive behaviors is SMART recovery. SMART recovery is an alternative (or an addition to) 12-Step programs. It is a program that teaches people how to change self-defeating thinking, emotions and actions, and to work towards long-term satisfactions and quality of life (SMART Recovery, 2018). It incorporates principles of RET and CBT through self-help meetings and materials.

Another area that uses behavioral and cognitive terms is relapse prevention. Many times counselors will help a client identify what behavioral (going to the park) and cognitive (thinking I must smoke to keep my friends) experiences that "trigger" his/her craving to use. Once these are identified, the counselor and client would identify healthier behavioral activities and cognitive strategies to deal with triggers and cravings.

Strengths and Limitations of Learning Theory

The learning theory and cognitive approach are useful theories with addictions and substance use disorders. We can understand how the use of a drug might be initiated through observational learning and classical conditioning. Then the use is maintained through positive and negative reinforcement. The cognitive approach explains how our thinking about alcohol and other drugs impacts our substance use and addictive behaviors. Further, research has shown the effectiveness of CBT with people who are struggling with addictions (CSAT, 1999; McHugh et al., 2010).

The weakness of the theory is based in a statement by my co-author (Dr. C). It might explain why some people use alcohol and other drugs and become addicted, but it doesn't explain why some people use and do not become addicted. However, behaviorists might challenge this line of thinking, stating that the drug wasn't reinforcing enough to sustain behaviors associated with substance use disorder or addiction.

In this chapter, there was a discussion of such terms as "classical" and "operant" conditioning, and "observational learning." Further, we learned about the cognitive approach. The last area we covered is how to apply these terms to counseling people with substance use disorders.

Case Study

Jenny is 21 years old. She has an opiate use disorder (heroin). She has overdosed twice.

In terms of her past, Jenny reports a happy childhood. She was pregnant at 16 and decided to give the child away as she thought it would be best if someone older and more stable (employed, etc.) were able to take care of the child. She says she felt empty and sad when this happened. She started thinking, then, that she was a bad person.

Jenny started snorting heroin at age 17. The heroin took away "everything" and she found her "best friend/worst enemy" at the same time. She does not work. She asks for and gets money from her family, who feel bad that she had an addiction. To support her habit, she started stealing. She was arrested once for stealing.

Case Conceptualization

Jenny starts doing heroin at 17 and removes "everything" negative. This is negative reinforcement. As she uses the drug it removes an aversive stimulus (negative emotional feelings and thoughts related giving her child away etc.) and therefore, increases the likelihood that she will do it again.

The family positively reinforces Jenny's behavior of asking for money (which she later uses for drugs). Jenny asks for money, the family gives her the money (reinforcer), which increases the likelihood that Jenny will ask for money again.

Jenny's arrest for stealing and then being asked to leave her family's home weren't strong enough punishments. Punishments are immediate consequences that make it less likely that a person (Jenny) will repeat a behavior in a similar situation in the future.

Best treatment may be CBT or RET so it focuses on her thoughts ("I'm a bad person"), feelings (feeling empty) and her drug-taking behavior (use of drugs). The counselor may work with Jenny on her cognitive distortions. Additionally, Jenny may complete a contingency management contract regarding her use of heroin.

Recommended Reading and Resources

Bandura, A., Ross, D., & Ross, S.A. (1961). Transmission of aggression through imitation of aggressive models. *Journal of Abnormal and Social Psychology, 63*, 575–582.

Bandura and the Bobo Doll study. Retrieved from www.youtube.com/watch?v=dmBqwWlJg8U

CSAT (Center for Substance Abuse Treatment. (1999). *Brief interventions and brief therapies for substance abuse.* Treatment Improvement Protocol Series No. 34. Rockville, MD: Substance Abuse and Mental Health Services Administration.

Higgens, S.T., & Petry, N.M. (1999). Contingency management: Incentives for sobriety. *Alcohol, Research and Health, 23(2),* 122–127.

References

CSAT (Center for Substance Abuse Treatment). (1999). *Brief interventions and brief therapies for substance abuse.* Treatment Improvement Protocol Series No. 34. Rockville, MD: Substance Abuse and Mental Health Services Administration.

Dryden, W., & Neenan, M. (2004). *The rational emotive behavioral approach to therapeutic change.* Thousand Oaks, CA: Sage.

Ellis, A., McInerney, J.F., DiGiuseppe, R., & Yeager, R.J. (1988). *Rational-emotive therapy with alcoholics and substance abusers.* Needham Heights, MA: Allyn and Bacon.

Engler, B. (2014). *Personality theories: An introduction* (9th edn). Belmont, CA: Wadsworth/Cengage Learning.

Koob, G.F., Caine, S.B., Parsons, L., Markou, A., & Weiss, F. (1997). Opponent process model and psychostimulant addiction. *Pharmacology, Biochemistry and Behavior, 57(3),* 513–521.

Lamb, R.J., Schindler, C.W., & Pinkston, J.W. (2016). Conditioned stimuli's role in relapse: Preclinical research on Pavlovian instrumental transfer. *Psychopharmocology, 233,* 1933–1944.

McHugh, R.K., Hearon, B.A., & Otto, M.W. (2010). Cognitive-behavioral therapy for substance use disorders. *Psychiatric Clinics of North America, 33(3),* 511–525.

Miltenberger, R.G. (2012). *Behavior modification: Principles and procedures* (5th edn). Belmont, CA: Wadsworth.

NIDA (National Institute of Drug Abuse). (2012). *Principles of drug addiction treatment: A research-based guide.* Washington, DC: Author.

NIDA (National Institute of Drug Abuse). (2014). *Principles of drug addiction treatment for criminal justice populations: A research-based guide.* Washington, DC: Author.

NIDA (National Institute of Drug Abuse). (2018). *Community reinforcement approach plus vouchers (alcohol, cocaine, opioids).* Retrieved from www.drugabuse.gov/publications/principles-drug-addiction-treatment-research-based-guide-third-edition/evidence-based-approaches-to-drug-addiction-treatment/behavioral-1

SMART Recovery. (2018). *Smart Recovery: Self management and recovery training.* Retrieved from www.smartrecovery.org/

Solomon, R.L. (1980). The opponent process theory of acquired motivation: The costs of pleasure and the benefits of pain. *American Psychologist, 35,* 691–712.

Solomon, R.L., & Corbit, J.D. (1974). An opponent process theory of motivation: 1. Temporal dynamics of affect. *Psychological Review, 81,* 119–145.

Steg, L., Van Den Berg, A. E., & De Groot, J. I. M. (Eds). (2012). *Environmental Psychology: An Introduction.* Hoboken, NJ: Wiley-Blackwell.

Thombs, D.L., & Osborn, C.J. (2013). *Introduction to addictive behaviors* (4th edn). New York: Guilford Press.

4 Family Systems Theory

Alan A. Cavaiola

Introduction

It's often said that substance use disorders do not occur in a vacuum and that for every one individual impacted by addiction, there are on average six others who are also affected. In this chapter we will be exploring the impact of substance use disorders on families and significant others (e.g. spouses, partners, couples, friends.) Although it may be common for a person impacted by alcohol or drugs to claim that a stressful job, a difficult boss or a nagging loved one "drove them to drink (or use drugs)," this is usually not the case. Therefore, the various family models we will be discussing fall under the heading of *sustaining models*, in that family members – often unintentionally – engage in behaviors that enable, sustain or reinforce their loved one's addiction. This may sound counterintuitive because most family members and significant others often want nothing more than to have their loved one to embark on recovery by becoming clean and sober. In this chapter we will be discussing some of the reasons why families often engage in behaviors that unintentionally may "support or reinforce" their loved one's drinking or drug use.

Families that are impacted by substance use disorders (SUDs) tend to share many similarities in terms of how their suffering and dysfunction plays out on a day-to-day basis. It's also important to point out that, when discussing families impacted by SUDs, we're not only referring to families where a parent or grandparent manifests an alcohol or drug problem but also families where an adolescent or adult son or daughter is experiencing an SUD as well as instances where one or both partners in a couple's relationship are experiencing alcohol and/or drug issues. Therefore, there are many situations where individuals are impacted by SUDs and so are his or her significant others.

To begin the exploration of families impacted by SUDs, it's important to examine what healthy families look like because we can then begin to understand how alcohol or substance abuse erode the very qualities or characteristics that allow families to function in a healthy way. As the famous author, Tolstoy remarked in *Anna Karenina*, "all happy families are alike, each unhappy family is unhappy in its own way." So, let's examine some of the traits that characterize healthy families:

(1) healthy family members trust one another
(2) healthy family members are able to communication with one another in a clear and direct manner and are able to express loving feelings towards one another
(3) healthy families value and validate each other's feelings
(4) healthy family are invested in the emotional growth of each individual family member member
(5) healthy family members value interdependence (i.e. they can count on one another)
(6) healthy families value independence and autonomy
(7) healthy families have appropriate rules and boundaries
(8) healthy families are invested in teaching younger family members
(9) healthy families value and enjoy leisure time together
(10) healthy families celebrate holidays, anniversaries, birthdays via special rituals
(11) healthy families value connection with extended family members (e.g. grandparents, aunts, uncles, cousins, etc.)

(adapted from Walsh, 1993)

Learning Opportunity 4.1

As you review the list of healthy family traits we just listed, are there any other traits that should be included? Also, what are some of the healthy traits in your family as you were growing up? Please list both and then discuss in small group or in your chat room.

As mentioned, all of the qualities that allow families to function in healthy ways can be affected and eroded when a family member is impacted by a SUD. For example, in healthy families, communication is often clear and direct whereas in families impacted by SUDs, communication suffers and becomes vague, confusing or convoluted. Take the following scenario as an example:

> Chris is 21 years old and is living at home with his parents after flunking out of college. He comes home very late every night after partying with his friends and one night he is confronted by his parents, who say to him, "You took $50. from my wallet before you went out." Chris responds, "No I didn't. I'm tired of your accusing me every time you lose something or something goes wrong. This is messed up." To which his father replies, "If we find any money missing again, we're throwing you out." Chris replies, "You said that last time money was missing, besides if you didn't nag me all the time, I wouldn't go out every night drinking with my friends."

This is an example of the type of conflictual communication that occurs in the families where SUDs are present. Nothing gets resolved or talked out and no real resolution to problems is ever reached. In the example above, Chris is obviously experiencing substance use problems but no real plan for addressing these problems is ever discussed or agreed upon. Also think about the frustration that Chris's parents are experiencing and how angry and frustrated Chris may feel, presuming that he may not have stolen the money. However, even when parents have an active alcohol or drug abuser living in their home, it's not usual that they lock the door to their bedroom and lock away any money, car keys, medications and any prized possessions. Their life becomes a far cry from the healthy family traits mentioned earlier. When examining the dynamics occurring in Chris's family we see very much the opposite of "healthy family traits." For example, in healthy families, family members trust one another, yet in Chris's family we see an erosion of trust between him and his parents. We also see dysfunctional communication patterns, as Chris's parents claim that they nag him because he is out drinking every night while Chris states that he goes out drinking all the time, in order to avoid his parents' nagging. This is what's known as a *negative feedback loop*.

Healthy families also have appropriate rules and boundaries. Yet, if Chris did take money out of his mother's purse, this is clearly a boundary violation. Also, when Chris's father threatens to throw him out of the house if money is missing again, it's totally opposite to healthy family trait #6, "Healthy families value independence and autonomy." In healthy families, sons or daughters begin their autonomy by going off to college, joining the military or finding a job that affords them enough money pay for rent and other expenses. Not surprisingly, research indicates that healthy family functioning represents a protective factor against sons and daughters developing alcohol problems (Leonard & Homish, 2008.)

With regard to communication patterns in families impacted by SUDs, it's often said that there are three "unwritten rules" of living in a home impacted by alcohol or drug addiction: "Don't trust, don't talk and don't feel." These are often the rules whereby sons or daughters living in homes with a parent or parents impacted by substance use disorders learn not to trust anyone with family secrets surrounding Mom or Dad's alcohol or drug problem, and not to talk about anything that goes on at home, behind closed doors. In order to survive in such a dysfunctional system, sons or daughters also learn to suppress or stuff away their feelings, which usually tend to be invalidated or dismissed if expressed. It wouldn't be unusual for a son or daughter who is crying because of being upset about their parent's being intoxicated to hear, "Stop crying or I'll give you something to cry about!"

It's important to point out that families experiencing SUDs vary in the intensity and level of dysfunction they experience. For example, research into alcoholic families concludes that those families who experience less interference with important family rituals (e.g. family dinnertime, family vacations, Christmas holiday rituals) tended to have children who were better adjusted and less likely to become alcoholics as adults (Steinglass, 1981; Steinglass, Bennett, Wolin, & Reiss, 1987). Wolin, Bennett, Noonan and Teitelbaum (1980) also found there were three types of ritual patterns in alcoholic families: (1) *intact rituals* where important family rituals were maintained in spite of alcoholism; (2) *subsumptive rituals*, which existed in families that made adjustments or modifications in order to accommodate the drinking; and (3) *disrupted family rituals*, which were found in those families who were most impacted by their loved one's drinking. Families that managed to maintain *intact rituals* or *subsumptive rituals* tended to have better-adjusted children and there was less likelihood of sons and daughters developing SUDs later in life.

Brown and Lewis (1999) found the following characteristics among families impacted by alcohol use disorders: (1) families experience distinct developmental stages as they progress from active drinking to recovery; (2) the environment or context of the drinking family is often traumatic and very harmful to children and adults; (3) the family system of the drinking family is often restrictive, rigid and closed; and (4) in recovery, the unhealthy family system must collapse (i.e. the defensive structures that maintain the pathology of the entire family must change. In other words, once the alcoholic family member enters recovery, the entire family must also change and this may be accomplished by abandoning dysfunctional family roles (e.g. enabling behaviors). (5) With the collapse of the unhealthy family system, adults then turn their attention to their own individual recovery (which often takes years); (6) children may be just as neglected or abandoned in early recovery as they were during active drinking, especially as parents turn their attention away from the family and onto themselves; (7) families who embark on recovery are on a "dynamic process of difficult change which sometimes takes as a long as 10 years before all the pieces come together: a stable, healthy environment; a secure healthy family system and couple relationship …" (adapted from Brown & Lewis, 1999, pp. 17–24.)

It is important to take into consideration that families impacted by SUDs also experience progression, which runs parallel to the progression that the alcoholic or addict undergoes. According to Jackson (1954), families first experience *denial of the problem.* In this stage, families attempt to deny that their loved one has a drinking or substance use problem. They may blame external stressors (e.g. job stress, financial stress) for their loved one's drinking or drug use. This stage often coincides with the SUD family member's denial that his or her drinking or drug use is problematic. In the second stage, *attempts to eliminate the problem*, the non-alcoholic spouse or partner begins to isolate from friends and extended family members. Here the goal is try to maintain the illusion of having "a happy home" to the outside world. In the third stage, *disorganization*, the non-alcoholic spouse tries cope with the ever-increasing tension in the home. This stage often finds frequent arguments, which may result in violence between spouses and partners. This would also be the stage where behavior problems in the children may begin. In the fourth stage, *attempts to reorganize in spite of the problem*, the non-alcoholic spouse or partner tries to hold everything together by making sure the rent or mortgage is paid, bills are paid and basic needs are met (e.g. food, shelter, clothing). Usually in this stage the alcoholic spouse/partner is ignored based on resentful feelings that he or she can't be trusted or counted on. In the fifth stage, *efforts to escape*, decisions whether to divorce or separate are central to determining whether the marriage and family will continue to sustain the life they have been experiencing. This stage usually corresponds to the person with the alcohol use disorder, "hitting bottom," at which point he or she may seek treatment. If this occurs, this leads to the sixth stage, *recovery and reorganization of the whole family*, as the entire family hopefully will engage in the treatment process (the alcoholic attends treatment and AA, while the non-alcoholic spouse and children also attend counseling and Al-Anon and Alateen.) Even when the alcoholic spouse or partner enters treatment and begins recovery, not all families will engage in their own treatment. The seventh stage occurs if the alcoholic spouse does not "hit bottom" and either separation and divorce is sought. This stage is referred to as *reorganization of part of the family*, referring to the fact that the non-alcoholic spouse and children usually begin to reorganize as a single-parent family.

As mentioned earlier, Brown and Lewis's (1999) research into families impacted by alcohol use disorders also found evidence of progressive family stages which they define as: *drinking stage, transition stage, early recovery* and *ongoing recovery*. During the active *drinking stage*, the family is basically in survival mode, as "daily family life becomes dominated by the anxieties, tensions and chronic trauma of active alcoholism" (Brown & Lewis, 1999, p. 14.) Basically, the family is trying its best to cope and to hold things together. As the consequences of drinking become more visible to others and more difficult to resolve (e.g. DUI arrest, medical illness, physical abuse), there is a growing need for secrecy and isolation from others which, unfortunately cuts the family off from outside sources of help or input from extended family, friends and the community. As the family moves towards the *transition stage*, there is a great deal of tension and apprehension as family members move into the "unknowns" of recovery and what will happen next. Brown and Lewis (1999) suggest that the parents need to get a foothold on each of their individual recoveries first before being able to work on their relationship as a couple. Two scenarios are common as couples move into *transition*. The first is where the couple is in crisis (perhaps due to an arrest, disclosure of an extramarital affair, job loss, etc.) and often anger and hostility permeates the couple's bond with one another. The second scenario is where the couple has a workable, bonded relationship that had included active alcoholism, therefore this couple is not in crisis as one or both partners move towards recovery. As the alcoholic partner moves towards abstinence, the couple may feel a loss of closeness. In *early recovery* the family also faces many challenges as they experience many "firsts" without alcohol (e.g. first holidays, anniversaries, birthdays, etc.). Couples will begin to find healthier ways to differentiate (separate from one another) as they let go of enabling or controlling dysfunctional roles. Intimacy within the couple's relationship needs to be redefined. Parenting roles and responsibilities also need to be redefined and sometimes this is a difficult transition as the non-alcoholic parent had often assumed major responsibility for parenting responsibilities and may resent the now sober parent interfering with parenting. Finally, in *ongoing recovery*, families begin to experience a sense that thing have slowed down and calmed down. But this does not happen with the passage of time alone. There are distinctions made between being "dry" versus "sober." An alcoholic who is "dry" has stopped drinking but they have not really embraced recovery, nor have they embraced the need for change. For example, a recovering alcoholic who has been working the 12 Steps of AA, has probably looked within by making a "fearless moral inventory" of themselves (4th Step) and has probably made some attempts at "making amends" to their family for their inappropriate or destructive

Table 4.1 Sample Treatment Regimen for Families and Significant Others

Sessions 1–3
- family members introduce themselves and discuss their goals
- psychoeducation: understanding why substance use disorders are considered chronic diseases
- identifying enabling/controlling behaviors
- identifying ways to support recovery
- introduction to family support groups:
  Al-Anon (www.al-anon.alateen.org)
  Nar-Anon (www.naranon.com)
  Families Anonymous (www.familiesanonymous.org)

Sessions 4–6
- identifying feelings and attitudes regarding your loved one's substance use
- developing alternate responses to your loved one's behavior
- creating an environment at home that supports recovery (e.g. socializing without substances)
- identify co-dependent behaviors and how to develop new ways to communicate
- characteristics of healthy families and how to create a healthy family environment
- role play: new ways to communicate

Sessions 7–10
- keeping expectations realistic
- becoming aware of "dry drunk" behaviors/attitudes and how to respond effectively
- creating a healthy balanced lifestyle and the importance of self-care

behavior during active addiction (8th Step). A person who is "dry" never gets close to looking within or making amends to those they may have hurt. Families in ongoing recovery will still experience problems; however, the recovering family now has a framework by which to discuss and resolve problems in such a way that every family member can be heard and respected. This would also be the point at which the family can seek treatment.

Families in ongoing recovery can embrace the healthy family traits that we presented at the beginning of this chapter. Table 4.1 provides a sample agenda for families participating in family treatment programs.

Key Terms

alliances: these are unspoken agreements between family members to support one another especially during times of family conflict. Alliances can be supportive and healthy or dysfunctional, e.g. "I'll protect your drinking if you protect mine."

boundaries: boundaries are usually physical as well as psychological barriers that exist both within families and with the outside world. Each individual family member may have their own physical boundary or physical space or comfort level.

collusion: similar to alliances, collusion implies that two family members are colluding or allying together against other family members.

enabling: when family members inadvertently support their loved one's drinking or drug use by providing him or her with money or by providing excuses to others for their behavior. For example, a husband might enable his wife's drinking by calling her boss to say she's sick when in fact she's hungover from drinking the night before.

emotional cutoffs: when a family member refuses to communicate with or have contact with another family member or someone outside the family.

family roles: it's common for family members in homes impacted by SUDs to take on certain roles. Spouses or partners may take on the role of the enabler or the placater. While children may take on the role of the hero or scapegoat

family of origin: the family that an individual grows up in.

identified patient (IP): when families seek treatment there's usually a person who becomes the symptom-bearer within the family. This may or may not be the individual who is experiencing a SUD, but may be a family member who is experiencing behavioral or emotional adjustment problems.

negative feedback loop: circular communication that often represents a no-win type of situation. For example, a spouse telling their wife, "I drink because you yell at me." While the wife may respond with "If you didn't drink so much, I wouldn't yell at you."

triangulation: when an unstable dyad (like a husband and wife or life partners) as a result of experiencing conflict or instability in their relationship, draw in a third party (like a son or daughter or other family member) who then becomes the target of their conflict.

Family Models Relevant to Substance Use Disorders

Just as there are theoretical models and counseling techniques pertaining to individuals (e.g. psychoanalytic, behavioral, gestalt, cognitive behavioral), there are models which are specific to working with couples and families. In this section, we will be presenting those family theoretical models which are most relevant to treating individuals with SUDs.

Family Systems Model

The Family Systems Model was originally developed by well-known theorists such as Jay Haley and Murray Bowen. According to Bowen (1978), families are essentially social systems that are bound by a precise and predictable set of rules or dynamic which function throughout the entire family often for up to three generations (Bradshaw, 1995). What is essential to this model when applied to substance use disorders is that any disturbance to part of the family (or system) will impact all family members. Therefore, whenever there's a problem, the entire family reacts in an attempt to try to maintain balance or *homeostasis*. What's interesting about the concept of homeostasis is that these attempts by the family to maintain balance can either be around healthy goals or they can reflect dysfunction within the family system. Here are two examples of family homeostasis:

Scenario 1: Susan is a 17-year-old high school senior who currently lives with her parents, Bob and Jane and her younger 15-year-old brother, Tom. Susan has been the star player on her school's lacrosse team and has been scouted by several prestigious universities, all of whom have offered her scholarships. In order to help pay for Susan's extra coaching and strength training. Susan's father, Bob has been working extra hours at the glass products factory and Jane has also been taking time off from work, to drive Susan to practices and the extra coaching sessions. Tom doesn't mind the extra attention that Susan is receiving, as he knows she will be going off to college soon and that she's worked hard to obtain scholarships, given that her family could probably not afford to send her away to college. Tom is musically talented and plays trumpet in the high school band and especially likes playing in the school's jazz band.

Scenario 2: In the last scheduled game of her high school lacrosse season, Susan suffers a major injury which requires that she have extensive knee surgery. Both Susan and her parents are worried that this will jeopardize her lacrosse scholarships. Susan is anxious that she needs to get back to practicing and strength training in order to be ready to play once she selects a university and reports for practice in August. Susan's doctor prescribes an opiate-based analgesic (painkiller) in order to help her with the pain following her surgery. Susan goes through the prescription quickly and asks her doctor for a refill which he reluctantly prescribes. Within a month, Susan is dependent on the painkiller in order to walk. Her parents are worried that Susan is pushing herself too hard and taking too many pills. Susan's grades began to slip but she rationalizes that most universities don't really look at last semester grades. Within a few months, Susan's doctor refuses to prescribe more painkillers and recommends more physical therapy sessions. Susan becomes frustrated and impatient. Her boyfriend offers to buy some "Roxies" from a kid in school, however the pills are expensive. Her father has been giving Susan money, thinking that she's using it to buy things she'll need for college; however, he just found out that the factory where he works is closing in a couple of months. Susan's mother is frantic and overwhelmed with stress. She develops high blood pressure and suffers a mild stroke. Because Susan's "Roxies" cost so much, Susan's boyfriend suggests she switch to snorting (intranasal) heroin which is much less expensive.

In the two scenarios described above we see a family trying to maintain homeostasis. In the first scenario, Susan's family is doing everything to support her goals of attending a Division 1 university on a lacrosse scholarship. This is an example of a healthy homeostasis in which the entire family is supportive of one another and therefore, supportive of Susan's goals to obtain an athletic scholarship. Also, in this first scenario, Susan's family embodies many of the healthy family traits described earlier in this chapter. However, in the second scenario Susan suffers an untimely injury, turns to opiate painkillers and her life begins to unravel as her opioid use disorder progresses. As with most families impacted by SUDs her parents are at a loss as to how to help their daughter. Her father enables her by giving her money, under the assumption she is using it to buy things for her dorm room. Instead, Susan uses the money to buy "Roxies" (Roxicette or "blues," which is a prescription opiate popular on many college campuses) and later heroin. Compounding the financial woes of the family are worries that Bob's factory will be shutting down soon. There's a saying, "When the factory moves out, heroin moves in," which describes what has been taking place in many towns across America and has been chronicled in recent books such as *Dreamland* by Sam Quinones (2016) and *Glass house* by Brian Alexander (2017). Susan's mother, Jane has developed a stress-related stroke and her younger brother Tom, quits the high school band to join a punk rock band. Tom is later arrested for stealing an expensive microphone from a local music store. From a Family Systems perspective, Tom's acting out (i.e. his arrest) would be an example of his unconscious attempt to take the focus off of his sister's progressive drug use (which is causing his parents a lot of stress) by diverting the focus to him. In doing so, Tom has adopted the role of the family "scapegoat" which we will describe later in this chapter.

One of the basic principles of the Family Systems Model (and a healthy family trait) that Bowen proposes is the concept of differentiation and separation. Healthy families value independence and autonomy and we see this in the first scenario, where Susan's parents are doing everything possible to prepare to successfully "launch" her off to college. In ideal circumstances sons and daughters are encouraged to "leave the nest" as part of their overall development into emerging adulthood. However, think about how SUDs impact on the differentiation process.

Learning Opportunity 4.2 – Differentiation

See what you can find out about the concept of differentiation. Given what you know about Susan's family from the second scenario, what do think will happen to both Susan and Tom? Will they experience a healthy separation from their family? What would you predict? Discuss with your small group or in your chat room.

The Family Systems Model can also be applied to couples. We see this both in active addiction as well as in recovery. During active addiction, as difficult as that may be for a couple, there is also a homeostasis that develops, whereby the non-addicted spouse or partner may become the enabler or caretaker to their addicted loved one. Those homeostatic patterns may exist over the course of many years. Now consider what happens when the addicted partner becomes clean and sober. During active addiction, homeostasis suggests that there will be a certain predictability to how problems are managed. However, recovery becomes an unknown and with it comes a great deal of anxiety and apprehension for both partners. For the non-addicted spouse or partner, they may fear their partner may no longer need him or her, or may fear they may meet someone in AA or NA and fall in love with that person. It's not unusual for the non-addicted partner to resent their loved one's going to AA or NA meetings, "First I lost you to alcohol or drugs and now I've lost you to AA/NA!" is a common frustration expressed by non-addicted partners. In response to these fears, apprehensions and frustrations, a wife of an alcoholic who was newly sober and attempting to do a "90 in 90" (i.e. attending 90 meetings in 90 days), had purchased a monogrammed whiskey flask for her husband for a Christmas present. Although to an outside observer this seems insane, the purchase of the whiskey flask was actually an attempt to return to the dysfunctional homeostasis that existed prior to the husband getting sober and attending AA.

It's important to consider that there are many instances where both partners are actively using alcohol or drugs. This was the focus of the HBO documentary *Dope Sick Love* which chronicles three couples impacted by SUDs. What becomes obvious is that it's often impossible for couples to recover together. As one partner makes attempts to recover, the other partner often becomes frightened or threatened by this change and they will pull their partner back into using again. Again this is an example of how powerful dysfunctional homeostasis can be.

The Family Systems Model was initially developed as a generalist theory, meant to describe all families, it wasn't until the 1970s that this model began to influence the drug and alcohol treatment field. Steinglass was one of the first researchers to notice repetitious, patterned family interactions among his clients, which led him to conclude that substance use disorders had a stabilizing or adaptive function within these families which helped maintain equilibrium (or homeostasis) and also helped solidify family roles and the ways in which these families interacted (e.g. expression of emotions, conflicts, etc.) (see Steinglass, Davis, & Berenstein, 1977; Steinglass, 1981; Steinglass et al., 1987). He also found that in instances where a parent was actively using alcohol, that these families tended to be more rigid both in terms of family roles and interactions.

Family Disease Model

The Family Disease Model grew out of Al-Anon, the 12-Step program which began in the 1950s to assist families and friends of individuals suffering from alcohol use disorders. According to folklore, when Alcoholics Anonymous was in its early beginnings, Lois Wilson, the wife of Bill Wilson (one of the co-founders of AA along with Dr. Bob), would meet with the wives and girlfriends of the men attending the AA meeting (which at the time were being held in Bill and Lois's home.) The essence of the Family Disease Model is that alcoholism not only impacts the alcoholic but everyone in his or her immediate social circle (i.e. family and friends.) These family members and friends often fall into roles of co-dependency which is viewed as a "recognizable pattern of personality traits, predictably found within most members of chemically dependent families" (Cermak, 1986, p. 1). Co-dependency traits often include: (a) low self-esteem or self-esteem that's based on controlling the alcoholic loved one; (b) feeling responsible for meeting the needs of other's before oneself; (c) experiencing anxiety and boundary issues around intimacy and separation; (d) being enmeshed in relationships with the alcoholic loved one; (e) having other symptoms such as denial, depression, anxiety or hypervigilance (Cermak, 1986). The Family Disease Model also hypothesizes that families adopt several different types of co-dependency roles as coping strategies. These roles are often seen as survival roles in the dysfunctional alcoholic family. For examples, spouse or partner roles include the enabler, the controller, the placater, the waiverer, the martyr. The enabler attempts to hold the family together by making excuses when their loved one is unable to make it into work or unable to pay bills. Some parents even supply their addicted sons or daughters with drugs in order to avoid them needing to purchase drugs from dangerous drug dealers. The controller tries to regulate their loved one's substance use by controlling his or her access to money or transportation to go out to purchase drugs or alcohol. The placater attempts to reduce tension in the home by acquiescing to their loved one's every demand. The placater will do anything to keep the peace within the home. The waiverer, on the other hand, will threaten their loved one with dire consequences (e.g. kicking him or her out of the house), if he or she drinks or uses drugs "one more time," only to acquiesce or cave once the next substance use episode occurs. The waiverer talks a good game but usually doesn't hold to their threats. The martyr uses guilt trips in order to get their loved one into stopping their alcohol or drug use. He or she will usually complain incessantly to others how their life has been ruined by their addicted loved one, but rarely, if ever, do anything about it. What's common in any of the aforementioned spousal or partner roles, is that although the behaviors are meant to somehow try to change their loved one, these strategies usually don't work, which then just adds to their already-existing stress levels. Co-dependents often are plagued by many stress-related illnesses (Whitfield, 1989).

The child roles are also considered to be survival roles or attempts to cope in a dysfunctional family system that has been ravaged by alcoholism and/or drug addiction.

For example, the family hero will try to detract from parental conflicts or tension by calling attention to their latest accolade or award. Family heroes are often the oldest child within the family and as adults it's common for them to assume leadership roles or other positions of responsibility or to go into helping professions (e.g. medicine, social services, counseling, etc.) The family scapegoat is basically the "screw up" of the family. His or her knack for getting into trouble at the most inopportune moments also becomes a way of diverting attention from battling parents. If Mom and Dad are fighting at the dinner table, it's the scapegoat who will knock their milk over in an effort to draw attention away from the argument. The family clown-mascot role is characterized by attempts to diffuse parental conflicts by joking or comic stunts to draw attention away from whatever tension the family may be experiencing at the moment. The lost child is the quiet child, who withdraws from family conflict, hides in their room and otherwise keeps a low profile. These children tend to internalize family tensions and conflicts. Although these alcoholic family roles are often attributed to Sharon Wegsheider-Cruze (Wegsheider, 1981), they were originally developed by well-known family therapist, Virginia Satir (Satir, 1988; Satir, Bitter, & Krestensen, 1988) who was working with families impacted by cancer. She discovered that children would adopt these roles after one of their parents had been diagnosed with cancer. This coincides with the disease model perspective, in that with both cancer or alcoholism, children tend to take on similar survival roles.

Behavioral and Cognitive Behavioral Couples and Family Models

In chapter 3 in this textbook, we presented a variety of behavioral models that were designed to describe how individuals develop alcohol or drug problems. Now we will examine the role of couples and families in sustaining SUDs. Generally, we will be looking at the different ways in which families or partners inadvertently or unintentionally reinforce their loved one's drinking or drug use behaviors. There have been several research studies which have determined that verbal communication, verbal output and attention *increases* around the topic of drinking in couples where there is an alcoholic partner (Becker & Miller, 1976; Hersen, Miller, & Eisler, 1973; Billings, Kessler, Gomberg, & Weiner, 1979; Frankenstein, Nathan, Sullivan, Hay, & Cocco, 1985). Interaction patterns also differed depending on the gender of the person with the alcohol use disorder. For example, Haber and Jacob (1997) found that women's alcoholic drinking tended to be reinforced by relationship consequences whereby these couples experienced more negative interactions than male alcoholics when NOT drinking, but fewer negative interactions when they were drinking. It is also common for spouses to withdraw from their alcoholic spouse when he or she is drinking, believing that this will somehow encourage abstinence. Research suggests quite the opposite, i.e. that assertive and engaged spousal coping was associated with reduced drinking (McCrady, Hayaki, Epstein, & Hirsch, 2002; Moos, Finney, & Cronkite, 1990; Orford, Guthrie, Nicholls, Oppenheimer, Egert, & Hensman, 1975).

McCrady has done extensive clinical and research work with couples experiencing SUDs and has developed several techniques for working with couples where one or both partners are actively using. Her stance is that couples treatment begins with the very first contact or first session. (The prevalent view in the addictions treatment field, for many years, was that the addict or alcoholic needed to establish stable and consistent abstinence/recovery first before any couples or family counseling could be initiated.) Working with couples from the onset of treatment however, provides several advantages. First, it allows both partners to participate in the behavioral change process rather than focusing on one individual partner. Second, couples therapy also allows the couple to reinforce one another (both in session and between sessions) for positive behavior change and to find shared activities that do not revolve around drinking. Third, couples find they are able to communicate more positively with one another, Fourth, couples who participated in couples therapy were better able to identify the role each other plays in maintaining substance use. Fifth, couples therapy allows partners to problem-solve and resolve conflicts together (McCrady, Ladd, & Hallgren, 2012; McCrady, Owens, & Brovko, 2013). Here, research indicates that couples who have participated in counseling together had lower rates of domestic violence than those who participated in individual therapy alone (O'Farrell, Murphy, Stephan, Fals-Stewart, & Murphy, 2004; Schumm O'Farrell, Murphy, & Fals-Stewart, 2009). McCrady, Ladd and Hallgren (2012) discovered that similar to how an individual will make several key changes as he or she is going through addictions treatment, so too does the significant other or partner. For example, family members and significant others who participate in couples/family counseling often benefit by: (a) recognizing that their loved one has a substance use disorder that requires change; (b) understanding and supporting positive behavioral changes in their partner; (c) raising their awareness of family members' patterns of behaving and thinking that might trigger substance use in their loved one; (d) developing emotional, cognitive and behavioral skills that enhance motivation to change and to support positive changes and (e) developing expectations of positive behavioral changes (McCrady, Ladd, & Hallgren, 2012; McCrady, Owens, & Brovko, 2013).

Structural Family Theory

Structural Family Theory was originated by Salvador Minuchin and his colleagues at the Philadelphia Child Guidance Clinic (PCGC) in the 1980s. Initially, Structural Family Therapy was utilized to treat a number of child/adolescent behavioral problems, everything from bedwetting to eating disorders to fire-setting. Essentially, Structural Family Therapy addresses problems in functioning within a family. In order to bring about change within the family Structural Family therapists will first "join" with the family in order in order to understand the invisible rules which govern its functioning. The counselor takes note of how family members relate to one another, which is referred to as *mapping*. The therapist then ultimately attempts to change the dysfunctional relationships within the family, causing it to stabilize into healthier patterns.

When M. Duncan Stanton and Thomas C. Todd (Stanton, 1979; Stanton & Todd, 1982) joined the PCGC team, Structural Family Theory was applied to work with heroin-addicted young adults and their families in Philadelphia. In their work with families, Stanton and Todd (1982) made several important observations regarding this heroin-addicted population. First, they found that although they were often counseling young adult men and women, these individuals often had a great deal of contact with their family of origin (i.e. parents). It's often assumed that as a person becomes more deeply involved in his or her addiction, they become more isolated from others. This was not the case, however, with families impacted by opioid use disorders according to Stanton and Todd (1982). This finding generally holds true with individuals impacted by SUDs other than opioid use disorders, especially for individuals younger than 35 years old. Here it was discovered that 60–80% of these young adults had contact with one or both parents on a daily basis (e.g. Bekir, McLellan, Childress, & Gariti, 1993; Cervantes, Sorenson, Wermuth, Fernandez, & Menicucci, 1988; Stanton, 1997). We will explore more Structural Family Therapy techniques later in this chapter.

Family Theory Models and Applications to Addiction Counseling: Assessment, Techniques/Interventions and Clinical Implications for Counselors

Assessment

You're probably familiar with the popular expression, "a picture's worth a thousand words." This familiar phase is very much applicable to the use of genograms as an assessment tool that can be used with families. Later we will describe *medically oriented genograms* in the Biological Models chapter. There, we emphasize that genograms could be used to look at genetic patterns within families that might serve to indicate genetic markers of substance use disorders. In this chapter, however, we are advocating for the use of family genograms to look at interactional and behavioral patterns within the family milieu. For example, by gathering information about how the family interacts, we may begin to see enabling patterns. We may see examples of who colludes or allies with whom, or whether there may be enmeshed relationships between a father and teenage daughter or a mother and teenage son. Enmeshed relationships are also ripe for triangulation as "third parties" unwittingly get drawn in to conflicts between parents and their teenage sons or daughters. The genogram can also tell us about family roles as we begin to hear which children have taken on roles of hero, scapegoat, clown-mascot or lost child. Figure 4.1 provides you with the format and symbols that are used to write a genogram. Where Figure 4.2 provides you with a sample of a three-generation genogram using a fictitious client, John G. There is also a narrative explanation given to explain the various symbols depicted in John G.'s genogram.

Techniques/Interventions

We will not go over some of the family therapy techniques and interventions that can be used with families impacted by SUDs. In order to accomplish this goal, we will begin by presenting a case and then we will discuss some of the ways those techniques can be applied when working with Tara and her family. We will then provide you with some other techniques that fall outside the realm of the family therapy models we presented.

Case Example: Tara

Tara is a single woman in her early 20s who is currently living at home with her biological mother and father, her grandmother, and an older brother and younger sisters in West Virginia. Tara began using alcohol and marijuana when she was around 13 years-old however, she then progressed to using OxyContin (an opioid analgesic or painkiller) which she ingests orally.

   West Virginia is one of the states that has been impacted especially hard by the opioid epidemic. There have been times when Tara would "cook" the OxyContin pills down to liquid form in order that she could inject it intravenously. Although Tara has used other substances in the past eight years, she identifies OxyContin

Format for family genogram

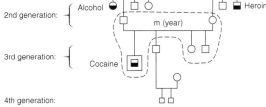

Symbols useful for genograms

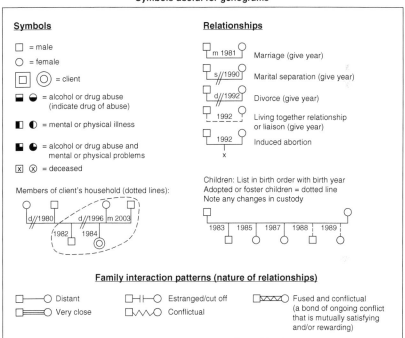

Figure 4.1 Family Genogram

The genogram is useful for engaging the client and significant family members in a discussion of important family relationships. Squares and circles identify parents, siblings, and other household members, and an enclosed square or circle identifies the client. Marital status is represented by unique symbols, such as diagonal lines for separation and divorce. Different types of connecting lines reflect the nature of relationships among household members. For instance, one solid line represents a distant relationship between two individuals; three solid lines represent a very close relationship. Other key data, such as arrest information, are written on the genogram as appropriate.

Source: New Jersey Division of Addiction Services, New Jersey Department of Health and Senior Services.

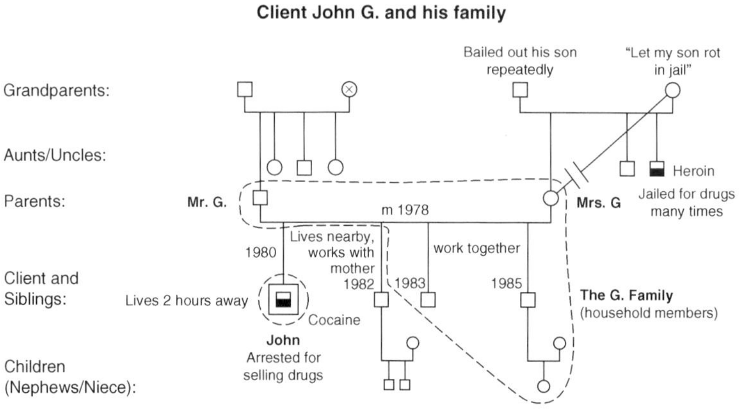

Figure 4.2 Sample Genogram of Client John G.

This sample genogram depicts a family that initially was seen as a close, loving family unit. The son, John, had come under the influence of some "bad friends" and had become involved in abusing and selling substances. While expressing their willingness to help, the family denied the seriousness of the situation and minimized any problems in the nuclear or extended family.

When the discussion was extended to one of John's maternal uncles, Mrs. G. admitted that her brother had been arrested a number of times for heroin possession. Questions about the maternal grandmother's reaction to John's "problem" caused the united family front to begin to dissolve. It became apparent that Mrs. G.'s mother took an "insensitive position" regarding John's substance use disorder and there was a serious estrangement between her and her daughter. In discussing the details of the uncle's criminal activity (which was a family secret that even John and his brothers did not know), it emerged that Mrs. G. had for years agonized over her mother's pain. Now, desperately afraid of reliving her parents' experiences, Mrs. G. had stopped talking to her mother. John's brothers felt free to open up and expressed their resentment of their brother for putting the family in this position.

Mr. G., who had been most adamant in denying any family problems, now talked about the sense of betrayal and failure he felt because of John's actions. It was only through the leverage of the family's experience that the family's present conflict became evident.

Source: New Jersey Division of Addiction Services, New Jersey Department of Health and Senior Services (Public Domain)

as her current drug of preference. Her entire family is aware of her prescription opioid use and are very worried that she will overdose or be harmed when she goes out to buy the drug on the street from drug dealers. Tara also admits to having used black tar heroin when OxyContin is unavailable. She also admits to stealing pain medication from her father who sustained a work-related injury while working as a coal miner.

Case Conceptualization

Tara's opioid use disorder seems to be maintained by several core issues. First, is that Tara reports that she was sexually molested by an older, cousin when she was around 13 years old, which coincides with the initial onset of her using alcohol and marijuana. Tara was afraid to tell her parents because she worried that they wouldn't believe her. The other core family issue is that when Tara was 11 years old, her older brother Jon had been murdered in a drug deal gone bad. This had a devastating impact on Tara's parents, who blamed themselves for Jon's death because he had been living at home at the time, and the parents felt they could have done more to get Jon into treatment or somehow motivate him to accept help. Now, every time Tara leaves the house, her parents go into "panic mode," as they fear that Tara will end up being murdered like Jon was. Another core issue is that Tara had been raped by three men from whom she had purchased heroin. She has very little recollection of that night and thinks she may have been given a "date rape drug" like GHB or Rohypnol. Finally, Tara admits that the more her parents try to restrict her from going out of the house, the more she rebels by sneaking out of the house at all hours of the day or night.

Tara's family lives with death hanging over them on a daily basis. They never really forgave themselves or grieved Jon's death and now they live in utter fear that the same thing will happen to Tara. Tara's parents had gone into a deep depression after Jon was murdered. As a result, Tara's father has rationalized that if he gives her his painkillers, it's better than her going out on the street to buy heroin from a drug dealer who might end up raping or murdering her. This is a family who find themselves in what is sometimes referred to as a "family crucible," in which all members are locked into a pattern of destructive behaviors from which they see no way out. Tara's siblings very much want her to seek help. Her older brother, Frank especially feels that his parents have unintentionally become enablers to Tara's addiction and has concluded that "Nothing will change, unless Mom and Dad wake up and begin to make major changes." Tara's younger sister, Eva is also very worried about Tara and constantly worries that something horrible will happen to her. Eva tends to keep these feelings bottled up and binge eats when she feels anxious.

Learning Opportunity 4.3 – Family Counseling

If you were a family counselor and you were seeing Tara, her parents and siblings for the first time, what would be some of the important issues you would want to address with this family? If Tara were agreeable to entering treatment at a residential addictions treatment program, what treatment would you recommend for Tara's family?

Family Systems Model and Structural Family Model

As described earlier, according to Family Systems theory, substance use may symbolize a maladaptive attempt to maintain a dysfunctional homeostasis. It's not coincidental that problems related to substance use may arise during critical periods in which the family is attempting to negotiate key developmental milestones (e.g. like "launching" an adult son or daughter into the world). As mentioned earlier, in healthy families, differentiation or separation between an young adult son or daughter and his or her parents is encouraged and supported. However, when an SUD impacts a son or daughter, healthy differentiation becomes impossible and is often replaced by enmeshment (or fusion) as parents find themselves in constant fear of overdose or imprisonment and are convinced their son or daughter will never be able to make a successful transition towards becoming an independent young adult. Because of these tensions and conflicts, this may be a time at which the son or daughter acts out and gets arrested or gets a DUI. Nothing stops healthy differentiation dead in its tracks like an arrest or some other substance-related crisis. It's at this point that the family often rallies around their son or daughter to try to fend off potential jail or prison time. When family counselors begin to counsel families in the aftermath of an arrest, the therapeutic work must eventually shift the focus away from the arrest to how the family can address the substance use issues in order to move forward. In order to accomplish this goal, family counselors utilize a few different techniques. The first is *joining.* Here, the Family Systems counselor is attempting to develop a therapeutic alliance with the family in order to gain their trust and confidence. The counselor joins the family in two ways. The first of these is supporting the family system and its members (by making a connection with each family member). Joining also involves the family counselor asking each family member what his or her perception of the problem is. (This is why it's very important to have all family members present, as we've witnessed instances where a younger sibling correctly perceives the dysfunction within the family and speaks the truth, while other family members may be invested in maintaining a dysfunctional homeostasis. We once had an 8-year-old younger sister, tell us "Nothing will change as long as Dad and my older brother are drinking buddies." The younger sister was pointing out an unhealthy alliance between her father and older brother.) Once a connection is made and the family gains trust in the counselor, the counselor can then challenge the family system. The counselor must be able to tell each family member that he or she understands their perception of the problem and also can state with confidence that there are ways to address the problems (Stanton, Todd et al., (1978).

The second technique used by Family Systems counselors is called *restructuring.* Here the family counselor attempts to challenge the homeostasis by changing the bonding and power alignments among various family members. In order to accomplish these goals, counselors will use techniques such as *contracting* (an agreement to work on particular substance use issues before proceeding to work on other problems), *reframing* (here the counselor encourages family members to understand how the substance use serves an important function or purpose within the family) and *enactment* (here the family counselor is asking the family to discuss the substance use problem with one another as they might at home, while the counselor observes the dynamics between family members.)

There are several ways these Family Systems techniques can be utilized in working with Tara's family. Given the murder of Tara's older brother, Jon; Tara's parents have tried to stabilize the dysfunctional homeostasis created by Tara's opioid use by focusing all of their efforts on making certain that Tara does not meet a similar untimely death. Yet, just as Tara is powerless over her opioid use disorder, so too are her parents and siblings. Because the parents are so focused on Tara, it's almost as if their other daughter and son do not exist. Also, a Structural Family counselor might try to *restructure* the family by placing Tara's older brother in charge of Tara and giving permission for her parents to focus on themselves by attending Nar-anon or Al-anon groups specific to parents and grandparents. The family counselor might *contract* with the family to refrain from providing Tara with money and pain medication. Finally, a family counselor might *reframe* the parents' enabling behavior as being an example of their willingness to do just about anything to keep Tara alive. When the counselor feels that he or she has sufficiently joined with this family, she may introduce another "life-saving" approach, which would be to seek other forms of intervention even if it means that Tara will be court-mandated to treatment.

The real challenge for Tara's parents and siblings will come once Tara completes detox and residential treatment and begins to work on her recovery. Often parents and siblings are at a loss as to how to best help their now-recovering loved one, so the tendency is to go back to old roles or ways of relating to one another. Parents often become hypervigilant, watching their son or daughter's every move, instead of focusing on their own recovery. There is also a tendency to go to back to the old *homeostasis*, mostly because it's familiar. No wonder that family counselors often refer to this initial period when a loved one comes home from treatment, as *walking on eggshells* because of the tension created by not knowing how to act towards one another in healthier ways.

Family Disease Model

Since this model examines how substance use disorders impact on all family members, which then results in all family members adopting particular roles in order to cope with the impact of the disease, it is important that counselors first explore how these roles play out with each particular family member without blaming or judging the family. Instead, it's important that the counselor empathizes with the family's attempts to cope with the SUD before asking them to change these attitudes and behaviors. For example, trying to get a spouse or partner to attend Al-anon or Nar-anon will be a difficult task if he or she doesn't see a rationale for the recommendation that they attend meetings.

The essential message that would be given to the non-alcoholic, non-addict spouses, partners and/or family members would be "detach with love, take care of yourself while letting go and allowing your loved one to take care of him or herself." That can be a tall order to someone who's been accustomed to being the caretaker. Therefore, it's important that the counselor exercise patience as well as empathy.

With regard to Tara's family, using a Family Disease Model perspective, it becomes clear to the counselor that both Tara's parents and her siblings have adopted particular roles in response to her opioid use disorder. Her parents have obviously become Tara's enablers while her older brother, Frank, stepped into the "hero" role shortly after his brother's death, and Tara's sister, Eva has become the "lost child" of the family. Frank is usually very outspoken about how "Tara has ruined the family" while Eva usually does not express her apprehensions. The role of the family counselor would be to try to encourage the family to adopt healthier roles. For example, rather than enabling Tara by giving her money and painkillers, they could help her by encouraging her to go for treatment. Overall, the message to the family members is "take care of yourself first." This is not dissimilar to Al-anon or Nar-anon's recommendation that family and significant others "detach with love."

Behavioral and Cognitive Behavioral Models

From a behavioral perspective, family counselors are interested in how the family may be inadvertently *positively reinforcing* alcohol or drug use behaviors. The best example of this would be how Tara's parents give her money and painkiller medications, in order to dissuade her from going down to bad neighborhoods to purchase prescription opioids and/or black tar heroin.

A behavioral family counselor would focus on changing the reinforcement patterns such that Tara would be rewarded for any positive behaviors (e.g. days when Tara doesn't use, or she goes out looking for a job). It's important that Tara not be given money as a reward because that may be a trigger for her to go and purchase prescription opioids or heroin, so instead it would be recommended that the parents reward Tara with verbal praise or making her favorite dinner or taking her out to a movie. Behavioral family counseling would be especially helpful once Tara detoxes and completes a residential treatment program by helping the family to develop new ways to relate to one another in which the parents could reinforce Tara's efforts to work on her recovery such as going to NA meetings or talking with her sponsor. Often, when a son or daughter comes home from residential treatment, there's a tendency for families to go back to old ways of relating to one another rather than to try new behaviors.

From a cognitive behavioral perspective, a CBT family counselor would begin by exploring irrational beliefs that Tara and her family may hold. For example, Tara's parents may express irrational beliefs that "Tara will never change and she will end up like her brother, Jon." Tara's brother may express beliefs such as "Tara is a loser and she's unwilling to help herself." It would be important to help the parents and Tara's brother, Frank to change these distressing beliefs to more rational alternative beliefs such as "Tara can change if we try to motivate her towards treatment" or "Tara is not a loser, she is sick and suffering and needs our help and compassion."

Other Family Models and Approaches: CRAFT, Johnsonian Interventions, Civil Commitment and Adolescent Family Treatment Models

CRAFT (Community Reinforcement and Family Training)

CRAFT was originated by Robert Meyers, PhD (Meyers, Miller, & Smith, 2001), for the purposed of helping families cope with a loved one's SUD. CRAFT utilizes several techniques to help families cope. First, CRAFT helps families to refrain from contentious arguing and criticisms and instead to use more positive communication skills and to look for "windows of opportunity" when concerns about alcohol or drug use can be expressed without criticism, anger or judgment. Instead of "You came home drunk last night, you're going to end up just like your father," CRAFT would recommend to wait for a receptive moment to say something like "I'm worried because you seemed to have a lot to drink last night." By teaching families how to communicate more positively, they are thereby avoiding critical name-calling, blaming and other negative statements. Instead, family members are encouraged to utilize the following communication skills: (1) be brief (i.e. avoid lengthy lectures or preaching, instead make statements brief and to the point); (2) be positive (state what behaviors you want, rather than criticizing, blaming or overgeneralizing); (3) be specific (rather than making vague statements, describe the behaviors you would like to see); (4) describe your feelings in a calm, non-judgmental, non-accusatory way; (5) offer an understanding statement (e.g. express empathy and understanding to your loved one and their struggle with SUDs); (6) accept partial responsibility for your loved one's behavior (family members may cite a small piece of the problem for which they can take responsibility, e.g. "I know I've been too lenient and looked the other way, hoping that things would get better, that's my fault.") and (7) offer to help (by asking your loved one, "How can I best help you?" especially in an honest, genuine way) (Smith & Meyers, 2004).

CRAFT also emphasizes the use of *natural consequences*. For example, instead of getting the intoxicated loved one into bed when he or she comes home under the influence, it's suggested to leave the person wherever he or she passes out. This strategy is designed to help stop enabling behaviors. Also, CRAFT utilizes positive reinforcement by finding alternative behaviors or activities that do not involved alcohol or drug use and helping to promote those alternatives. In the HBO video series *Addiction* (Meyers, 2007) there's a segment on CRAFT in which a grandmother is coached on how to utilize CRAFT principles with her young adult grandson, Doug. In coming up with ways to reinforce Doug for non-using behaviors, the grandmother mentions that Doug used to play the guitar and had expressed in interest in playing the drums. The counselor and grandmother then discuss how to use these interests as positive reinforcement for the grandson.

Finally, the CRAFT approach is really about helping family members. Meyers provides a list of Five Things to Know About Coping with a Loved One's Unhealthy Behavior which are as follows:

(1) Your love has power.
(2) You are not alone.
(3) You can catch more flies with honey than with vinegar.
(4) You have as many tries as you want. Relationships are a process.
(5) You can live a happier life whether or not your loved one sobers up.

(Meyers in Hoffman & Froemke, 2007, p. 159)

These coping statements are really about empowering family members and providing hope (family members can learn techniques that can help motivate their loved one to recovery) and that they are not alone in their struggles. The emphasis is also on helping family members to try to new approaches and techniques in order to break old ways of communicating that had become totally ineffective.

Advantages and Disadvantages to the CRAFT Approach

There are several advantages and disadvantages to CRAFT. The main advantage is that this approach is considered one of the least coercive approaches to help motivate family members or other loved ones to accept treatment. CRAFT also offers several ways to help loved ones on how best to communicate concerns about alcohol or drug use. CRAFT is also very advantageous in supporting loved ones and making them aware that they are not alone in their struggle. The main disadvantage is that this approach is not applicable to everyone. For example, in the case of Tara, where the danger of overdose is more imminent and inpatient detox is the safest choice, there may not be enough time to teach the basics of CRAFT in order to bring about positive change. This is not to say that CRAFT might not be useful in supporting the family once their loved one is in recovery because it really does help dysfunctional communication patterns.

Johnsonian Intervention

An intervention is a technique which is designed to motivate individuals with substance use disorders to accept treatment. Originated by Vernon Johnson (1973), interventions are a means to present "reality in a receivable way" in an effort to help combat denial. Johnson concludes that people with alcohol use disorders (and other substance use disorders) do not purposely deny the impact that his or her drinking or drug use is having on their lives. Instead he feels that there are three factors that account for this tendency to negate or refute the serious impact of substance use: *denial, euphoric recall* and *repression*. Denial is what counselors most often hear from clients who are caught up in the downward progression of alcohol and/or drug use. Statements such as "I can't be an alcoholic because I never had two DUI's" or "I know about a dozen people who drink or drug much more than I do" are common expressions of denial. Euphoric recall refers to the tendency to think back to the pleasurable aspects of drinking or drug use, for example the initial "buzz" or pleasant/euphoric effect of drinking not vomiting at 2 or 3 a.m. from "room spins" or the hangover and inability to make it to work or school the next day. According to Johnson, *repression* is described somewhat similarly to how Anna Freud characterized this defense mechanism back in the 1950s, that is, the tendency to put out of one's mind that which is distressing or embarrassing. Johnson, however, points out that repression can also be the result of blackouts (i.e. alcohol- or benzodiazepine-induced amnestic episodes) whereby the individual is unable to recall things he or she may have said or did while under the influence.

Because of *denial, euphoric recall* and *repression*, Johnson (1973) felt that family members, friends, co-workers should be asked to list two or three examples where their loved one's drinking or substance use had caused them concern, in order that these incidents could be presented to their significant other in a loving, concerned manner. Again, the goal of an intervention is not to emotionally "beat up" or guilt-trip the loved one into agreeing to enter treatment, but rather to express these incidents and concerns in a loving way or as Johnson describes it, "to present reality in a receivable way."

The key factor in carrying out a successful intervention is preparation. In the first meeting with an intervention counselor, the concerned parties are asked to think about who else should be included in the intervention? Are there other individuals who are as concerned about this loved one's substance use other than those who are present? As mentioned earlier, not only are family members included, but also friends, co-workers, bosses, and sometimes former spouses/partners. Not everyone is suited to be part of an intervention. For example, those who are current drinking or drug use "buddies" of the person would be excluded. Similarly, individuals who hold so much anger or resentment towards the alcoholic that they would be unable to maintain the spirit of love and concern should also be excluded. Prior to the conclusion of this first meeting, loved ones and significant others would be asked to list two specific incidents in which the loved one's drinking or drug use caused them the most concern or worry.

In the second meeting, these incidents will be reviewed with everyone present. From having done several interventions, it's always surprising that family members report being totally unaware of some of the horrific drinking incidents described by other family members living in the same house. However, this really is an example of the "conspiracy of silence" that often exists in families impacted by SUDs – that no one is allowed to talk about the "drinking or drug problem." Once everyone has had a chance to talk about the incidents, those present will decide on what order they will go in, on the day the intervention takes place. The family and counselor will then decide when and where the intervention will be held. It's preferable to do the intervention at a time when the loved one is not actively under the influence of alcohol or drugs. If the loved one were to be under the influence, he or she may have no recollection of the intervention or may easily misconstrue the nature and purpose of the intervention. For this reason, interventions are sometimes done early in the morning or even at the person's workplace, especially when co-workers or bosses are involved in the intervention. Prior to the conclusion of this second meeting, a family member is asked to call several detox or inpatient programs to reserve a bed for their loved one. This can be a tedious process, given that health insurance will need to be checked and pre-approvals given. Also, be aware that not all health insurance policies will cover all programs, so it's important to find a treatment program that's considered to be "in-network" in order to avoid the family being billed for unpaid expenses.

The third meeting provides an opportunity to role play the intervention. In some instances, the counselor may have a colleague come in to the session to play the role of the loved one. Family members are often fearful of the reactions of their loved one, so the role play provides an opportunity desensitize the concerned significant others regarding their worst fears. Also in this session, friends and family members will be asked to come up with "consequences" should their loved one refuse to go into treatment. Examples of consequences would be to refrain from any future enabling behaviors. For example, one son told his father that if he got behind the wheel of the family car after drinking, he would call the police. A spouse told his wife that if anyone called looking for her, he would promptly tell them that she was too intoxicated to come to the phone. A daughter refused to let her children see their grandfather until he got help. Tara's parents may refuse to give her any more money and painkillers. Consequences often sound harsh but the message is clear, "If you seek help, we will be there with you every step of the way."

On the day of the actual intervention, the role of the counselor is to ask the SUD loved one to listen to what their family and friends have to say and that he or she will be given time to respond, once everyone has expressed their concerns. Where interventions often get derailed is when the SUD loved one begins to pick apart specifics of what is being said, (e.g. "I never said or did that!!!") Or one of the friends or family members jumps the gun and begins to plead with their alcoholic or addicted loved one to seek help. Hopefully, if the loved one does accept help, consequences will not have to be used, but be aware that the SUD loved one may begin to strike bargains with their family. For examples, "Just let me try to stop on my own and if I can't do it, I'll go into rehab," or "I'll check myself into rehab tomorrow. I have to get my affairs in order before I leave." No wonder Vernon Johnson titled his book, *I'll Quit Tomorrow*. I had the opportunity of taking a class with Vernon Johnson when he taught at the Rutgers Summer School of Alcohol Studies. On the first day of class, he described how he was asked to do an intervention on Betty Ford, who was First Lady during the time when her husband, Gerald Ford, was President of the United States. It sounded like an intimidating task to say the least. Johnson explained that he not only had a lot of support from the entire Ford family and friends but especially from the White House staff, who were well-aware of where Betty hid bottles or would sneak drinks. Obviously, the intervention was successful and the rest, as they say, is history! Betty Ford not only got sober, but became one of the staunchest advocates for alcohol and drug treatment. The Betty Ford Centers are known the world over for providing quality SUD treatment.

Advantages and Disadvantages to Johnsonian Interventions

From the perspective of breaking through denial, euphoric recall and repression, interventions make a lot of sense, as does the concept of interventions becoming a way of "presenting reality in a receivable way." If interventions are done in a spirit of love and concerns and participants follow their "script" of what they need to say, interventions can make a difference. As I've always told families, nothing is ever the same after an intervention. For one thing, the conspiracy of silence is broken and family members and friends often bond together. It's important that these family and friends are seen for follow-up sessions following an intervention. If the intervention does not go as planned, they will need support to avoid drifting into the "would've, could've and should'ves" or things they would have said if given another chance. If the intervention goes well, follow-up sessions will be needed to provide the family with support and perspective on what to expect when their loved one returns home, newly sober.

The main disadvantage of interventions is that they are considered coercive (i.e. essentially the family is saying, "Do what I say or else") and many question the use of surprise tactics (i.e. the loved one is never told ahead of time that the intervention will take place). However, most interventionist counselors will likely tell you that if someone were to be invited to their intervention, they probably wouldn't show up. There are other less coercive methods of intervention in which the SUD loved one is invited to attend the family sessions and sometimes they do, even if for nothing more than out of curiosity. This raises another disadvantage to interventions in which the SUD loved one holds onto resentment towards those who arranged and participated in the intervention. This would be more likely to occur in situations where the SUD loved one has refused treatment. An alcoholic father felt he had been "sandbagged" by his family for having done an intervention. Eventually, he did get into recovery and was able to let go of his resentments when he realized how much his family loved him in order to go to the time and expense to do an intervention.

Before concluding this section, we'd like to mention that interventions have been depicted in TV and movies, some good and some not-so-good. Probably one of the more realistic interventions was depicted in the film, *Stuart Saves His Family*, which stars Al Franken, as Stuart and Vincent D'Onfrio as Donnie, Stuart's older brother. The character of Stuart Smalley was based on a NBC *Saturday Night Live* skit which Al Franken had played for several years. In the movie, Stuart and Donnie's father has a severe alcohol use disorder. After a hunting accident, in which the father accidentally shoots Donnie, the family decides to do an intervention. The father is depicted as being very intimidating and mean-spirited and when he begins to attack his family verbally for doing the intervention, Donnie gets angry and confronts his father, by blaming intoxication for the hunting accident.

Most of you are probably familiar with the reality TV program *Intervention* on the A & E. station We recommend that you watch several episodes, not only to get an idea of what interventions look like but also to give you some important insight into family dynamics. There are several controversies and ethical concerns regarding the intervention series which have been noted by Kosovski and Smith (2011). Of particular concern is that the series depicts SUD individuals who are engaging in very dangerous behaviors even while being filmed. Another ethical concern is the use of deception, (i.e. participants in the program are told they are being filmed for a documentary on addiction and are unaware they will be facing an intervention.)

Adolescent Family Treatment Models

Adolescents who develop substance use disorders are especially problematic and therefore require specialized treatment. Just as there are various types of inpatient or residential SUD treatment programs for adults, so too, there are residential treatment programs specifically for adolescents. Adolescent treatment programs, in general, tend to be more highly structured and activity-oriented. In addition, it is imperative that adolescent treatment programs contain a strong family counseling component because without the help and support of the teenager's family, relapse becomes more likely. Through treatment, families can make changes towards becoming part of the solution rather than being part of the problem. The following are a few examples of adolescent family treatment models.

Multisystemic or Multidimensional Family Therapy

This approach is primarily a family-based outpatient SUD model that requires close collaboration between the adolescent and his or her family as well as contacts with the adolescent's school and juvenile justice system (if they are mandated to treatment by the courts.) The family counselor is responsible for meeting with the adolescent, with the adolescent and their family members, and also with school counselors and juvenile justice officers on an ongoing basis throughout the week. The goal of these sessions is to provide structure to the adolescent's life by helping to reinforce the family, school and community's rules and expectations. The other goal is to help prevent the adolescent's SUD from progressing or escalating to a point where residential treatment would become necessary. The HBO video series *Addiction* (2007) provides a good illustration of the Multisystemic Family Therapy approach.

Functional Family Therapy (FFT)

The Functional Family Therapy approach was created by therapists Alexander and Parsons (1982) who, at the time, were working with youth who exhibited a variety of conduct disorders. FFT utilizes a combination of behavioral techniques along with a family systems perspective. From the very outset, FFT family therapists work with both the adolescent and his or her parents and siblings with the goal of examining how their day-to-day interactions function to regulate their relationships. The behavioral aspect of FFT explores the "payoffs" or reinforcers that maintain or reinforce certain maladaptive behaviors between family members (Waldron, Slesnick, Brody, Turner, & Peterson, 2001; Waldron & Turner, 2008). Alexander and Parsons (1982) describe three behavioral "payoffs": (1) *merging*: which is meant to increase closeness and contact (e.g. even in arguing with one another, family members are engaged or connected to one another); (2) *separating*: which is meant to create distance and autonomy (e.g. an adolescent may have very little interaction with his or her parents in order to obtain more independence); and (3) *midpointing*: which involves a combination of both merging and separating behaviors (e.g. the adolescent may at one time say, "Pay attention to me, listen to me" while at other times he or she may be saying, "Go away, leave me alone"). According to the FFT model, it is the very nature of these interpersonal family relationships that causes problems within the family. The challenge of the FFT approach is to encourage family members to gain a new perspective, in which they can look at their own roles in maintaining certain dysfunctional behaviors.

Most of the research on FFT has focused on its impact on acting out or externalizing behaviors (i.e. criminal behaviors) (e.g. Sexton & Turner, 2011, who found significant reductions in felony and violent crimes following FFT). One study focused specifically on FFT with substance use (Waldron, Slesnick et al., 2001) found significant reductions in marijuana use as a result of FFT therapy. The greatest reductions in marijuana use occurred in the group that participated in a combination of both FFT and cognitive behavioral therapy.

Civil Commitment of Individuals with Substance Use Disorders

Finally, civil commitment is not a family treatment model; however it is an option available to families who are concerned about the well-being of a loved one experiencing severe substance use disorders. Similar to mental health commitment laws, whereby individuals who are in danger of hurting themselves or others can be committed by the courts to an inpatient mental health facility, civil commitment laws for individuals with SUDs are designed to provide a safe inpatient environment (e.g. a medically supervised detoxification) for purposes of screening and stabilization. Most addiction treatment in the United States is initiated by voluntary admission (i.e. people voluntarily sign themselves into a treatment program having either "hit bottom" or at the urging of family or significant others). Currently 38 states and the District of Columbia have some form of civil commitment laws (Cavaiola & Dolan, 2016), however, in those remaining 12 states that lack a civil commitment option, people must voluntarily sign themselves into treatment. The problem with voluntary admissions is that it assumes that individuals who have been drinking or using drugs for many years will have the motivation and clear-headed reasoning necessary in order to make an informed, rational decision to voluntarily enter treatment. In many instances this is not a reasonable option and, if one takes into account how alcohol and drugs impact on behavior, cognitions and emotions. Also, this contributes to the problem of "revolving door" admissions, whereby individuals may decide to sign themselves into treatment one day, only to sign themselves out AMA (against medical advice), the next day. In addition, when taking into account the number of deaths resulting from overdoses, physical complications resulting from alcohol and drug use, accidents and other causes, waiting for someone to "hit bottom" does not seem like a compassionate option. Civil commitment provides an option for families who fear their loved one may overdose or cause harm to themselves or others.

There are several disadvantages to civil commitment. First, many consider civil commitment to be a violation of one's Constitutional civil liberties guaranteed under the 14th Amendment. The 14th Amendment guarantees that American citizens are not deprived of their freedom (in this instance by being confined against his or her will). Civil commitment is therefore considered by some to be coercive and paternalistic and thereby takes away the person's right to voluntarily consent to treatment (Rustad, Junquera, Chaves, & Eth, 2012). All models discussed in this chapter have their advantages and disadvantages (Table 4.2).

Table 4.2 Advantages and Limitations to Family Model

Limitations

- families are unique, so not every model is applicable to all families
- couples often present with dysfunction and problems that are different from the type of dysfunction experienced by families
- not all families are supportive of their SUD loved one and may decline to have involvement in his or her treatment
- family models are NOT *causal models* but rather are *sustaining models*, i.e. families may engage in behaviors that support or reinforce the SUD (e.g. enabling)

Advantages

- family models provide an excellent framework for understanding how SUDs impact on the entire family as well as significant others
- family models provide descriptions of the dynamics with families impacted by SUDs
- family models provide methods for assessing families (e.g. genograms) and also provide techniques for treating families impacted by SUDs
- family models emphasize the importance of families in supporting recovery
- family models also emphasize how family members can work on their own wellness even if their loved one does not get sober
- in some instances family counseling may be more effective than individual counseling approaches

---

Learning Opportunity 4.4 – Civil Commitment

What are your opinions about coercive approaches like Johnsonian Interventions and Civil Commitment? Can you think of situations where such approaches might be justified? Discuss in small groups or in your chat room.

Summary

Substance use disorders do not occur in a vacuum. Not only does the SUD person suffer but so do his or her families and significant others. Families can often become part of the solution or part of the problem when it comes to substance use disorders, therefore it is imperative that families and significant others be involved in motivating loved ones to enter treatment, as well as while they are in treatment and then when they return home. This chapter reviews some of the major theoretical models that conceptualize how SUDs impact on family members and how these models can be utilized to help bring about change. In addition to presenting basic conceptualization of Family Systems, Structural Family Theory, the Family Disease Model and Behavioral/Cognitive Behavioral Theory, we also present information on the CRAFT approach, Johnsonian Intervention and the use of civil commitment as other options for families who are concerned about the well-being of their loved ones.

Recommended Reading and Resources

Bekir, P., McLellan, T., Childress, A.R., & Gariti, P. (1993). Role reversals in families of substance misusers: A transgenerational phenomenon. *International Journal of Addictions*, *28(7)*, 613–630.

Brown, S., & Lewis, V. (1999). *The alcoholic family in recovery: A developmental model*. New York: Guilford Press.

Jackson, J.K. (1954). The adjustment of the family to the crisis of alcoholism. *Quarterly Journal of Studies on Alcohol, 15*, 562–586.

Johnson, V. (1973). *I'll quit tomorrow*. New York: Harper & Row.

McCrady, B.S., Owens, M.D., & Brovko, J.M. (2013). Couples and family treatment methods. In B.S. McCrady & E.E. Epstein (Eds). *Addictions: A comprehensive guidebook* (2nd edn, pp. 454–481). Oxford: Oxford University Press.

Stanton, M.D., & Todd, T.C. (1982). *The family therapy of drug abuse and addiction*. New York: Guilford Press.

Steinglass, P., Bennett, L.A., Wolin, S.J., & Reiss, D. (1987). *The alcoholic family*. New York: Basic Books.

Wegsheider, S. (1981). *Another chance: Hope and health for the alcoholic family*. Palo Alto, CA: Science & Behavior Books.

Resources

Families and Addictions (website): This website was developed by the Substance Abuse and Mental Health Services Administration (SAMHSA) and lists a number of publications. www.samhsa.gov/find-help/national-helpline

Family Genogram Programs (websites): These websites provide programs for writing creating genograms. Some sites provide free samples, others charge usage fees. www.genogramanalytics.com/index.html; www.genopro.com/genogram/

What is a genogram? (YouTube video): This brief video describes what a genogram is and how it can be used in counseling. www.youtube.com/watch?v=MuXvG9tbUMs

How to Make a Genogram (website): This is from WikiHow.com and provides a step-by-step model for creating a genogram. www.wikihow.com/Make-a-Genogram

Substance Abuse Treatment and Family Therapy (website): This one of SAMHSA's Treatment Improvement Protocols which provides in depth information on family therapy. www.ncbi.nlm.nih.gov/books/NBK64269/

Family Behavior Therapy (website): This guide to behavioral family therapy is presented by the National Institute of Health's (NIH) National Institute on Drug Abuse (NIDA) www.drugabuse.gov/publications/principles-drug-addiction-treatment-research-based-guide-third-edition/evidence-based-approaches-to-drug-addiction-treatment/behavioral-5

References

Alexander, B. (2017). *Glass house: The 1% economy and the shattering of the All-American town*. New York: St. Martin's Press.

Alexander, J., & Parsons, B.V. (1982). *Functional family therapy*. Monterey, CA: Brooks/Cole Publishing.

Becker, J.V., & Miller, P.M. (1976). Verbal and nonverbal marital interaction patterns of alcoholics and nonalcoholics. *Journal of Studies on Alcohol, 37,* 1616–1624.

Bekir, P., McLellan, T., Childress, A.R., & Gariti, P. (1993). Role reversals in families of substance misusers: A transgenerational phenomenon. *International Journal of Addictions, 28(7),* 613–630.

Billings, A.G., Kessler, M., Gomberg, C.A., & Weiner, S. (1979). Marital conflict resolution of alcoholic and nonalcoholic couples during drinking and nondrinking sessions. *Journal of Studies on Alcohol, 40,* 183–195.

Bowen, M. (1978). *Family therapy in clinical practice.* New York: Jason Aronson

Bradshaw, J. (1995). *Family secrets: What you don't know, won't hurt you.* New York: Bantam Books.

Brown, S., & Lewis, V. (1999). *The alcoholic family in recovery: A developmental model.* New York: Guilford Press.

Cavaiola, A.A., & Dolan D. (2016). Considerations in civil commitment of individuals with substance use disorders. *Substance Abuse, 37,* 181–187. http://dx.doi.org/10/1080/08897077.2015.1029207

Cermak, T. (1986). Diagnostic criteria for codependency. *Journal of Psychoactive Drugs, 18(1),* 15–20.

Cervantes, O.F., Sorenson, J.L., Wermuth, L., Fernandez, L., & Menicucci, L. (1988). Family ties of drug abusers. *Psychology of Addictive Behaviors, 2,* 34–39.

Frankenstein, W., Nathan, P.E., Sullivan, R.F., Hay, W.M., & Cocco, K. (1985). Asymmetry of influence in alcoholics' marital communication: Alcohol's effects on interaction dominance. *Journal of Marital and Family Therapy, 11,* 399–411.

Haber, J.R., & Jacob, T. (1997). Marital interactions of male versus female alcoholics. *Family Process, 36,* 385–402.

Hersen, M., Miller, P.M., & Eisler, R.M. (1973). Interactions between alcoholics and their wives: A descriptive analysis of verbal and nonverbal behavior. *Quarterly Journal of Studies on Alcohol, 34(2),* 516–520.

Hoffman, J., & Froemke, S. (2007). *Addiction: New knowledge, new treatments, new hope.* New York: Rodale Books & New York: HBO Home Box Office.

Jackson, J.K. (1954). The adjustment of the family to the crisis of alcoholism. *Quarterly Journal of Studies on Alcohol, 15,* 562–586.

Johnson, V. (1973). *I'll quit tomorrow.* New York: Harper & Row.

Kosovski, J.R., & Smith, D. C. (2011). Everybody hurts: Addiction, drama and the family in the reality television show. *Intervention. Substance Use & Misuse, 46,* 852–858.

Leonard, K.E., & Homish, G.G. (2008). Predictors of heavy drinking and drinking problems over the first 4 years of marriage. *Psychology of Addictive Behaviors, 22,* 25–35.

McCrady, B.S., Hayaki, J., Epstein, E.E., & Hirsch, L.S. (2002). Testing hypothesized predictors of change in conjoint behavioral alcoholism treatment for men. *Alcoholism: Clinical and Experimental Research, 26,* 463–470.

McCrady, B.S., Ladd, B.O., & Hallgren, K. (2012). Theoretical bases of family approaches to substance abuse treatment. In F. Rotgers & S. Walters (Eds). *Treatment of substance abusers: Theory and technique* (3rd edn, pp. 224–255). New York: Guilford Press.

McCrady, B.S., Owens, M.D., & Brovko, J.M. (2013). Couples and family treatment methods. In B.S. McCrady & E.E. Epstein (Eds). *Addictions: A comprehensive guidebook* (2nd edn, pp. 454–481). Oxford: Oxford University Press.

Meyers, R.J., Miller, W.R., & Smith, J.E. (2001). Community reinforcement and family training (CRAFT). In R.J. Meyers & W.R. Miller (Eds). *A community reinforcement approach to addiction treatment* (pp. 147–160). Cambridge: Cambridge University Press.

Moos, R.H., Finney, J.W., & Cronkite, R.C. (1990). *Alcoholism treatment: Context, process and outcome.* Oxford: Oxford University Press.

O'Farrell, T.J., Murphy, C.M., Stephan, S.H., Fals-Stewart, W., & Murphy, M. (2004). Partner violence before and after couples-based alcoholism treatment for male alcoholic patients: The role of treatment involvement and abstinence. *Journal of Consulting and Clinical Psychology, 72,* 202–217.

Orford, J., Guthrie, S., Nicholls, P., Oppenheimer, E., Egert, S., & Hensman, C. (1975). Self-reported coping behavior in wives of alcoholics and its association with drinking outcome. *Journal of Studies on Alcohol, 36,* 1254–1267.

Quinones, S. (2016). *Dreamland: The true tale of America's opiate epidemic.* New York: Bloomsbury Press.

Rustad, J.K., Junquera, P., Chaves, L., & Eth, S. (2012). Civil commitment among patients with alcohol and drug abuse: Practical, conceptual and ethical issues. *Addictive Disorders and Their Treatment, 11,* 136–154.

Satir, V. (1988). *The new peoplemaking.* Palo Alto, CA: Science & Behavioral Books.

Satir, V., Bitter, J.R., & Krestensen, K.K. (1988). Family reconstruction: The family within – a group experience. *Journal for Specialists in Group Work, 13(4),* 200–208.

Schumm, J.A., O'Farrell, T.J., Murphy, C.M., & Fals-Stewart, W. (2009). Partner violence before and after couples-based alcoholism treatment for female alcoholic patients. *Journal of Consulting and Clinical Psychology, 77,* 1136–1146.

Sexton, T., & Turner, C.W. (2011). The effectiveness of functional family therapy for youth with behavioral problems in a community practice setting. *Couple and Family Psychology: Research and Practice, 1(S),* 3–15.

Smith, J.E., & Meyers, R.J. (2004). *Motivating substance users to enter treatment: Working with family members.* New York: Guilford Press.

Stanton, M.D. (1979). Family treatment approaches to drug abuse problems: A review. *Family Process, 18,* 251–280.

Stanton, M.D. (1997). The role of family and significant others in the engagement and retention of drug dependent individuals. In L.S. Onken, J.D. Blaine, & J.J. Boren (Eds). *Beyond the therapeutic alliance: Keeping the drug dependent individual in treatment* (pp. 157–180). National Institute on Drug Abuse Research Monograph. Rockville, MD: National Institute on Drug Abuse.

Stanton, M.D., & Todd, T.C. (1982). *The family therapy of drug abuse and addiction.* New York: Guilford Press.

Stanton, M.D., Todd, T.C., Heard, D.B., Kirshner, S., Kleiman, J.I., Mowatt, D.T., & Vandeusen, J.M. (1978). Heroin addiction as a family phenomena: A new conceptual model. *American Journal of Drug and Alcohol Abuse, 5,* 125–150.

Steinglass, P. (1981). The alcoholic family at home: Patterns of interaction in dry, wet, and transitional stage of alcoholism. *Archives of General Psychiatry, 38,* 578–584.

Steinglass, P., Bennett, L.A., Wolin, S.J., & Reiss, D. (1987). *The alcoholic family.* New York: Basic Books.

Steinglass, P., Davis, D.L., & Berenson, D. (1977). Observations of conjointly hospitalized "alcoholic couples" during sobriety and intoxication: Implications for theory and therapy. *Family Processes, 16,* 1–16.

Waldron, H.B., & Turner, C.W. (2008). Evidenced-based psychological treatments for adolescent substance abuse. *Journal of Clinical Child & Adolescent Psychology, 37,* 238–261.

Waldron, H.B., Slesnick, N., Brody, J.L., Turner, C.W., & Peterson, T.R. (2001). Treatment outcomes for adolescent substance abuse at 4- and 7-month assessments. *Journal of Consulting and Clinical Psychology, 69,* 802–813.

Walsh, F. (1993). *Normal family processes* (2nd edn). New York: Guilford Press.

Wegsheider, S. (1981). *Another chance: Hope and health for the alcoholic family*. Palo Alto, CA: Science & Behavior Books.

Whitfield, C. (1989). Co-dependence: Our most common addiction: Some physical, mental, emotional and spiritual perspectives. *Alcoholism Treatment Quarterly, 6(1),* 19–36.

Wolin, S.J., Bennett, L.A., Noonan, D.L., & Teitelbaum, M.A. (1980). Disrupted family rituals: A factor in the intergenerational transmission of alcoholism. *Journal of Studies on Alcohol, 41,* 199–214.

5 Biological Models of Addiction

Alan A. Cavaiola

Introduction

A long-held assumption in the addiction treatment field is that genetic factors can increase one's likelihood of developing a substance use disorder (SUD). In other words, alcoholism and drug dependencies tend to "run in families." It's important to consider that other mental health and medical conditions are also known to have heritability risk factors, such as particular types of cancer or essential hypertension (high blood pressure). For example, schizophrenia is about 50% heritable, while autism is about 70% heritable. Interestingly, there is a great deal of overlap in the genes involved in several distinct mental disorders such as schizophrenia, bipolar disorder, ADHD and depression (Winerman, 2019). Therefore, just as one inherits particular traits from one's biological parents (e.g. eye and hair color, height, weight, athletic, musical or artistic talents), one can also inherit predispositions to develop a substance use disorder and perhaps even process addictions like gambling disorders.

Although there are several caveats to these genetic theories of addiction, the general consensus is that, for many individuals, his or her substance use disorder might best explained by genetics. One such caveat is that if substance use disorders are indeed inherited, what exactly is inherited that might predispose a person to becoming addicted? Are there differences in one's basic physiology that are somehow inherited from parents or grandparents? Also, although there has been a great deal of research which examined the possibility of there being an "addictive personality" that pre-determines whether one develops a SUD, the majority of research has focused on inherited physical characteristics (e.g. variations in how alcohol is metabolized or broken down in the body, or depletions in particular neurotransmitters such as dopamine).

Suffice to say, genetic and other biomedical models of addiction are truly etiological models because their main contention is that genetics will determine whether one becomes addicted to alcohol or drugs. Therefore, it's important to keep in mind, that when we consider the Nature–Nurture controversy, that the biomedical models clearly fall under the "Nature" side of the debate because physical predisposing traits are thought to be internal and therefore are *not* considered part of environmental (i.e. Nurture) influences.

It's also important to point out that the biological models that we will be presenting are synonymous with the disease model in that they put forth the notion that similar to how diseases such as cancer, cardiac conditions and sickle cell anemia are thought to be inherited, so too are SUDs. The disease model is also synonymous with the Minnesota Model, which emphasizes the use of the 12 Steps of Alcoholics Anonymous/Narcotics Anonymous as part of the standard treatment protocol. The majority of 28-day inpatient programs for SUD operate on the basis of the Minnesota Model. These include well-known programs such as Hazelden in Minnesota and the Betty Ford Center in Palm Springs, California.

In this chapter, we will also be exploring other biological factors that may help to explain the etiology of substance use disorders. With the advent of advanced neurological imaging techniques like CT scans and PET scans, neuroscientists are better able to look "inside the brain" in order to see how it responds to alcohol and other mood-altering substances. We will therefore be discussing the role of neurotransmitters and particular hormonal imbalances as possible causes of substance use disorders.

Key Terms

concordance rate: the probability or likelihood that twins or two family members will have the same trait of characteristic based on genetic inheritance.

monozygotic twins: also referred to as "identical twins," occurs when the male sperm fertilizes one egg (or zygote) of the mother. Monozygotic twins have the exact same DNA.

dizygotic twins: also referred to as "fraternal twins," occurs when male sperm fertilizes two separate eggs of the mother. Dizygotic twins do not have the exact same DNA.

phenotype: the observable physical and biochemical characteristics of an individual, determined both by genetic make-up and environmental influences.

genotype: the genetic make-up of an individual organism (as distinguished from their physical appearance. The genetic constitution of an individual.

genetic marker: refers to a particular gene or DNA sequence that can be used to identify a particular genetic trait which can be traced back through one's pedigree.

genetic predisposition: an inheritable characteristic, such as the risk of acquiring a disease like alcoholism or Huntington's Disease.

Human Genome Project: an international human genetic research project conducted between 1990 and 2003, which determined the base pair sequences in human DNA with the purpose of storing this information in computer databases.

genetic variants: each gene pool contains pairs of DNA pairs. The variations occur both within and among members of a population. Genetic variation is brought about through mutation which then produces a permanent change in the chemical structure of a chromosome.

allele: an alternate or abnormal form of a gene.

alcogene: a specific gene which genetically transmits alcohol use disorders to offspring (e.g. sons and daughters).

CT scan: also known as a computed tomography scan (and formerly known as computerized axial tomography scans or CAT scans), makes use of many computer-generated X-ray measurements taken from many cross-sectional images to produce cross-sectional images of bones, organs and other tissue.

PET scans: also known as positron emission tomography, makes use of radio-active dyes to observe metabolic processes within the body. Three-dimensional computer-generated images are then produced which allows for detection of diseases and metabolism (e.g. brain activity).

evoked potentials: a technique used to measure electrical activity in the brain in response to specific stimulation (e.g. a flashing light) of specific sensory nerve pathways.

epigenetics: modifications that regulate the activity of DNA, involving RNA as "messengers" that determine how genes are expressed.

Genetic Theories of Addiction

Biological or biomedical models tend to look at physical causes for addiction. Perhaps the most well-researched paradigm with the biological model are the genetic models (see Bohman, Sigvardsson, & Cloninger, 1981; Cotton, 1979; Cloninger, Sigvardsson, & Bohman, 1988; Cloninger, Bohman, & Sigvardsson, 1981; Goodwin, 1988; Hesselbrock, 1986; Hesselbrock & Hesselbrock, 1992; Schuckit & Smith, 1997). Much of the early research which examined genetic links to alcoholism was done in Scandinavian countries (because of open adoption records). These studies sought to rule out the environmental impact of modeling that might occur if one were to grow up with their alcoholic parent by following monozygotic twins who were raised apart by non-alcoholic, adoptive parents.

According to Donald Goodwin (1988), one of the leading researchers in the field of genetics and alcohol use disorders, the contention that alcoholism runs in families can be traced back to the Bible, Aristotle and Plutarch. The well-known Greek philosopher, Plutarch is quoted as writing, "Drunkards beget drunkards." However, one of the major challenges in determining whether substance use disorders have a genetic basis is to rule out the impact of environmental influences; that is, do sons or daughters learn to drink or use substances in ways similar to their parent because of modeling their parents' behavior? This is the true essence of the nature–nurture debate: how much of a particular trait can be accounted for by genetic (nature) influences versus environmental (nurture) influences. Physical traits such as eye color or hair color indisputably have a genetic basis. Yet, let's take a behavioral trait like acting ability or musical talent. Would we say that John David Washington's success as an actor (he starred in *BlacKKKlansman*, 2018) was the result of genetic influence or from having grown up in a household with his famous actor father, Denzel Washington? The same problem holds true with substance use disorders also. If a son or daughter develops an opioid use disorder at age 18, could we definitively say whether this was the result of growing up in a household where the mother or father abused substances or the result of genetics? Goodwin (1988) points out that some of the earliest family studies of alcoholism were done in Germany in 1929 and 1933. These studies found that rates of alcoholism were higher in male relatives (25–50%) than female relatives (5–8%), which appeared to coincide with the suspected rates of alcoholism in the general population of Germany at the time. Interestingly, the 1933 study also compared alcoholics with individuals who were addicted to morphine and found that offspring of morphine-addicted individuals were more likely to develop addictions to morphine than to alcohol. Goodwin cautions however that this is not conclusive evident to suggest that there is "a drug-specific proneness to addiction" (1988, p. 67).

Learning Opportunity 5.1

Think about different physical characteristics (body size, weight, hair/eye color) and personality traits (sense of humor, calm, restless, tenacious, resilient) that are similar to your biological parents; then make a list of those traits and share them with a group of three or four other students. With regard to the personality similarities, would you say those might have been inherited or the result of role-modeling from your mother or father? Discuss with your group.

In order to try to shed light on the nature–nurture conundrum, researchers began to study twins, particularly monozygotic or identical twins because they shared identical DNA, and ideally to study monozygotic twins who were reared apart (e.g. twins who were separated from their biological parents and raised by adoptive parents.) Many of these early studies (e.g. Cadoret, O'Gorman, Troughton, & Heywood, 1985; Cadoret, Troughton, & O'Gorman, 1987; Cloniner, Bohman, & Sigvardsson, 1981; Goodwin, Schulsinger, Hermansen, Guze, & Winokur, 1973) were done in Scandinavian countries (e.g. Sweden, Norway) because they keep open adoption records, therefore it was easier for researchers to follow up on twins who were separated and raised by adoptive parents. The results of these early adoption studies found significantly higher rates of alcohol abuse and dependence among biological sons of alcoholic parents when compared to sons who were adopted at birth by non-alcoholic parents.

Learning Opportunity 5.2

Why did researchers prefer to study monozygotic twins as opposed to dizygotic twins? Also why was it important that researchers studied twins who were adopted at birth by non-alcoholic parents?

Later studies which examined families, twins and adopted twins definitively demonstrated that genetic influences had contributed to the development of alcohol use disorders in 50–60% of both men and women (McGue, 1999).

For example, studies done at the Minnesota Center for Family Twin Research (MCTFR) (often referred to as the "Minnesota Twins" research), studied 1,400 pairs of monozygotic twins beginning at either age 11 or 17. At the time of the 12-year follow-up, this research identified several genetic markers which were predictive of later alcoholism. These include personality factors such as impulsivity, sociability, rebelliousness and becoming easily bored; family background such as father having a high tolerance to alcohol; and a low P300 brainwave pattern (a smaller P300 at age 17 was predictive of those who would develop alcohol and drug problems by age 20). Finally, precocious experimentation with alcohol (before age 15) was also predictive of later alcoholism (Legrand, Iacano, &McGue, 2005).

When looking at addiction etiology from a genetic perspective, it's important first to accept the fact that not all people who have substance use disorders are alike. For example, Cloninger (1987) concluded that there were two distinct types of alcoholics among the population they studied. Type 1 alcoholics tended to develop excessive drinking patterns later in life and were more prone to depression, situational stress and anxiety disorders. Whereas Type 2 alcoholics had biological parents and other relatives who had alcohol use disorders. This group often began drinking in their teens, had histories of antisocial behavior and tended to be impulsive sensation-seekers who often ran into legal problems. The Type 2 group was also less responsive to treatment. Interestingly, another genetic marker of the Type 2 groups was that they were also more likely to be left-handed. In a 40-year follow-up study of individuals considered to be at high-risk for alcoholism because of paternal alcoholism (i.e. having a father who was diagnosed as alcoholic), it was determined that sons of alcoholic fathers were more likely to develop "a more severe form of alcoholism, i.e. alcohol dependence, may be under greater genetic influence" (Knop, Penick, Nickel, Mednick, Jensen, Manzardo, & Gabrielli, 2007, p. 391). These findings suggest that Type 2 alcoholic fathers are more likely to have Type 2 alcoholic sons.

Overall, the genetic research has generally concluded: first, that alcohol use disorder (alcoholism) tends to run in families; second, that adopted children tend to be more similar to their biological parents than their adoptive parents in terms of alcohol use (Dodgen & Shea, 2000); and, third, that alcoholism rates tend to be higher in monozygotic twins who share identical genetic make-up, than in dizygotic twins (ranging from .47 to .77 concordance for monozygotic twins versus .33 and .54 for dizygotic twins (Heath et al., 1997; Kender, Neale, Heath,

& Kessler, 1994; Kendler, Prescott, Neale, & Pedersen, 1997; McGue, Pickens, & Svikis, 1992; Pickens et al., 1991; Prescott, Aggen, & Kendler, 2000.) Also, children born to both an alcoholic mother and father have a great likelihood of developing an alcohol use disorder than those born to either an alcoholic mother *or* father. Cotton (1979) reviewed over 39 genetic studies and found that generally, alcoholics were six times more likely (than general population samples) and twice as likely (than psychiatric populations) to have one or both biological parents who were diagnosed as alcohol dependent. Also, Cotton found that rates of alcohol use disorders were higher in the families of women than male alcoholics, and in close as opposed to distant blood relatives, and in fathers and brothers as opposed to mothers and sisters. Sons of alcoholics are anywhere from four to seven times more likely to be alcoholic than sons of non-alcoholic parents.

All the research sounds pretty convincing, yet there are two important questions that need to be taken into account. First, if substance use disorders are indeed genetic, then what exactly is inherited that predisposes one to develop a SUD? Second, the genetic research usually provides a range of inheritability probability (e.g. male offspring will have a 40–70% chance of developing a SUD if their father was an alcoholic). Yet that means that approximately 30–60% of male offspring will *not* develop a substance use disorder. Therefore, it would be unlikely that there will ever be a 100% chance that a son or daughter will develop an SUD based on their genetic inheritance. The same holds true for inheritability factors of other diseases/disorders as for other inherited physical and personality traits. Therefore, genetic inheritance may put one at risk for a substance use disorder but does not destine one to become an alcoholic or addicted person.

We will now examine some of the research that has uncovered several *genetic markers* which may help to answer the question of "What exactly gets inherited that determines if a person will be at risk for developing a SUD?" For example, there are differences in brain-wave activity of sons of alcoholics versus sons of non-alcoholics. Sons of alcoholics produce more alpha wave brain activity when EEG (electroencephalogram) studies are performed after they drink alcohol. Alpha brain waves are often associated with being very relaxed, and with serenity and creativity. Some speculate that sons of alcoholics may go on to develop alcohol use disorders because alcohol boosts alpha waves in the brain, therefore enhancing feelings of relaxation and serenity (Pollock, Gabrielli, Mednick, & Goodwin, 1988). Another possible genetic marker is the finding that sons of alcoholics do poorly on tests of conceptual or abstract thinking and the ability to categorize (Schuckit, Butters, Lyn, & Irwin, 1987). In a related study of intellectual performance using the WISC IQ scales it was determined that lower scores on Verbal IQ may be an antecedent to alcoholism (Gabrielli & Mednick, 1983). Another marker which seems to suggest a biologically inherited predisposition is that sons of alcoholics have moderately elevated levels of acetaldehyde after drinking alcohol. Acetaldehyde occurs when alcohol is being metabolized or broken down (Schuckit & Rayse, 1979; Agarwal & Goedde, 1989; Foroud & Li, 1999). These modest levels of acetaldehyde are often associated with increased drinking, whereas increased or high levels of acetaldehyde are considered to be a deterrent to drinking. In fact, the alcohol-antagonist medication Antabuse produces the highest levels of acetaldehyde, which is why if any person taking Antabuse ingests alcohol, they will have a very horrible reaction, similar to being poisoned. This aversive reaction serves as a deterrent to drinking. Another group of studies found that sons of alcoholics tend to feel less intoxicated when given the same amount of alcohol to drink than sons of non-alcoholics. Finally, the research done by Henri Begleiter (e.g. Porjesz & Begleiter, 2003) at Downstate Medical Center in Brooklyn, New York, found that sons of alcoholics responded differently to flashes of light or clicking sounds according to differences in their P300 brain waves, with decreased amplitude responses. The sons of alcoholics did not respond with the same degree of efficiency.

Advantages and Limitations of the Genetic Model

Although the research on genetic factors that predispose one to developing substance use disorders is very convincing, as indicated earlier, there is rarely, if ever, a 100% concordance rate (or likelihood) that one will develop an SUD, even if both parents are diagnosed with severe SUDs. Think of it this way: it is unlikely that you will inherit *all* of your parents' traits or characteristics. This point was raised by Gabor Maté in his bestseller, *In the realm of hungry ghosts* (2010). He hypothesizes that addictions are rooted in trauma from our past, emotional pain, failure to connect in meaningful ways with others, and societal values which overemphasize consumerism and external goods as a way to soothe one's distress or misery. Maté points out that workaholism and addiction to shopping are at their all-time high and represent an attempt to feel good by acquiring tangible objects rather than seeking solace or peace in our connections with loved ones. Maté (2010, p. 38) exclaims:

> Not all addictions are rooted in abuse and trauma, but I do believe they can all be traced to painful experience. A hurt is at the center of all addictive behaviors. It is present in the gambler, the Internet addict, the compulsive shopper, and the workaholic. The wound may not be as deep and the ache not as excruciating, and it may even be entirely hidden – but it's there.

The other limitation of the genetic model surrounds the uncertainty of *what exactly gets inherited* that predisposes one to become addicted. Although the aforementioned research performed on sons of alcoholics is also convincing in explaining what appear to be essential differences between sons of alcoholics compared to sons of non-alcoholics, it has yet to be determined what exactly gets inherited that predisposes individuals to develop SUDs.

It is important to take note that in trying to answer the question "How exactly do SUDs get genetically transmitted?" there has been another body of research that was developed by Dr. Ernest Noble at UCLA's Neuropsychiatric Institute and Dr. Kenneth Blum and Dr. Peter Sheridan from the University of Texas (Blum et al., 1990) which attempted to identify the actual gene variations (or anomalies) that might explain why certain biological offspring (e.g. identical twins) were at high risk for alcohol use disorders. It is estimated that there are approximately 3,000 human genetic diseases which get passed down from one generation to the next generation. These genetic diseases are caused by defects in the DNA (the substance in the chromosomes that carries the genetic code for the production of genes; Blum & Payne, 1991). This search for an "alcogene(s)" has yielded some interesting findings. According to Blum and Payne (1991) "each cell contains a billion pairs of DNA which are stored in 46 packages called chromosomes. These chromosomes act in pairs, so there are 23 pairs in each cell. At conception, half of the chromosomes of each pair are derived from the egg of the mother and half from the sperm of the father. Each chromosome is made up of many genes …" (1991, p. 227. Without getting into the rather complex details of the experimental research, what Noble, Blum and their colleagues thought they discovered was *the* specific gene variation which results in alcoholism. They hypothesized that the A1 allele gene transmitted an unusual pattern (possibly a genetic defect) in the dopamine D2 receptor gene. This research was very promising in that it seemed to locate both the specific gene variation that causes alcoholism and how it does so (i.e. by causing disruptions in dopamine production; dopamine is one of our "feel-good" neurotransmitters that gets released when we ingest alcohol or drugs). Unfortunately, attempts to replicate these findings had failed; there have since been other attempts to find specific gene variations that are predictive of alcohol use disorders in the offspring of alcoholic parents, however (see McGue & Irons, 2013). However, Dr. Judith Grisel (2019) author of *Never enough: The neuroscience and experience of addiction* concludes that the years of research in trying to find specific gene variations that would put to rest, once and for all, the claim that substance use disorders are genetic in origin has not conclusively found the "smoking gun" of gene variations or genetic sequences that are present in alcoholics but not present in social drinkers or abstainers.

Learning Opportunity 5.3

If a specific gene were to be definitively identified that was thought to genetically transmit substance use disorders and let's say you were considered to be at high risk for developing an SUD, would you be willing to be genetically tested using a DNA saliva test? If so, why or why not? Would you encourage your biological loved ones to be tested?

Grisel (2019) concludes that the research which sought to find specific alcogenes in DNA strands may have been too simplistic. She points out that more cutting-edge research in the area of epigenetics may be more fruitful in determining the role of genetics in substance use disorder transmission from one generation to the next. Epigenetics (literally means "on top of genetics") examines the role of RNA, which acts as messengers, which may "communicate" how DNA will express itself. In other words, it's not simply that one inherits particular DNA gene variants but how those DNA variants become expressed, which is where RNA and epigenetics comes in.

Case Example: Bill and Ted – A Family Impacted by Addiction

Bill and Ted are identical twins who live in Portsmouth, Ohio. They are 24 years old and both are homeless and unemployed. Both Bill and Ted are addicted to heroin; because both brothers are unemployed, however, they support their heroin addiction by panhandling and selling drugs. Ted began drinking and smoking and cannabis while in high school. He struggled in high school and was never as talented in sports like his twin brother Bill. Bill was the star of the high school football and baseball teams. Sports came naturally to him. When he suffered a torn knee ligament in his senior year, however, his dreams of obtaining an athletic scholarship to a Division 1 university were crushed. Bill was prescribed opioid painkillers after his first knee surgery and, when his doctor would no longer prescribe any more pills, Ted purchased some black tar heroin (which has been plentiful in many parts of Ohio; see Quinones, 2016) and soon they were both using heroin intravenously. Bill and Ted's parents, George and Karen never envisioned that their sons would become "homeless drug addicts." Initially, Bill and Ted started to work in the family's auto collision repair business, which had been developed by George's father, Henry, the paternal grandfather of Bill and Ted. It was Henry's hope that his son (George) and grandsons would carry on the family's collision repair business once he retired. However, this dream was never realized. George and Karen were both battling with their own substance use disorders (Karen was addicted to benzodiazepines and George was addicted to alcohol and would occasionally use cocaine). Because of George and Karen's struggles with addiction, Bill and Ted were essentially raised by their paternal grandparents, Henry and Martha. Interestingly, both Henry and Martha also had their own struggles with drinking over the years and at one point both started to go to AA meetings. Henry stopped going to AA meetings but managed to remain abstinent; Martha relapsed, however, and continued to drink excessively. Henry's brother had expressed concerns about Henry and Martha's drinking and had encouraged them to attend AA. Henry was hopeful that he could retire and turn the auto collision business over to his son, George and grandsons. However, because of George and his sons' addiction, they were unable to properly manage the business and it eventually went bankrupt.

Case Conceptualization

This family demonstrated three generations of substance use disorders. George was at high risk for developing a SUD given that both his parents (Henry and Martha) experienced problems with drinking. Henry was more open about admitting that his drinking had become problematic which is why he decided to stop drinking totally. Bill and Ted are also considered to be at high risk for an SUD given that both of their parents (George and Karen) admit to problems with alcohol and cocaine. Interestingly, when George and Karen were first married, they appeared to be enthusiastic, devoted parents; as they become more involved in drinking and cocaine use, however, they were unable to take care of their sons. This is an all-too-common occurrence in families impacted by substance use disorders where grandparents are required to step into the role of primary caregivers for their grandchildren.

Neurotransmitter Models of Addiction

Key Terms

neurotransmitters: are substances manufactured in the neuron that aid in synaptic transmission of nerve impulses in the brain. Neurotransmitters are of two types: monoamines (e.g. serotonin, dopamine, norepinephrine, GABA and neuropeptides (e.g. endorphins, enkephalins and dynorphins)

synapse: the junction or space between two neurons across which neural electrical impulses are transmitted.

synaptic cleft: the area through which nerve impulses cross from axon to dendrite.

endorphins: includes any group of neuropeptides that bind to opioid receptor sites in the brain and throughout the body. Endorphins are thought to be the body's own analgesic or pain-reliever. Endorphins are also involved in craving behavior, and sexual functioning.

CNS: stands for central nervous system, which is composed of the brain and spinal cord.

axon: or thin nerve fiber that that carries messages away from the nerve cell body dendrite: or thin nerve fiber that carries messages towards the cell body.

synaptic transmission: the process by which a electrochemical nerve impulse is transmitted or jumps from one end of the synapse to the next synapse.

synaptic vesicles: sac-like structures located at the end of a synapse that contain the various neurotransmitters.

synaptic re-uptake: after a nerve impulse is transmitted from one synapse to another, the neurotransmitter that is released into the synaptic cleft or juncture is then re-absorbed back into the synaptic vesicles (see Figure 5.1).

At the simplest level, whenever one ingests alcohol or any mood-altering substance the euphoric high or "buzz" that one feels is produced by neurochemical changes in the brain. The same holds true however, for other things that produce pleasure or reward such as eating chocolate cake, winning a bet, having sex, getting a promotion, purchasing new clothes or getting an "A" on an exam. You may have noticed that some of the aforementioned pleasurable events or rewards fall within the framework of what we call "process addictions." For example, sex addiction, gambling, workaholism, shopping addiction, food addiction (such as overeating or

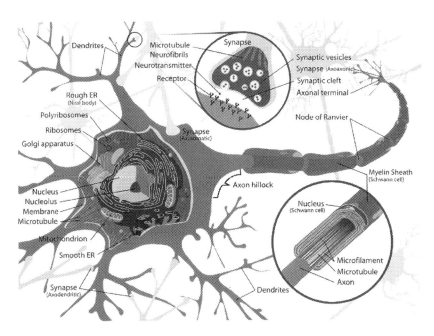

Figure 5.1 Neurotransmitter Release at the Nerve Synapse
Courtesy: Pixabay https://pixabay.com/vectors/red-science-diagram-cell-neuron-41524/

addiction to sweets or high carb foods) share in common the fact that some individuals experience incredible pleasure in these activities because they flood the brain with dopamine.

The aforementioned neurochemical change (e.g. enhanced dopamine production) takes into account both the "what" and the "where." When you drink a shot of tequila (or any alcohol-containing beverage), dopamine gets released in the brain. Dopamine is the "*what*," it's the neurotransmitter that helps to produce that anticipated pleasurable buzz (along with other neurotransmitters like GABA and serotonin). *Where* in the brain these neurotransmitters are released is also very important because it's in an area known as the nucleus accumbens, which is located about three inches behind the bottom of our eye sockets. The nucleus accumbens is part of the brain involved in emotions and reward. This area, known colloquially as the "reward center" of the brain, is called the *mesolimbic pathway* by neuroscientists (Grisel, 2019). You may be thinking that while alcohol, benzodiazepines and opioid substances all tend to slow down the mind and produce a feeling of calm, what about substances like methamphetamines, crack or cocaine which produce incredible energy and elated mood? Alcohol, benzos and opioids are all central nervous system depressants while methamphetamines and cocaine are considered CNS stimulants and these depressant versus stimulation effects are produced by combinations of neurotransmitter and neuropeptide release at the synapses of particular nerve cells throughout our brains. For example, drinking a few shots of tequila will result in an increase in dopamine in the brain; however, GABA production is also increased along with glutamate. GABA is an inhibitory neurotransmitter, which means it will slow down (or depress) the nervous system, thereby producing feelings of relaxation, reduced anxiety/worry and sleepiness. Glutamate, on the other hand, is an excitatory neurotransmitter which is responsible for helping the brain form memories (which helps explain why excessive drinking results in memory "blackouts"). Both GABA and glutamate are pervasive throughout the brain (Grisel, 2019), which may account for why those neurotransmitters have such a profound effect when people drink alcohol. Alcohol ingestion also impacts on endorphin release, which is why (prior to the discovery of other pain analgesics such as opioid "painkillers") alcohol was used to reduce pain. Alcohol has such a pervasive effect on brain chemistry, it's no wonder that Grisel (2019) likens its effect to a "sledgehammer." Also, it's important to consider that when a person drinks excessively and on a daily basis over the course of several years, they may develop neurological disorders such as Wernicke-Korsakoff syndrome, which is characterized by impaired cognitive (thought) processing, psychotic-like thinking, confusion and profound memory deficits, which is the result of a combination of brain cell damage and nutritional deficiency.

Let's examine the impact of mood-altering substances. If alcohol impacts the brain "like a sledgehammer," then cocaine and amphetamines impact the brain more "like a laser" (Grisel, 2019). Cocaine, methamphetamines and MDMA or ecstasy (ecstasy is referred to as a "psychedelic amphetamine" because it contains chemical properties of psychedelics like LSD and amphetamine or stimulants). This group of stimulants impact on the monoamine neurotransmitters which include: dopamine, serotonin, norepinephrine, epinephrine (or adrenalin) and melatonin (Grisel, 2019). All of the aforementioned neurotransmitters combine to produce a feeling of intense stimulation, incredible energy and grandiosity (as if one could do or accomplish anything). For those who go on cocaine binges (which often last for several days or a few weeks) or who use amphetamines daily over the course of several days, the stimulation thrill described earlier is replaced with psychotic-like, paranoid thoughts and something called stereotypy. A condition in which individuals repeat the same behaviors over and over again. In most instances, both conditions will resolve and people return to normal once he or she detoxes and becomes drug-free.

According to Grisel (2019), cannabis (marijuana) use is likened to the brain being hit by a can of red paint, in the respect that the psychological-emotional impact of cannabis is pervasive and widespread, impacting a variety of neurotransmitters in various locations within the brain. For example, glutamate neurotransmitter activation in the region of the hippocampus may account for why cannabis users have difficulty in forming short-term memories. Cannabis, like opioids, has its own special neural receptors in the brain called *endocannabinoids* (the prefix "endo-" refers to these receptors being endogenous or internal, within the brain). Therefore, in addition to the release of neurotransmitters like dopamine and serotonin, which produce a feeling a well-being, other neurotransmitter release produces sensory input (e.g. sound, taste, visual) that is perceived as totally new and therefore incredibly interesting to someone who's stoned. This accounts for why, after smoking or

---

Boxed Item 5.1 The Role of Neurotransmitters

Each of the neurotransmitters in the brain has specific functions and produces certain emotional states. As mentioned previously, various drugs of abuse will tend to increase production of combinations of the neurotransmitters. For example:

Serotonin promotes feelings of well-being and sleep (serotonin is made from the amino acid tryptophan. Certain foods such as turkey contain high levels of tryptophan, which is why people feel sleepy after Thanksgiving dinner). Serotonin also reduces aggressive and compulsive behaviors such as excessive alcohol or drug intake, and over-eating. Serotonin also helps to regulate the cardiovascular system.

Dopamine increases feelings of well-being and is associated with sexual arousal; however, dopamine may increase aggressive behavior and alertness. Excessive dopamine may actually cause psychotic behavior, while dopamine depletions are associated with anhedonia (i.e. the inability to experience pleasure.)

Norepinephrine also increases feelings of well-being and reduces compulsive behaviors; however, an excessive amount of norepinephrine may increase anxiety, heart rate and blood pressure, and may cause tremors in those withdrawing from alcohol or drugs.

GABA reduces anxiety and compulsive behavior and may help to elevate one's threshold for pain. GABA is considered an "inhibitory" neurotransmitter in that, it helps to reduce heart rate, blood pressure and breathing rate.

Glutamate is also an excitatory neurotransmitter which helps us to form memories and helps with learning and cognitive processing. Glutamate also send signals to other neurotransmitters and tends to be one of the most pervasive neurotransmitters throughout the brain. It is thought to also help in the development of neurons. Excessive glutamate has been found people with strokes, autism and intellectual disabilities.

Adenosine is an inhibitory neurotransmitter that produces drowsiness. Caffeine blocks this neurotransmitter, however as the impact of caffeine wears off, drowsiness develops as adenosine is naturally produced during the course of the day and is involved in the onset of sleep.

---

ingesting cannabis, every sensation (whether visual, auditory or gustatory) becomes amazing, as if being experienced for the first time. No wonder Foreigner's classic rock song is entitled, "Feels Like the First Time," not "Feels Like the 7th, 8th or 9th Time." However, the problem often encountered when individuals stop using cannabis is that *nothing* is very interesting, which may be akin to an extreme type of post-acute withdrawal syndrome (see Boxed Item 4.2). Cannabis withdrawal is said to be characterized by anhedonia, an emotional symptom often found in people who experience major depression, whereby nothing is experienced as being pleasurable.

Finally, opioids also have endogenous opioid receptors in the brain which accounts for their analgesic or pain-relieving impact. Prescription opioids (such as hydrocodone (Oxycontin®), hydromorphone [Vicodin®] and oxycodone [Percoset®]).

Biomedical Applications to Addiction Counseling: Assessment, Techniques and Interventions – Clinical Implications for Counselors

Assessment

When meeting with a new client who is requesting services for a substance use disorder, standard procedure is to conduct a thorough biopsychosocial assessment which examines ways in which the client's alcohol and/or drug use has impacted on him or her physically or biologically, psychologically (e.g. emotionally and cognitively) and socially (e.g. interpersonal relationships with family and friends). When doing a biopsychosocial assessment, it's important to gather information pertaining to family history, not only to explore how substance use has impacted on important familial relationships but also to explore possible genetic influences or genetic risk factors. Based on the genetic theory, the supposition is "the more blood relatives one has who have substance use disorders, the higher the risk in their sons or daughters." So how do we collect family history? The best way is to use a genogram (McGoldrick & Gerson, 1985). A genogram is a shortcut way to gather family history using a series of symbols (see Figure 4.1; see also Figure 5.2) According to Monica McGoldrick and Randy Gerson (1985), who originated this technique for gathering family history, it's best to begin by asking clients to provide the names and approximate ages of their immediate family: parents, siblings, grandparents, aunts, uncles cousins, etc. It's important to note who's deceased by placing an X through their circle (for women) or square (for men) and then asking what caused his or her death. It's then important to ask about any divorces, separations or other disruptions in family structure. McGoldrick suggests that it's best to begin by then asking about the client's family history of medical problems (e.g. diagnosed medical disorders as well as hospitalizations or other treatments he or she may have received), before asking about more personal information such as histories of mental health or substance use disorders. In gathering family history on substance use disorders rather than starting off with a question like, "So, does anyone in your family have drinking or drug problems?" it's more helpful to begin with less threatening questions, such as "Tell me something about what was considered acceptable drinking in your family when you were growing up." Or, "Was alcohol usually a part of celebrations like holidays or birthdays?" and "If so, what was considered acceptable use of alcohol?" The questioning would then move to asking if anyone in the family was considered to have an alcohol or drug problem by other family members. Also, did anyone in the family ever go for help for a drink or drug use problem? Or, "Has anyone in your family ever gone for help by attending Alcoholics Anonymous (AA) or Narcotics Anonymous (NA)?"

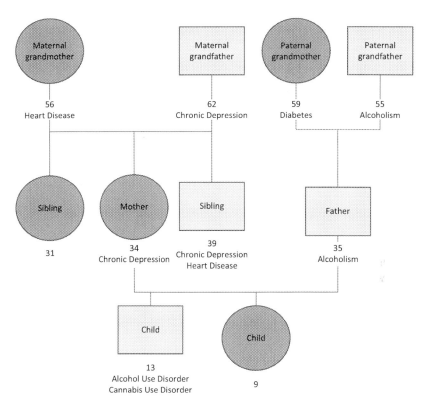

Figure 5.2 Genogram Illustrating Alcoholism on Paternal Side
Source: www.pinterest.com/pin/80009330860167913/

By exploring the family's mental health history, we are also trying to find risk factors for substance use disorders. As mentioned earlier, there are particular mental health disorders which tend to correlate or coexist with SUDs, such as bipolar disorder, PTSD, eating disorders and depressive disorders. McGoldrick recommends starting off with less threatening questions. Start by asking if any family members ever experienced any problems with coping with daily life? Then ask if any family members had experienced any emotional coping problems. Then ask if any family members had ever received help for emotional problems, whether they may have been hospitalized and whether any family member was ever prescribed medication for emotional problems? Be aware that if a client were to say, "My Aunt Mabel was hospitalized for a 'nervous breakdown' back in 1987" it would then be necessary to ask what types of problems Aunt Mabel might have been experiencing. A "nervous breakdown" can mean anything (e.g. a suicide attempt, major depression, a manic episode or detoxification for alcohol or drug dependence). There is no such diagnosis as a "nervous breakdown" in the *DSM-5* or any of its earlier editions. Therefore, it's important that counselors try to decipher what clients means when using this colloquial term. In the Family Models chapter, we discussed the use of genograms. However, as opposed to focusing on the family's medical/substance use history, we also used genograms to assess family structure and dynamics.

We wish we could say there are definitive genetic tests for substance use disorder potential or risk, just as there is for Huntington's Disease and for certain developmental disabilities like Down syndrome. The best type of test available for SUDs is what is referred to as "an alcohol skin flush" genetic test which is available through genetic testing for medical problems by companies such as "23 and Me" and CriGenetics. The alcohol skin flush test determines which individuals are likely to experience a skin flush reaction when drinking alcohol. Those who experience this reaction are thought to be a lower risk for developing alcoholism. The flushing reaction is said to be very uncomfortable (face and neck become hot and red, nauseous feelings are also common) therefore drinking alcohol becomes an unpleasant or aversive experience. The skin flush is thought to be the result of a build-up of acetaldehyde (a by-product that's produced when alcohol is ingested). It is thought to be most common in people of East Asian ancestry, which may account for why Japanese, Burmese, Thai, and Chinese have lower rates of alcohol use disorders. The drug Antabuse, which is used to help treat alcoholism works by preventing the liver from breaking down acetaldehyde. Therefore, when a person taking Antabuse drinks alcohol, it is like they are poisoning themselves in that they experience an extreme skin flush reaction, nausea, vomiting and extreme discomfort.

Learning Opportunity 5.4 – Antabuse

Although Antabuse is not as popular today as when it was first developed back in the 1960s, it may still be useful with some individuals. See what you can find out about how Antabuse works and how it may be helpful in the treatment of alcohol use disorders. What model best explains how Antabuse works? If you had a close friend or relative who is diagnosed with an alcohol use disorder, would you recommend that they take Antabuse to help them manage cravings to drink?

Biological Model Treatment and Techniques

Genetic theory has not produced techniques that are applicable to treatment. However, if tests such as the skin flush test were developed which not only predicted alcoholism risk but also risk for other substance use disorders, those genetic tests might provide useful information about genetic risk factors. The question, is how can we use this "at risk" information? Promising advances in genetic engineering have been able to change the devastating impact of particular genetically transmitted disorders; based on our current understanding of the genetics of substance use disorders, however, it's probable that these disorders are not caused by one "alcogene" but rather a combination of several genes which makes genetic engineering more complex and outcomes are less assured. I (AAC) was fortunate to have met Dr. Kenneth Blum at a conference presentation. I asked him, if genetic engineering continues to make advances, would we one day see a time where alcoholism could be eliminated by genetic engineering surgery? He explained that there were two problems to consider. The first is whether this type of genetic engineering might be considered an attempt to create a "Master Race" (which was the goal of Adolf Hitler.) The second problem with genetic engineering is that, by tinkering with particular genes, we may be reducing the likelihood of someone developing a substance use disorder but we're not sure what other changes might take place. For example, the Pulitzer Prize winning author Ernest Hemingway was known to be a heavy, frequent drinker, probably an alcoholic. So, if Hemingway were to be subjected to genetic engineering, we might reduce his risk of developing alcoholism but would we also be taking away his incredible writing abilities?

Learning Opportunity 5.5 – Risk Factors

Imagine that you have a younger brother or sister or a close friend who recently had a baby who is determined to be at genetic risk for developing problems with drugs and alcohol when they grow up. What would you recommend to help reduce the possibility that your sibling or friend's baby will develop an SUD when they grow up?

Fortunately, there are several treatments that have evolved out of the research on neurotransmitters. Most of this research has focused on drugs that help with detoxification and help clients manage cravings. For example, given the recent opioid epidemic, medication-assisted treatments (MAT) using drugs such as buprenorphine (Suboxone® and Subutex®) and dolophine (Methadone) can be used both to detoxify people dependent on prescription opioids and heroin, and as a type of maintenance alternative to using opioids with high overdose potential. There are certainly controversies regarding Suboxone and Methadone (such as a potential to abuse these medications), however, when taken properly and when combined with counseling, these medications allow people to function on a daily basis.

Several medications have been developed which help reduce craving and, in some instances, help act as *agonists*. Agonists work by occupying the particular receptor sites that produce the mood-altering effect or buzz from taking drugs. Therefore, if someone takes a drug of abuse then the agonist blocks the mood-altering effect of that drug. Naltrexone is an example of an agonist drug that is thought to help reduce opioid and alcohol craving. If someone injects heroin or ingests a prescription opioid such as Percoset while taking Naltrexone, that person will not experience the "high" of taking the opioid drug.

Advantages and Limitations of the Neurotransmitter Model

Probably the most vocal critics of the neurotransmitter model are Satel and Lilienfeld (2013), co-authors of the book, *Brainwashed: The seductive appeal of mindless neuroscience.*

The basis of their criticisms comes from questions regarding the addictive nature of particular substances. For example, the National Institute of Drug Abuse (NIDA), under the leadership of Alan Leshner (1997) and more recently Nora Volkow (Goldstein & Volkow, 2002), have put forth the claims that substance use disorders are "chronic, relapsing brain diseases," and that the brain becomes "hijacked" by the powerful neurotransmitter changes (e.g. in dopamine, serotonin, norepinephrine) that occur during substance intoxication and alter brain chemistry long after drug use ceases (as evidenced by post-acute withdrawal). However, there are caveats or exceptions to these claims. Satel and Lilienfeld (2013) point out that the follow-up studies of Viet Nam veterans who were addicted to heroin while serving in Viet Nam found low rates of continued heroin dependence once these soldiers returned home to the United States. In these follow-up studies only 5% of the men who were addicted to heroin in Viet Nam relapsed within 10 months after returning to the US, and only 12% had relapsed briefly within three years of returning home. According to Robins (1993), who conducted these follow-ups, these results "ran counter to the conventional wisdom that heroin is a drug that causes addicts to suffer intolerable craving that rapidly leads to re-addiction if exposed to the drug" (p. 1052). These results also challenged the prevailing wisdom of the time which claimed, "once an addict, always an addict," which speaks to the chronic nature of substance use disorders. The Viet Nam follow-up studies also point to the powerful impact of environmental factors (Robins, Helzer, & Davis, 1975). Some theorists conclude the Viet Nam represented the perfect substance use experiment, in that combat troops were exposed to life-threatening, unpredictable dangers, lack of group cohesiveness (given US military policy of time-limited deployment with constantly shifting troop deployments), being isolated from friends and family, and with consistent and abundant drug availability.

This notion that mood-altering chemicals are inherently addicting and therefore irresistible even to casual users was challenged by Johann Hari (2015), author of *Chasing the scream.* He points to research that was well known in the 1970s in which rats could press a bar order to receive a drink of water containing morphine or a drink of plain water. Invariably, the rats would bar press for the morphine-laced water until eventually they would literally drop dead from morphine-overdose (e.g. Pickens & Plunkett, 1970; Smith & Davis, 1973; Smith, Werner, & Davis, 1975). Without doubt, morphine was considered to be a powerful, irresistible reinforcer even for rats! When Canadian researchers Alexander, Coambs and Hadaway (1978) replicated some of these earlier studies, they included two bottles of water (i.e. one containing morphine-laced water, the other plain water), however they also changed the rats' environment. These rat cages were filled with several "rat toys" like running wheels, balls, shiny objects and female and male rats. The findings were startling. The rats who were in "rat park" or the enriched environment did not prefer the morphine-laced water and therefore did not perish due to morphine overdose!

Learning Opportunity 5.6 – Rat Park

What do the Viet Nam follow-up study and the "rat park" studies have in common? See if you can figure out the commonalities and discuss within a small group or in your online chat discussion why the findings of both studies are important to describing limitation of the neurotransmitter model.

Satel and Lilienfeld conclude that "neurobiology is not destiny" (2013, p. 51) and, although mood-altering substances without doubt disrupt neural mechanisms, thereby constraining a person's capacity for choice, they do not destroy it. Most of the critics of biomedical models of addiction feel that while developments in neuroscience technology have advanced our understanding of addictions, they tend to downplay the important role of environmental factors (e.g. the impact of poverty, racism and traumatic experiences) (see Figure 5.3).

We mentioned earlier that one of the limitations of the genetic model of addiction is that there really hasn't been conclusive evidence that indicates what exactly "gets inherited" that predisposes one to become addicted. However, the neurotransmitter model may have provided a possible answer. For example, if individuals who develop SUDs are looking for the "rush" provided by the flooding of the neurotransmitter dopamine, or the pain relief from the flood of endorphins, then

---

Advantages

- genetic models are truly etiological or causal models (i.e. this model hypothesizes that people develop SUDs because they are at genetic risk); in other words, SUDs tend to be handed down from generation to generation
- genetic models are very much aligned with the disease model, which exonerates people from responsibility for becoming alcoholics or addicted individuals
- all drugs of abuse flood the brain with dopamine which impacts on the mesolimbic (or reward) system creating the "rush" or high from substance use
- all drugs of abuse disrupt dopamine, serotonin and endorphins which predisposes substance users to developing acute and post-acute withdrawal whenever the individual attempts to cease alcohol or drug use

Limitations

- not everyone who had a biological relative with a SUD will necessarily develop a SUD
- genetic research has not been able to isolate a gene by which SUDs are transmitted
- genetic research is unable to describe why SUDs can skip a generation
- if all drugs of abuse flood the brain with specific neurotransmitters (e.g. dopamine) why doesn't everyone who uses a mood-altering drug become addicted?

Figure 5.3 Summary of Advantages and Limitations of Biomedical Models

---

Boxed Item 5.2 Medications that Assist in Reducing Drug Craving

Drug Causing Craving	*Medications That Lessen Craving*
Alcohol	Topirimate (Topamax)
	Acamprosate (Camprel)
	Naltrexone (ReVia)
Cocaine	Baclofen
Heroin/prescription opioids	Naltrexone
	Vivitrol (injectable Naltrexone)
Nicotine	Chantix
	Zyban (Wellbutrin)

---

perhaps these individuals are deficient in these neurotransmitters prior to the onset of alcohol or drug use that then places these individuals at greater risk for SUDs. That seems logical, right? Blum and Payne (1991) point to a study done in Milan, Italy (Gennazzini et al., 1982), which looked at endorphin levels in the cerebral spinal fluid in a group of individuals with long-term alcohol use disorders. Although the results of the study had suggested there were indeed beta-endorphin depletions, there was no possible way to measure the beta-endorphin levels prior to the onset of alcohol use in this group of individuals. Therefore, at best, the researchers could only conclude that excessive, continuous drinking had depleted beta-endorphin levels. Several more recent studies have also concluded that repetitive substance use will deplete neurotransmitter levels and that this contributes to "the chronic relapsing nature of the disease" (Reed, Butelman, & Kreek, (2017, p. 199). Long-term, prospective studies (i.e. studies that begin to acquire dopamine and endorphin measures in childhood and continue these measurements up through adulthood), are needed to prove this dopamine-endorphin deficiency theory is valid.

Case Example: Tina

Tina is a 21-year-old single mother of two children (a newborn and a 3-year-old). She began using alcohol and smoking cannabis when she was around 14 years old but did not experience many problems as a result of her substance use at that time. When Tina was a senior in high school, she began dating a guy that she really fell in love with and hoped that one day they would get married and start a life together. Although she and her boyfriend, Josh, did not plan to start having children until they both graduated high school and had steady jobs, Tina became pregnant with her first child. She was able to abstain from alcohol and cannabis throughout the time she was pregnant. Josh was unable to find work, so he joined the National Guard as a way to earn money and hopefully pay for college. Unfortunately, Josh's battalion was deployed to Afghanistan and during his second deployment he was killed when his Humvee was hit by a rocket-propelled grenade (RPG). Tina had just given birth to their second child. Because her parents were against Tina getting married, she rarely spoke with them. She found herself isolated, alone and depressed. She began drinking and smoking cannabis again, only this time on a daily basis after the kids were in bed for the night. Tina would often wake up feeling hungover and even more depressed, feeling that she couldn't face another day. After a neighbor called Child Protective Services on Tina for leaving her children unattended, she tried to stop drinking and smoking but found it very difficult. She reports that she would begin to experience "shakiness and sweats" which are common symptoms of alcohol withdrawal. She would eventually give in to drinking and smoking again.

Case Conceptualization

Tina is struggling with both depression as well as alcohol and cannabis use disorders. Although initially Tina felt that drinking and smoking pot would relax her and help her unwind from the stress of taking care of her children, she soon found that her drinking and smoking made her feel worse. This was most likely the result of dopamine and serotonin depletions that she began to experience as a result of several months of continuous substance use. Even when Tina tried to stop using, she would find herself feeling worse, initially because of acute withdrawal and then, after a few days or weeks, she would begin to experience post-acute withdrawal (often characterized by anxiety, lethargy, depressed affect, anhedonia, irritability, impatience and low frustration tolerance.) Post-acute withdrawal is thought to come about as a result of dopamine and serotonin depletions in the brain and often results in high relapse rates during the initial weeks/months of sobriety.

Boxed Item 5.3 Post-Acute Withdrawal (PAW)

Each of the various mood-altering substances that result in substance use disorders produce "substance-specific" withdrawal symptoms. Generally, the withdrawal symptoms for CNS depressant substances (e.g. alcohol, benzodiazepines, opioids) tend to produce withdrawal symptoms that are opposite to the depressant impact of these substances, which in this case is agitation, restlessness and overstimulation. Stimulant drugs of abuse (e.g. cocaine, methamphetamine, amphetamines), on the other hand, tend to produce withdrawal symptoms of depression, lethargy and malaise. All of the aforementioned withdrawal symptoms comprise what we know as "acute withdrawal," which generally lasts for a few days; at most, several days. However, there is also a phenomena called *post-acute withdrawal*, which is thought to be the result of dopamine depletions in the brain. The thinking is that during the time a person is using mood-altering substances, they are essentially flooding their brain with dopamine. However, because of tolerance, the brain adapts and eventually stops producing dopamine on its own. It's hypothesized that it takes several months (sometimes 6 to 12 months of total abstinence) before the brain begins to produce its own dopamine again. Not surprisingly, PAW is characterized by anhedonia (an inability to experience pleasure), lethargy and lack of motivation to accomplish things.

Boxed Item 5.4 Can Brain Scans Predict Relapse?

Recent research being conducted at Stanford University is seeking to predict who will relapse and who won't by using fMRI brain scans. Researchers MacNiven, Knutson and colleagues were able to accurately predict those individuals who would relapse in 75% of the cases they studied. Their sample was composed of veterans who had completed a 28-day residential treatment program for stimulant use disorders (cocaine and methamphetamines.) This research is based, in part, on the findings that while self-reported drug craving is often not an effective predictor of relapse, brain activity as measured by fMRI scans does predict relapse. In this study, participants were shown several images of everyday objects like food and office supplies, but interspersed were images of drugs and drug paraphernalia. Those participants who experienced more intense brain activity in the mesolimbic (reward) center of the brain, and especially in the area known as the nucleus accumbens, were found to have relapsed within three months.

Collins, N. (2018, Dec. 28). Brain scans help predict drug relapse, Stanford researchers find. *Stanford News.* http://news.stanford.edu

Boxed Item 5.5 Chemical Imbalances

Many mental health and substance use disorders are thought to be the result of chemical imbalances in the brain. However, according to author Kelli Maria Korducki (2019) and Harvard Medical historian Anne Harrington (2018), this type of oversimplified thinking may have resulted in "the wholesale failure of mental health care in America," which has become "a rigid and restrictive system that leaves even the reasonably privileged … with little to work with and so many others with nothing" (Korducki, 2019, p. 4). Too much emphasis seems to have been placed on searching for biological answers to mental health and substance use disorders at the expense of other forms of "talk therapy." In today's world, psychiatrists have become medication managers who rarely spend more than 15 minutes with patients discussing their response to medications and side effects. Korducki does concede, however, that, for many, psychotropic medications are necessary and do provide relief. Yet she also points out that for many with complicated mental health and co-occurring disorders, simplified medication management solutions do not work.

Harrington, A. (2018). *Mind fixers: Psychiatry's troubled search for the biology of mental illness.*

Korducki, K.M. (2019, July 28). It's not just a chemical imbalance. *New York Times, Sunday Review.*

Boxed Item 5.6 The Epigenetics of Chronic Cocaine Use

Chronic cocaine use or cocaine addiction often results in strong associations between cocaine use and environmental triggers (e.g. using with certain people or in particular places, drug paraphernalia such as mirrors, razor blades, etc.). This type of associative learning is thought to occur as a result of classical conditioning, by pairing an unconditioned stimulus (UCS) or cocaine with a conditioned stimulus (CS) such as people, places or things (mirrors, razor blades). Recent research indicates that this type of associative learning actually results in changes in gene expression in the region of the brain known as the hippocampus. The hippocampus is involved in learning and memory. Researchers Gajewski, Eagle et al. (2019) have demonstrated that chronic cocaine exposure in mice resulted in modifications in the epigenetic profile of the *FosB* in the hippocampus, which was hypothesized to account for the associative learning of cocaine triggers. Also, when the researchers blocked the changes made to the *FosB* in the hippocampus, the mice were unable to form associations between cocaine use and environmental triggers! This research has important implications for relapse prevention for those with cocaine use disorders.

Gajewski, P.A., Eagle, A.L., Williams, E.S., Manning, C.E., Lynch, H., McCornack, C., Maze, I. et al. (2019, Sept. 2). Epigenetic regulation of hippocampal *FosB* expression controls behavioral responses to cocaine. *Journal of Neuroscience.* doi: 10:1523/JNEUROSCI.0800-19.2019

Society for Neuroscience (2019, Sept. 2). Chronic cocaine use modifies gene expression. Retrieved from https://medical express.com/news/2019-09-chronic-cocaine-gene.html

Summary

Biological models of substance use disorders include both genetic and neurotransmitter explanations for how and why some individuals are at greater risk for developing alcohol and drug problems while others are not. There is a great deal of research supporting genetic models of addiction; it remains to be seen, however, what exactly is "inherited" that places one at higher risk for developing these disorders. Also, although genetic research is empirically supported not everyone born to a parent with a SUD will necessarily be destined to become addicted. Similarly, recent advances in brain imaging have provided fascinating insights into the functioning of the brain and how our brains are "hardwired" to respond to alcohol and drugs of abuse. Neurotransmitters play a key role in producing the euphoric sensations that one feels when drinking alcohol or taking drugs; it remains to be seen, however, why some people develop substance use disorders while others don't, given the predictable changes in brain chemistry produced by drugs and alcohol. Recent research into pre-morbid dopamine and endorphin depletions may provide some answers.

Recommended Reading and Resources

Carter, A., Hall, W., & Illes, J. (2016). *Addiction neuroethics: The ethics of addiction neuroscience research and treatment.* New York: Elsevier Science.

Grisel, J. (2019). *Never enough: The neuroscience and experience of addiction.* New York, NY: Doubleday.

Maté, G. (2010). *In the realm of hungry ghosts: Close encounters with addiction.* Berkeley, CA: North Atlantic Books.

McGue, M. (1999). Behavioral genetic models of alcoholism and drinking. In K.E. Leonard & H.T. Blane (Eds). *Psychological theories of drinking and alcoholism* (2nd edn, pp. 372–421). New York: Guilford Press.

Quinones, S. (2016). *Dreamland: The true tale of America's opiate epidemic.* New York: Bloomsbury Press.

Reed, B., Butelman, E.R., & Kreek, M.J. (2017). Endogenous opioid system in addiction and addiction-related behaviors. *Current Opinion in Behavioral Sciences, 13,* 196–202.

Robins, L.N. (1993). Vietnam veterans rapid recovery from heroin: A fluke or normal expectation? *Addiction, 88,* 1041–1054.

Satel, S., & Lilienfeld, S.O. (2013). *Brainwashed: The seductive appeal of mindless neuro-science.* New York: Basic Books.

Resources

The Neurobiology of Drug Addiction (website): This website was developed by NIDA and presents a multi-part series on neurobiology and addiction. www.drugabuse.gov/neurobiology-drug-addiction

The Neuroscience of Addiction & Recovery (website): This information on brain plasticity and recovery was developed by The Best Brain Possible, an independent organization. www.thebestbrainpossible.com/neuroplasticity-addiction-recovery-brain/

Addiction & the Brain (website/newsletter): This newsletter is sponsored by the Harvard Mahoney Neuroscience Institute and contains very up-to-date, useful information. https://neuro.hms.harvard.edu/harvard-mahoney-neuroscience-institute/brain-newsletter/and-brain-series/addiction-and-brain

Addiction Neuroscience (Bing video): This video contains useful, basic information on the brain. www.bing.com/videos/search?q=addiction+neuroscience&view=detail&mid=1D607913C039FB7D35DD1D607913C039FB7D35DD&FORM=VIRE

Addiction and the Brain (YouTube video): This YouTube video contains very useful information on addiction neuroscience. The video lecture was developed by Dr. Marc Lewis. www.youtube.com/watch?v=aOSD9rTVuWc

References

Agarwal, D.P., & Goedde, H.W. (1989). Human aldehyde dehydrogenase: Their role in alcoholism. *Alcohol, 6,* 517–523.

Alexander, B.K., Coombs, R.B., & Hadaway, P.F. (1978). The effects of housing and gender on morphine self-administration in rats. *Psychopharmacology, 58(2),* 175–179.

Blum, K., & Payne, J. E. (1991). *Alcohol and the addictive brain: New hope for alcoholics from biogenetic research.* New York: Free Press.

Blum, K., Noble, E.P., Sheridan, P.J., Montgomery, A., Ritchie, T., Jagadeeswaran, P., Nogami, H. et al. (1990). Allelic association of human dopamine D2 receptor gene in alcoholism. *Journal of the American Medical Association, 263,* 2055–2067.

Bohman, M., Sigvardsson, S., & Cloninger, C.R. (1981). Maternal inheritance of alcohol abuse: Cross-fostering analysis of adopted women. *Archives of General Psychiatry, 38,* 965–969.

Cadoret, R.J., O'Gorman, T.W., Troughton, E., & Heywood, E. (1985). Alcoholism and anti-social personality. *Archives of General Psychiatry, 42,* 161–167.

Cadoret, R.J., Troughton, E., & O'Gorman, T.W. (1987). Genetic and environmental factors in alcohol abuse and antisocial personality. *Journal of Studies on Alcohol, 48,* 1–8.

Cloninger, C.R. (1987). A systematic method for clinical description and classification of personality variants: A proposal. *Archives of General Psychiatry, 44(6),* 573–588.

Cloninger, C.R., Bohman, M., & Sigvardsen, S. (1981). Inheritance of alcohol abuse: Cross-fostering analysis of adopted men. *Archives of General Psychiatry, 38,* 861–868.

Cloninger, C.R., Sigvardsson, S., & Bohman, M. (1988). Childhood personality predicts alcohol abuse in young adults. *Alcoholism: Clinical & Experimental Research, 12,* 494–505.

Cotton, N.S. (1979). The familial incidence of alcoholism. *Journal of Studies on Alcohol, 40,* 89–116.

Dodgen, C.E., & Shea, W.M. (2000). *Substance use disorders: Assessment and treatment.* San Diego, CA: Academic Press.

Foroud, J.C., & Li, T.K. (1991). Genetics of alcoholism: A review of recent studies in human and animal models. *American Journal on Addictions, 8,* 261–278.

Gabrielli, W.F., & Mednick, S.A. (1983). Intellectual performance in children of alcoholics. *Journal of Nervous and Mental Diseases, 17(7),* 444–447.

Gajewski, P.A, Eagle, A.L., Williams, E.S., Manning, C.E., Lynch, H., McComack, C., Maze, I. et al. (2019). Epigenetic regulation of hippocampal *FosB* expression controls behavioral response to cocaine. *Journal of Neuroscience, 39(42),* 8305–8314.

Gennazzini, A.R., Nappi, G., Facchinetti, G.L., Mazzella, D., Parrini, E., Sinforiani, F., Petraglia, F. et al. (1982) Central deficiency of beta-endorphin in alcohol addicts. *Journal of Clinical Endocrinology and Metabolism, 55,* 583–586.

Goldstein, R.Z., & Volkow, N.D. (2002). Drug addiction and its underlying neurobiological basis: Neuroimaging evidence for the involvement of the frontal cortex. *American Journal of Psychiatry, 159(10),* 1642–1652.

Goodwin, D.W. (1988). *Is alcoholism hereditary?* New York: Ballantine Books.

Goodwin, D.W., Schulsinger, F., Hermansen, L., Guze, S.B., & Winokur, G. (1973). Alcohol problems in adoptees raised apart from alcoholic biological parents. *Archives of General Psychiatry, 28,* 238–243.

Grisel, J. (2019). *Never enough: The neuroscience and experience of addiction.* New York: Doubleday.

Hari, J. (2015). *Chasing the scream: The first and last days of the war on drugs.* New York: Bloomsbury.

Heath, A.C., Bucholz, K.K., Madden, P.A.F., Dinwiddie, S.H., Slutzke, W.S., Bierut, L.J., & Martin, N.G. (1997). Genetic differences and environmental contributions to alcohol dependence risk in a national twin sample: Consistency of findings in women and men. *Psychological Medicine, 27,* 1381–1396.

Hesselbrock, M.N. (1986). Childhood behavior problems and adult antisocial personality disorder in alcoholism. In R.E. Meyer (Ed.). *Psychopathology and addictive disorders* (pp. 78–94). New York: Guilford Press.

Hesselbrock, M.N., & Hesselbrock, V. (1992). Relationship of family history, anti-social personality disorder and personality traits among young men at risk for alcoholism. *Journal of Studies on Alcohol, 53,* 619–625.

Kendler, K.S., Neale, M.C., Heath, A.C., Kessler, R.C., & Eaves, L.J. (1994). A twin family study of alcoholism in women. *American Journal of Psychiatry, 151,* 707–715.

Kendler, K.S., Prescott, C.A., Neale, M.C., & Pedersen, N.L. (1997). Temperance Board Registration for alcohol abuse in a national sample of Swedish male twins born 1902 to 1949. *Archives of General Psychiatry, 54,* 178–184.

Knop, J., Penick, E.C., Nickel, E.J., Mednick, S.A., Jensen, P., Manzardo, A.M., & Gabrielli, W.F. (2007). Paternal alcoholism predicts the occurrence but not the remission of alcoholic drinking: A 40-year follow-up. *Psychiatrica Scandinavica, 116,* 286–393.

Legrand, L.N., Iacono, W.G., & McGue, M. (2005). Predicting addiction. *American Scientist, March–April,* 140–147.

Leshner, A.I. (1997). Addiction is a brain disease and it matters. *Science, 278,* 45–47.

Maté, G. (2010). *In the realm of hungry ghosts: Close encounters with addiction.* Berkeley, CA: North Atlantic Books.

McGoldrick, M., & Gerson, R. (1985). *Genograms in family assessment.* New York: W.W. Norton.

McGue, M. (1999). Behavioral genetic models of alcoholism and drinking. In K.E. Leonard & H.T. Blane (Eds). *Psychological theories of drinking and alcoholism* (2nd edn, pp. 372–421). New York: Guilford Press.

McGue, M., & Irons, D.E. (2013). Etiology. In B.S. McCrady & E.E. Epstein (Eds). *Addiction: A comprehensive guidebook* (2nd edn, pp. 36–72). New York: Oxford University Press.

McGue, M., Pickens, R.W., & Svikis, D.S. (1992). Sex and age effects on the inheritance of alcohol problems: A twin study. *Journal of Abnormal Psychology, 101,* 3–17.

Pickens, R.W., & Plunkett, C.R. (1970). Morphine reinforcement in rats: Confounding activity effects. *Proceedings of the Annual Convention of the American Psychological Association, 5(Part 2),* 823–824.

Pickens. R.W., Svikis, D.S., McGue, M., Lykken, D.T., Heston, L.L., & Clayton, P.J. (1991). Heterogeneity in the inheritance of alcoholism. *Archives of General Psychiatry, 48,* 19–28.

Pollock, V.E., Gabrielli, W.F., Mednick, S.A., & Goodwin, D.W. (1988). EEG identification of subgroups of men at risk for alcoholism? *Psychiatry Research, 26(1),* 101–114.

Porjesz, B., & Begleiter, H. (2003). Alcoholism and human electrophysiology. *Alcohol Research and Health, 27(2),* 153–160.

Prescott, C.A., Aggen, S.H., & Kendler, K.S. (2000). Sex-specific genetic influences on the co-morbidity of alcoholism and major depression in a population-based sample of U.S. twins. *Archives of General Psychiatry, 57,* 803–811.

Reed, B., Butelman, E.R., & Kreek, M.J. (2017). Endogenous opioid system in addiction and addiction-related behaviors. *Current Opinion in Behavioral Sciences, 13,* 196–202.

Robins, L.N. (1993). Vietnam veterans rapid recovery from heroin: A fluke or normal expectation? *Addiction, 88,* 1041–1054.

Robins, L.N., Helzer, J.E., & Davis, D.H. (1975). Narcotic use in Southeast Asia and afterward. *Archives of General Psychiatry, 32,* 955–961.

Satel, S., & Lilienfeld, S.O. (2013). *Brainwashed: The seductive appeal of mindless neuro-science.* New York: Basic Books.

Schuckit, M.A., & Rayse, V. (1979). Ethanol ingestion: Differences in blood acetaldehyde concentrations in relatives of alcoholics and controls. *Science, 2003,* 54–55.

Schuckit, M.A., & Smith, T.L. (1997). Assessing the risk of alcoholism among sons of alcoholics. *Journal of Studies on Alcohol, 58(2),* 141–145.

Schuckit, M.A., Butters, N., Lyn, L., & Irwin, M. R. (1987). Neuropsychologic deficits and the risk for alcoholism. *Neuropsychopharmacology, 1(1),* 45–53.

Smith, S.G., & Davis, W.M. (1973). Behavioral control by stimuli associated with acquisition of morphine self-administration. *Behavioral Biology, 9(6),* 777–780.

Smith, S.G., Werner, T.E., & Davis, W.M. (1975). Intravenous drug self-administration in rats: Substitution of ethyl alcohol for morphine. *Psychological Record, 25(1),* 17–20.

Winerman, L. (2019). What can we learn from our DNA? *APA Monitor, March,* 38–45.

6 Sociocultural Model

Margaret Smith

Introduction

The sociocultural model of addiction examines substance use and substance use disorders in light of social and environmental influences. Social and environmental influences can include, but are not limited to peers, family, community and culture. In other chapters, we discussed how biological and psychological factors can place individuals at greater risk for developing substance use disorders. In this chapter we will examine the influence of "nurture" which encompasses all of the afore-mentioned environmental influences.

Learning Opportunity 6.1

Make a list of social and environmental factors that may contribute to sub-stance use or behavioral/process addictions. After making your list, get into groups of three or four and share your lists. Explain why these factors may contribute to substance use or behavioral/process addictions.

Key Concepts and Definitions

built environment: "The built environment includes all of the physical parts of where we live and work (e.g., homes, buildings, streets, open spaces, and infrastructure). The built environment influences a person's level of physical activity. For example, inaccessible or nonexistent sidewalks and bicycle or walking paths contribute to sedentary habits. These habits lead to poor health outcomes such as obesity, cardiovascular disease, dia-betes, and some types of cancer." (Centers for Disease Control [CDC], 2011, para. 1).

cultural competence: "Cultural competence is the ability to interact effect-ively with people of different cultures. In practice, both individuals and organizations can be culturally competent … Cultural compe-tence means to be respectful and responsive to the health beliefs and practices – and cultural and linguistic needs – of diverse population groups." (Substance Abuse and Mental Health Services Administration [SAMHSA], 2016, paras 2–3)

environmental influences: environmental influences can include but are not limited to peers, family, community, the built environment, and culture

ethnicity: in the United States, ethnic categories for the purposes of surveys and related matters are as follows:

> Hispanic or Latino: A person of Cuban, Mexican, Puerto Rican, South or Central American, or other Spanish culture or origin, regardless of race. The term, "Spanish origin", can be used in addition to "Hispanic or Latino".
>
> (State Library of Iowa, n.d., para. 4).

Historically, we also refer to ethnic groups in terms of their country's background such as Italian-Americans, Irish-Americans, etc.

race: "What we call 'race' are social categories ... There is currently one biological race in our species: Homo sapiens. However, that does not mean that what we call 'races' (our society's way of dividing people up) don't exist. Societies, like the USA, construct racial classifications, not as units of biology, but as ways to lump together groups of people with varying historical, linguistic, ethnic, religious, or other backgrounds." (Fuentes, 2012, paras 2–3).

In the United States, the racial categories are as follows:

> American Indian or Alaska Native: A person having origins in any of the original peoples of North and South America (including Central America), and who maintains tribal affiliation or community attachment.
>
> Asian: A person having origins in any of the original peoples of the Far East, Southeast Asia, or the Indian subcontinent including, for example, Cambodia, China, India, Japan, Korea, Malaysia, Pakistan, the Philippine Islands, Thailand, and Vietnam.
>
> Black or African American: A person having origins in any of the black racial groups of Africa. Terms can include "Black or African American".
>
> Native Hawaiian or Other Pacific Islander: A person having origins in any of the original peoples of Hawaii, Guam, Samoa, or other Pacific Islands.
>
> White: A person having origins in any of the original peoples of Europe, the Middle East, or North Africa
>
> (State Library of Iowa, n.d., para. 3)

racism: prejudice, discrimination, or antagonism directed against someone (or a group of people) of a different race based on the belief that one's own race is superior (Coalition for Racial Equality and Rights, 2019).

Sociocultural and Environmental Influences

As stated in the introduction, there are sociocultural and environmental influences related to alcohol and other drug use, misuse and addiction. This chapter addresses peers, family, community and culture. Further, we will discuss racism and poverty as sociocultural aspects that influence alcohol and other drug use and addiction. Lastly, we will address lessons learned from the environment, strengths and weaknesses of this model and we will end with a case example.

Learning Opportunity 6.2

Think of your child/young adulthood. Who impacted your decisions, actions and behaviors? How did they influence you? Were there more positive or more negative influences? And/or discuss the following: How much did your peers play into your decisions, actions and behaviors? And/or discuss the following: How much did family play into decisions, actions and behaviors? And/or address this question: How much did your community policies, laws and norms influence your decisions, actions and behaviors?

Peer Impact

Peer influences can include peer pressure, peer norms and peer deviance; socializing with substance using peers can contribute to substance use problems (Getz & Bray, 2005; Institute of Medicine (US) Committee on Opportunities in Drug Abuse Research, 1996; Shih et al., 2017; Sudhinaraset, Wigglesworth & Takeuchi, 2016; Walden, McGue, Iacono, Burt, & Elkins, 2004; White, Bates, & Johnson, 1991). Additionally, peer influences may be stronger than parental effects (Hansen et al. as cited in Whites et al., 1991).

Interestingly, adolescents are susceptible to the perception of the peers' drinking behaviors and tend to drink according to their *perception* of the norm as opposed to the actual norm (Perkins, 1997). In this case, high school and college students tend to drink more based on their misperception of use among their peers. Therefore, prevention, intervention and treatment programs should incorporate accurate norms in any materials to correct misperceptions of heavier use than actual (lower) use.

Adolescents' reasons for using alcohol include socializing with their friends, alleviating tension and anxiety (particularly in mixed-gender situations), getting high, to "cheer up" and reducing boredom (Segal & Stewart, 1996 in McGrady & Epstein, 1999, p. 63).

Family

Familial factors that relate to alcohol and other drug use problems can include, but are not limited to, poor parent–child relationships, divorce, poor parenting, parent or sibling use, pro-alcohol and other drug use attitudes, social deprivation, negative role models, and use of alcohol and other drugs to cope (Institute of Medicine (US) Committee on Opportunities in Drug Abuse Research, 1996). Important to keep in mind is that not all children who grow up with these factors are "doomed" to addiction. As much of the resilience research points out, many children have the ability to "bounce back" from bad experiences.

While family models do not address causes of alcohol or other drug addiction, they do indicate that families "unintentionally allow the addiction to progress" in attempts to maintain family balance (homeostasis) (Cavaiola, 2009, p. 840). For more information on family and addiction, refer to Chapter 4.

Community

Research and related literature indicate that there are community influences on alcohol use (Sudhinaraset, Wigglesworth, & Takeuchi, 2016), e-cigarette and cigarette use (Shih et al., 2017) and drug use (Kendler Maes, Sundquist, Ohlsson, & Sundquist, 2014).

Community, which includes neighborhoods and their built environments, can influence alcohol use. "For example, one study found that individuals who lived in a neighborhood with a poorly built environment, characterized by inferior building conditions, housing, and water and sanitation indicators, were 150 percent more likely to report heavy drinking compared with those living in better built environments" (Bernstein et al., 2007 in Sudhinaraset et al., 2016, p. 9). Increased alcohol advertising in minority communities (versus white communities), violence (including drug dealing), and community disorganization contribute to increased alcohol use and related problems (Sudhinaraset et al., 2016).

Learning Opportunity 6.3

Break into groups and discus how might race and ethnicity factor into substance use disorders or behavioral/process addictions?

Race and Ethnicity

In examining race and ethnicity, it can be helpful to know the current use and addiction rates among racial and ethnic groups.

In the United States, among racial and ethnic groups, Whites report the highest overall alcohol *use* among persons age 12 and over (57.4%). American Indian/Alaska Natives report the highest levels of *binge drinking* (30.2%), followed by Whites (23.9%), Hispanic/Latinos (23.2%), African-Americans (20.6%), and Asians (12.7%) (SAMHSA, 2013).

In 2013, among persons aged 12 or older, the rate of past month drug *use* was 3.1 percent among Asians, 8.8 percent among Hispanics, 9.5 percent among whites, 10.5 percent among blacks, 12.3 percent among AI/AN, 14.0 percent among Native Hawaiians or Other Pacific Islanders, and 17.4 percent among persons reporting two or more races.

(SAMHSA, 2015, para. 7)

The prevalence of past month use of tobacco product was 10.1% for Asians, 18.8% for Hispanics, 25.8% for Native Hawaiians or Other Pacific Islanders, 27.1% for Blacks, 27.7% for Whites, 31.2% for persons reporting two or more races, and 40.1% for American Indians or Alaska Natives. The rate of past month tobacco use among American Indians or Alaska Natives was higher than the rates for all other groups except persons reporting two or more races. The rate of past month tobacco use among Asians was lower than the rates among other groups (SAMHSA, 2015, para. 5).

The rate of:

substance dependence or abuse was 4.6 percent among Asians, 7.4 percent among blacks, 8.4 percent among whites, 8.6 percent among Hispanics, 10.9 percent among persons reporting two or more races, 11.3 percent among Native Hawaiians or Other Pacific Islanders, and 14.9 percent among American Indians or Alaska Natives. Except for Native Hawaiians or Other Pacific Islanders, the rate for Asians was lower than the rates for the other racial/ethnic groups (SAMHSA, 2015, para. 4).

Why are there higher rates among some groups over others? Here we need to look back on peers, family and now look at culture, racism and poverty.

Culture

"Culture is a system of shared beliefs, values, customs, behaviors, and artifacts that the members of a society use … and … [are] transmitted from generation to generation through learning" (Bates & Plog, 1990, p. 7). There are a variety of cultures based on the following examples: countries, race, sexual orientation, gender, and religion.

In terms of alcohol-related issues, a culture's attitudes, norms, and drinking patterns are linked to negative consequences and other problems. Cultural factors that contribute to alcohol problems include solitary drinking, overpermissive norms of drinking, lack of specific drinking norms, tolerance of drunkenness, adverse social behavior tolerated when drinking, utilitarian use of alcohol to reduce tension with anxiety, lack of ritualized and/or ceremonial use of alcohol, alcohol use apart from family and social functions with close friends, lack of child socialization into drinking patterns, drinking with strangers, which increases violence, drinking pursued as recreation, drinking concentrated in young males, and the cultural milieu that stresses individuals, self-reliance and high achievement (Kinney, 2015, p. 130).

Culture is also linked to drug use. One researcher (Westermeyer, 1987) who examined the environmental aspects of drug use found that ethnic groups might partially identify themselves by using a specific drug, or a specific mode of drug use, or participate in cultural events involving drugs. Additionally, drugs have different meanings for different ethnic groups. For example, one group might use a drug for religious purposes while another uses it as an aphrodisiac. Further, some groups may use a drug to alleviate stress arising from certain societal roles and responsibilities. Rites of passage, for example, during adolescence, may explain some periods of alcohol and other drug use. Additionally, "special social relationships that may be formalized or reaffirmed by drug use include the transition of casual acquaintances into close friendships, the establishment of important commercial or political agreements, or initiation into fictive kinship, such as through adoption or blood-brotherhood" (Westermeyer, 1987, para. 13). Lastly, cultural groups may use alcohol or drugs during religious ceremonies (wine during mass, peyote use during some Native American ceremonies). However, there is indication that use of alcohol and other drugs for religious ceremonies are considered sacred and therefore not abused within that context.

Further, historical cultural experiences can impact alcohol and other drug use. For example, while some Native American communities have high rates of abstinence, there are some tribes where there are rates of heavy binge drinking among the males, particularly those living on reservations (Inaba and Cohen, 2014). There are several theories about the reason for high binge drinking and alcoholism rates among some Native American tribes. The first is that stronger forms of alcohol were not part of Native American's lives until European colonists introduced them to wine and distilled spirits. Consequently, their bodies weren't as adapted as those of European colonists to the effects of alcohol. Oftentimes trading negotiations were conducted under the influence of heavy and violent drinking. Further, the colonists were heavy drinkers, therefore offering poor role models for the use of alcohol to those using wine and distilled spirits for the first time (Beauvais, 1998). Further, there is the stress of acculturation which is the demand to integrate into and identify with the dominant culture (Stevens & Smith, 2009). Lastly, as addressed in the next section, poverty and racism play a part.

Impact of Poverty and Racism

In the United States, poverty, racism and the lack of educational and occupational opportunities are linked to substance use problems (Cavaiola, 2009, p. 841). In terms of socioeconomic status, those of low socioeconomic status drink in larger quantities than those of higher socioeconomic status (Caswell, Pledger, & Hooper, 2003).

Systemic racism perpetuates such problems as few employment prospects, poor or limited educational opportunities, poverty-stricken neighborhoods, increased crime and violence, lack of recreational events and leisure activities, and poor built environments. Some theorize that these conditions then increase stress, which in turn increases alcohol and other drug use as a means to cope.

In a review of the recent literature, there are studies directly linking racial discrimination and increase in substance use. Gilbert and Zemore (2016, p. 188) found that, as experiences of discrimination increase, alcohol consumption, drinking-related problems, and risk of disorders also tend to increase. Further racism "fuels" drug use among minority groups. More specifically, in a pair of recent studies, Columbia University researchers Keyes and Hason (2017) "found that African-Americans who experienced racial discrimination … were each at least twice as likely to use illicit drugs like marijuana, heroin, cocaine, or pain pills without a medical reason" (para. 2). Being a member of a particular racial or ethnic group does not predestine one to develop a substance use disorder (SUD), however, it certainly can place individuals at greater risk.

"Other" Cultures

Other cultures to consider are the Lesbian/Gay/Bisexual/Transgender culture, women's culture, elder culture, and adolescent culture. Numbers indicate that LGBT culture men and women may abuse more alcohol and other drugs than their non-LGBT counterparts. While women drink less and have lower rates of addiction than men, they are "catching" up with men in terms of their numbers. Elder substance use problems are becoming more well known, but not studied nearly enough. Lastly, the adolescent subculture deals with their own issues of "rites of passage," biological and social developmental dynamics, and peer pressure.

Each culture deals with their own "isms" which impact substance use and related problems. For example, the LGBT culture deals with heterosexism, women deal with sexism, and elder cultures deal with ageism. These "isms' contribute to stress which in turn can increase substance use problems.

Learning Opportunity 6.4

Go to your online library and research scholarly peer-reviewed articles on race/ethnicity (and other cultures as discussed in this chapter) and substance use disorders. Read one article. Break into groups and discuss your article with your group members.

Lessons Learned from the Environment

We can't have volunteers enter a lab with available drugs and create stress-inducing environmental events to study the impact of social influences on drug use. That would be unethical. However, we do have a historical event that offers us a naturalistic study. In the 1970s in the context of the Viet Nam war, 20% of returning soldiers were addicted to heroin. Government officials were concerned, thinking that when they all returned the United States there would be a tremendous heroin problem affecting the country. However, almost a year later, of those returning soldiers, only 10% had used heroin and only 5% of those who became addicted relapsed within 10 months of their return to the United States (Becona, 2018; Inaba & Cohen, 2014). It was as if leaving a hostile environment (e.g. the war) and returning home "removed" addiction. This Viet Nam War study shows that addiction isn't just biological (as thought at that time) but also involves environmental factors.

Another study, now known as Rat Park, indicates that changing the environment reduces drug use. In several experiments, rats tend to prefer morphine sucrose over water when isolated in their cages. However, when freed into more of a "park" with cedar shavings and other rats (for socialization and sexual activity), the rats tended to use less morphine sucrose (Hadaway, Alexander, Coambs, & Beyerstein, 1979; Hari, 2015). These findings indicate that changing one's environment (from an isolated, lonely cage) to a park (with socialization and activities) reduces drug use.

Application to Addiction Counseling

There are several ways in which sociocultural and environmental factors should be addressed in addiction counseling. The first is to recognize that sociocultural and environmental factors do matter. Where someone "comes from" in terms of their context should be taken into account when assessing, diagnosing, treating, referring and supporting clients.

Counselors should be educated and trained in culturally competent counseling. However, this isn't a one-shot deal. As SAMHSA (2014, p. xvi) states:

> Cultural competence is not acquired in a limited timeframe or by learning a set of facts about specific populations; cultures are diverse and continuously evolving. Developing cultural competence is an ongoing process that begins with cultural awareness and a commitment to understanding the role that culture plays in behavioral health services.

Culturally competent counselors share the following attitudes and behaviors: respect, acceptance, sensitivity, commitment to equality, openness, humility, and flexibility (SAMHSA, 2014, pp. 49–50).

In terms of assessing and diagnosing, a counselor should be cautious in interpreting assessment and diagnostic tools in relation to someone's gender, age, sexual orientation and/or ethnicity/race as most screening, assessment and diagnostic tools do not take into consideration those aspects. According to SAMHSA, there are some tools available for adolescents, women, and African-Americans, for example, but they are limited. A culturally competent counselor needs to be looking for the research and evidence-based materials for assessing and diagnosing.

In terms of treatment and self-help resources there is a paucity of "specialized" programs and groups for people of diverse races and populations (such as Native American, African-Americans, Latino Americans and LGBT men and women).

However, the literature does indicate that programs that are culturally competent (that is, respectful of and responsive to diversity) tend to have better outcomes than those that are not (Campos, 2009).

Another way to make a difference in terms of sociocultural and environmental aspects is to advocate for polices, programs and treatment that support people of diverse backgrounds and those who struggle with the isms (racism, heterosexism, sexism, ageism, etc.), poverty and related socioeconomic issues.

Strengths and Limitations of Sociocultural Models

One of the strengths of the sociocultural and environmental model is that it focuses on the context of clients: Where are they from? What is happening around them? How do their peers, families and communities impact their use? Another strength is that this model focuses on the social and environmental pressures that clients may feel. What stressors do they experience from "isms" is their lives? How does poverty impact them?

One of the weaknesses of the model is that it excludes the impact of other risk factors such as genetics and biology/physiology aspects. With the scientific studies indicating a biological/chemical/physiological aspect, it seems important to include that in the understanding of substance use disorders and addiction.

Case Study

Sophie is a 14-year-old Latina female who lives in a poverty-stricken area. She is unable to play outside because there are no playgrounds and her parents are fearful of the crime and violence in the area.

While Sophie's community tries to invest in itself, the poor school system and few job opportunities impact the quality of the area in which she and her family live. She sees many advertisements for alcohol and tobacco on the billboards throughout her community.

In addition to those environmental influences, racism and discrimination contribute to stress. Sophie has heard people use derogatory names to refer to her and her family when they are outside of their neighborhood shopping or visiting their grandmother in another part of town. Further, Sophie's father who was just laid off from his carpentry job, has trouble finding a new job. He often hears that someone who is non-Latino was hired after he was denied. He is wondering if his race plays a part.

Sophia's friends have been smoking cigarettes and have just started sneaking beer they have found in their parents' refrigerators. Sophia finds that the alcohol makes her worries about her father's job and overall "yucky" feelings go away.

One afternoon, Sophia drank a little too much and her parents came home from work and found her vomiting in the bathroom. Worried about her use of alcohol, they contacted the school counselor who referred the family to an outpatient alcohol and other drug clinic for adolescent prevention and treatment of alcohol and other drugs.

Case Conceptualization

Sophia's peers and environment are contributing to her use of alcohol and cigarettes. While she may be feeling peer pressure to use, she is also dealing with racism (name calling, father's job insecurity) with the use of alcohol and cigarettes. As stated poverty, racism, and lack of job opportunities contribute to substance use problems. For "treatment" the best ways to deal with these problems is to change the system: reduce poverty and eradicate racism through policy, law and environmental change. The school counselor, in this case, is working on the individual aspect (education about alcohol and other drugs). But a counselor or other helper, using the sociocultural model, would focus more on the system that contributes to the problem. In this case, the counselor or helper would advocate for social change around poverty, racism and other environmental changes.

Recommended Reading and Resources

Culture Competence website via SAMHSA. www.samhsa.gov/section-223/cultural-competency/resources

Hari, J. (2015). *Chasing the scream: The first and last days of the war on drugs.* New York: Bloomsbury.

Substance Abuse and Mental Health Services Administration (SAMHSA) (2014). *Improving cultural competence.* Treatment Improvement Protocol (TIP) Series No. 59. HHS Publication No. (SMA) 14–4849. Rockville, MD: Substance Abuse and Mental Health Services Administration

Sue, D.W., & Sue, D. (2013). *Counseling the culturally diverse: Theory and practice* (6th ed). Hoboken, NJ: John Wiley and Sons.

References

Bates, D.G., & Plog, F. (1990). *Human adaptive strategies.* New York: McGraw-Hill

Beauvais, F. (1998). American Indians and alcohol. *Alcohol Research: Current Reviews, 22(4),* 233–290.

Becona, E. (2018). Brain disease or biopsychosocial model in addiction? Remembering the Vietnam veteran study. *Psicothema, 30(3),* 270–275.

Campos, M.D. (2009). Racial and ethnic minorities, issues in treatment. In D.L. Fisher & N.A. Roget. *Encyclopedia of substance abuse prevention, treatment and recovery.* Thousand Oaks, CA: Sage.

Cavaiola, A. (2009). Sociocultural models of addiction. In D.L. Fisher & N.A. Roget (Eds). *Encyclopedia of substance abuse prevention, treatment and recovery.* Thousand Oaks, CA: Sage.

Centers for Disease Control (2011). *Impact of the built environment on health.* Retrieved from www.cdc.gov/nceh/publications/factsheets/impactofthebuiltenvironmentonhealth.pdf

Coalition for Racial Equality and Rights (2019). Racism. Retrieved from www.crer.scot/what-is-racism

Fuentes, A. (2012). Race is real, but not in the way many people think: Busting the myth of biological race. *Psychology Today.* Retrieved from www.psychologytoday.com/us/blog/busting-myths-about-human-nature/201204/race-is-real-not-in-the-way-many-people-think

Getz, J.G., & Bray, J.H. (2005). Predicting heavy alcohol use among adolescents. *American Journal of Orthopsychiatry, 75(1),* 102–116.

Gilbert, P.A., & Zemore, S.E. (2016). Discrimination and drinking: A systemic review of the evidence. *Social Science & Medicine, 161,* 178–194.

Hadaway, P.F., Alexander, B.K., Coambs, R.B., & Beyerstein, B. (1979). The effect of housing and gender on preference for morphine-sucrose solutions in rats. *Psychopharmacology, 66,* 87–91.

Hari, J. (2015). *Chasing the scream: The first and last days of the war on drugs.* New York: Bloomsbury.

Inaba, D.S., & Cohen, W.E. (2014). *Uppers, downers, all arounders: Physical and mental effects of psychoactive drugs.* Medford, OR: CNS Productions.

Institute of Medicine (US) Committee on Opportunities in Drug Abuse Research. (1996). *Pathways of addiction: Opportunities in drug abuse research.* Retrieved from www.ncbi.nlm. nih.gov/books/NBK232972/

Kendler, K.S., Maes, H.H., Sundquist, K., Ohlsson, H., & Sundquist, J. (2014). Genetic and family and community environmental effects on drug abuse in adolescence: A Swedish national twin and sibling study. *American Journal of Psychiatry, 171(2),* 209–2017

Keyes, K., & Hason, D. (2017). Scientists present evidence that racism and sexism fuel drug use. Retrieved from www.mailman.columbia.edu/public-health- now/news/scientists-present-evidence-racism-and-sexism-fuel-drug-use

Kinney, J. (2015). *Loosening the grip* (11th edn). New York: McGraw-Hill.

McGrady, B.S., & Epstein, E.E. (Eds). (1999). *Addictions: A comprehensive guidebook.* New York: Oxford University Press.

Perkins, H.W. (1997). College student misperceptions of alcohol and other drug norms among peers: Exploring causes, consequences, and implications for prevention in U.S. Department of Education. *Designing alcohol and other drug prevention programs in higher education: Bringing theory to practice.* Washington, DC: US Department of Education.

Shih, R.A., Parast, L., Pedersen, E., Troxel, W.M., Tucker, J.S. Miles, J.N.V., Kraus, L. et al. (2017). Individual, peer, and family factor modification of neighborhood-level effects on adolescent alcohol, cigarette, e-cigarette, and marijuana use. *Drug and Alcohol Dependence, 180,* 76–85.

State Library of Iowa (n.d.). State data center. Retrieved from www.iowadatacenter.org/aboutdata/raceclassification

Stevens, P., & Smith, R.L. (2009). *Substance abuse counseling: Theory and practice.* Upper Saddle River, NJ: Pearson.

Substance Abuse and Mental Health Services Administration (SAMHSA) (2013). *National survey on drug use and health, 2011 and 2012.* Rockville, MD: Author, Center for Behavioral Health Statistics and Quality. Retrieved from http://media.samhsa.gov/data/NSDUH/2012SummNatFindDetTables/DetTabs/NSDUH-DetTabs Sect2peTabs1to42-2012.htm#Tab2.1A

Substance Abuse and Mental Health Services Administration (2014). *Improving cultural competence.* Treatment Improvement Protocol (TIP) Series No. 59. HHS Publication No. (SMA) 14–4849. Rockville, MD: Substance Abuse and Mental Health Services Administration.

Substance Abuse and Mental Health Services Administration (SAMHSA) (2015). SAMHSA American Indian/Alaska Native Data. Rockville, MD: Author. Retrieved from www.samhsa.gov/sites/default/files/topics/tribal_affairs/ai-an-data-handout.pdf

Substance Abuse and Mental Health Services Administration (SAMHSA) (2016). Cultural competence. Retrieved from www.samhsa.gov/capt/applying-strategic- prevention/cultural-competence

Sudhinaraset, M., Wigglesworth, C., & Takeuchi, D. (2016). Social and cultural contexts of alcohol use: Influences in a social–ecological framework. *Journal of the National Institute of Alcohol Abuse and Alcoholism, 38(1),* 35–45.

Walden, B., McGue, M., Iacono, W. G., Burt, S. A., & Elkins, I. (2004). Identifying shared environmental contributions to early substance use: The respective roles of peers and parents. *Journal of Abnormal Psychology, 113(30),* 440–450.

Westermeyer, J. (1987). Cultural patterns of drug and alcohol use: An analysis of host and agent in the cultural environment. *Bulletin on Narcotics, 39(2),* 11–27. Retrieved from www.unodc.org/unodc/en/data-and-analysis/bulletin/bulletin_1987-01-01_2_page003.html

White, H.R., Bates, M.E., & Johnson, V. (1991). Learning to drink familial, peer and media influences. In D.J. Pittman & H. R. White. *Society, culture, and drinking patterns reexamined.* New Brunswick, NJ: Rutgers Center for Alcohol Studies, Publications Division.

7 Solution-Focused Theory

Alan A. Cavaiola

Introduction

This chapter will focus on Solution-Focused Theory (SFT) which is a theory based on the concept of how and why people change. Therefore, SFT is not a theory of etiology or causation but rather a theory that explains how people change or find solutions to mental health and substance use disorder problems. What distinguishes SFT from other counseling therapies and theories is that it encourages clients to focus on a future in which alcohol or drug problems no longer exist. In this sense, it is a humanistic theory, in that it believes that people have the answers or solutions to their problems within themselves and it is the role of the counselor to draw out these solutions through a number of guided therapeutic strategies. SFT critiques other addiction treatment approaches in conceptualizing substance use disorders as incurable (i.e. chronic) diseases in which denial plays a key role in perpetuating the disease. SFT therefore, criticizes traditional addiction treatment as being overly focused on what is referred to as the *Three Ds: Disease, Denial and Dysfunction.*

The Three Ds: Disease, Denial and Dysfunction

The Three Ds are what SFT theorists refer to as the "problem-focused" approach to traditional treatment. Using this approach, the role of an addiction counselor is to convince clients that they have a disease (i.e. a substance use disorder), to break down the client's denial of the disease and to encourage the client to admit that their lives had become unmanageable or dysfunctional as a result of his or her excessive alcohol or drug use. Think about some of the well-known substance use disorder screening tools for example, the Addiction Severity Index which is a widely used structured interview, the Alcohol Use Disorders Identification Test (AUDIT), an alcohol screening measure, or the Michigan Alcoholism Screening Test for Alcohol & Drugs (MAST/AD). All of these screening/assessment tools focus on "problems" related to alcohol and drug use such as blackouts, arrests, difficulties with education or employment and medical issues. Rather than focusing on diagnosis and problems that come about as a result of drinking and/or drug use, SFT prefers to focus on future solutions to these problems.

One of the other criticisms that SFT theorists make of traditional addiction counseling approaches is the emphasis on the 12-Step approach as being the *only* means by which people can recover from substance use disorders (SUDs). Instead, SFT advocates that there are several paths to recovery, therefore the role of the SFT counselor is to match the client with the best approach towards change. Also, SFT theorists point to a recent and growing body of research that points to individuals who attain sobriety and recovery from SUD without accessing *any* formal intervention or treatment (Robbins, 1979; Misch, 2007; O'Malley, 2004; Curran, Muthen, & Harford, 1998).

One of the basic tenets of Solution-Focused Theory is that clients should be allowed to make choices regarding their treatment, rather than having a treatment plan imposed on them. According to Miller and Berg (1995), finding the "door to a solution" begins with making choices, a divergence from more traditional addiction counseling approaches, whereby treatment recommendations regarding abstinence, 12-Step group attendance (e.g. "attending 90 meetings in 90 days," "find a sponsor and a home group") and the need to change people, places and things in order to maintain sobriety are non-negotiable treatment recommendations. SFT uses a gentler approach by asking that clients consider change and by first examining how they would like their lives to be like in the future. According to Miller and Berg (1995, p. 66), "Finding the door to solution begins with the choice: I want my life to be different!"

Key Terms

Three Ds: the Three Ds refers to SFT's contention that traditional addiction counseling places too much emphasis on the Disease Model, the dysfunction caused by excessive drinking and/or drug use and the observation that people who have SUDs often use denial to avoid admitting to SUD-related problems.

Miracle Question: an SFT technique which asks that clients imagine what will be different once the "problem" no longer exists. This technique encourages clients to look to a future in which he or she is no longer plagued by addiction.

finding exceptions: an SFT technique whereby clients are asked to recall times when problems with alcohol or drugs were not present in the person's life.

scaling questions: an SFT technique whereby clients are asked to rate the impact of their drinking or drug use, or to rate the times when drinking or drug use was not causing problems (e.g. finding exceptions) on a scale from 1 to 10.

They suggest that in order to unlock the door to solutions there are six keys that the counselor needs to consider: (1) make sure the miracle or change is important to the client; (2) keep the change small; (3) make the change specific, concrete and behavioral; (4) be sure to state what he or she will do (i.e. state the change as something that's concrete and observable); (5) state how he or she will start their journey rather than how they will end it; (6) be clear about who, where and when but not necessarily why. These recommendations are very similar to how counselors collaboratively write treatment plans with their clients. In writing plans, there's a focus on goals that are small and concrete rather than vague and internal (e.g. improving self-esteem).

, Another key aspect to SFT, when applied to clients experiencing SUDs, is that it utilizes a 5-Step Treatment Model (Berg & Miller, 1991). This model is designed to provide counselors with a framework to help clients find solutions to problems arising from alcohol and/or drug use.

The 5-Step Treatment Model is described as follows:

Step 1: **Working with the problem drinker:** assessing and building the therapeutic relationship

Step 2: **Negotiating well-formed treatment goals:** beginning with the end in mind

Step 3: **Orienting the client towards a solution:** how to interview for change

Step 4: **Solution-focused intervention:** the components, types and delivery of treatment interventions

Step 5: **Goal maintenance:** strategies for maintaining progress

The 5-Step Model utilizes many of the techniques we will be presenting in this chapter. For example, in Step 4, the SFT counselor will introduce various SFT treatment techniques such as the Miracle Question and Finding Exceptions. Scaling Questions would be appropriately used in Step 3, where the counselor is examining the notion of change with the client. These techniques will be described in more depth in the next section.

Boxed Item 7.1 Principles of the Solution-Focused Approach

(1) no single approach works for everyone
(2) there are many possible solutions
(3) the solution and the problem are not necessarily related
(4) the simplest and least invasive approach is frequently the best medicine
(5) people can and do get better quickly
(6) change is happening all the time
(7) focus on strengths and resources rather than on weakness and deficits
(8) focus on the future rather than on the past

Miller, S.D., & Berg, I.K. (1995). *The Miracle Method: A radically new approach to problem drinking.* New York: W.W. Norton.

Solution-Focused Applications to Addiction Counseling: Assessment, Techniques and Interventions – Clinical Implications for Counselors

Assessment

When Solution-Focused counselors assess clients, they usually begin by discussing the client's reasons for entering treatment or what is referred to as the Presenting Complaint. The emphasis would be on *what* the client has been experiencing and *why now?* – that is, why has the client chosen this particular point in time to access treatment? The SFT counselor will also focus on what the client has tried in the past to manage or deal with the presenting complaint (including past attempts at counseling or treatment), with an emphasis on *what worked* as well as *what didn't work*. SFT counselors are interested in what internal resources the client possesses that can be brought to their current situation in a useful way. What's noteworthy is what the SLF counselor will refrain from focusing on, such as past developmental history (e.g. childhood history, educational history, family history). They will also refrain from asking about co-occurring mental health or medical problems. Similarly, they will refrain from focusing on social history or social functioning. Some of these areas may be explored, but only to the extent that they're relevant to the presenting problem. For example, if a client were to bring up that he or she will usually go on a binge after arguing with their boyfriend or girlfriend, then SFT counselors will explore the history of those relationships.

One of the main reasons for doing a thorough assessment of the problem is that it then allows the counselor and client to formulate treatment goals (see Boxed Item 7.2). Remember, SFTs are not interested in doing a more holistic Biopsychosocial Assessment. Rather SFT counselors are more interested in assessing the problem (or presenting complaint) that motivated the client to seek help. According to Berg (1992), well-formulated treatment goals would include the following:

Developing treatment goals from a SFT perspective has many of the qualities of good goal-setting (Perkinson, 2017) in that goals are described in simple, measurable, concrete terms rather than something vague like "Improving self-esteem." An example of a simple, concrete goal would be something like "Client will develop positive social supports who support his/her recovery" or "Client will develop leisure activities that support his/her recovery."

Treatment Techniques

There are three treatment techniques which are central to Solution-Focused Theory. The first technique we'll examine is the *Miracle Question*. The rationale of the Miracle Question is that it encourages clients to explore what the future will look like once his or her alcohol or drug use is no longer posing problems or difficulties. It's not unusual that when clients enter counseling they are looking for a miracle that will help bring about change, because they probably have tried

---

Boxed Item 7.2 Guidelines for Well-Formed Treatment Goals

(1) they are described in social interactional terms
(2) they have contextual or situational features
(3) they are described as including the presence of some behaviors as the start of something rather than the end of something.
(4) they are small rather than large
(5) they are salient (important) to the client and, through negotiation, salient to the therapist
(6) they are described in specific, concrete and behavioral terms
(7) they are described in terms of positive indicators of success rather than as an absence of problems
(8) they are both realistic and achievable
(9) they are perceived by the client as involving "hard work" on his or her part

Adapted from Berg (1992)

---

everything within their power to bring about change. Here's how the Miracle Question would be posed to the client:

> Suppose tonight, after you go to bed and fall asleep, while you are sleeping, a miracle happens. The miracle is that the problem or problems you are struggling with are solved! Just like that! Since you are sleeping however, you don't know that the miracle has happened. You sleep right through the whole event. When you wake up tomorrow morning, what would be some of the first things that you would notice that would be different and that would tell you that the miracle has happened and that your problem is solved?
>
> (Miller & Berg, 1995, p. 38)

As indicated above, the Miracle Question emphasizes what the future will look like when the problem or problems are no longer impacting on the client. The Miracle Question also asks the client to examine what their first indications would be that the miracle took place during the course of the night (i.e. "When you wake up tomorrow morning, *what would be some of the first things* that you would notice that would be different and that would tell you the miracle has happened …"). In a videotaped session (Berg, 1990a), Insoo Kim Berg is counseling a woman who has been in recovery from her substance use disorder for several years but has been struggling with being able to lose weight. In the beginning of the session, the client tells Insoo Kim Berg how she was able to lose weight in the past but had regained weight because of the stress of working and going back to school to earn her degree. When Insoo poses the Miracle Question to the client, her whole demeanor changes. The client goes from being very serious and somewhat negative to smiling and laughing and becoming fully engaged as she explains how she would know the miracle took place during the course of the night. Interestingly, the client states she would know the miracle took place because she would wake up and feel like exercising.

Learning Opportunity 7.1 – The Miracle Question

Think about a problem or issue that you're currently experiencing. Imagine someone were to pose the Miracle Question to you? Assuming a miracle occurs while you're sleeping tonight, how would you know the miracle took place? What would be different? What would you be feeling? Discuss in small groups or in your chat room.

The next technique that is central to Solution-Focused Theory is *Finding Exceptions*. Exceptions are "those times when people do not experience their usual pattern of problem drinking (Miller & Berg, 1995, p. 79), which would include instances where the client's drinking is greatly reduced and therefore becomes non-problematic, as well as periods of total abstinence and participation in treatment and/or 12-Step programs. Shining a light on exceptions helps to convey a sense of self-efficacy or self-confidence that positive change is possible. It's important to note, however, that not all clients have experienced "exceptions" or instances where they have abstained or reduced their drinking or drug use. For some clients, they may have only experienced exceptions during times of residential treatment, incarceration or hospitalization. Once "exception" periods have been identified, the counselor may then ask:

> What was different during those time when you weren't drinking or using drugs? What are you doing differently during those times of exception? What would others say you are doing differently during those times? What happens shortly before or after those times?
>
> (Berg, 1992)

There are also other questions that Miller and Berg (1995) recommend that counselors explore with clients as a means of helping to elucidate how periods of exceptions have come about:

> How have you managed to overcome the urge or temptation to drink to the problem stage in the past? What did you actually do that helped you to overcome the urge to drink at that time? What would others say you did? What exactly did you do the last time you thought you deserved a drink but decided not to have one? What have you done in the past in order to stay out of situations in which the temptation to drink to excess might outweigh your resolve to stay sober? How have you managed to stop drinking to the point of its being a problem in the past? What did you actually do that finally helped you to stop? What would others day you did? How did you manage

to get back on track the last time you experienced a setback in your efforts to solve your drinking problem? What was different about the last time you successfully managed to keep your drinking at an acceptable level to you and your loved ones? How did you do it? What would they say you did in order to be successful?

(Berg, 1992)

Learning Opportunity 7.2 – Exception Finding

What are some of the things that stand out in the Exception Finding questions that are listed above? Why do you think SFT counselors ask clients what his or her family or loved ones may have to say about periods of exception?

The next technique that SFT counselors may utilize with clients are *Scaling Questions*. Scaling questions are a means for clients to assess exceptions or times when drinking or drug use is not a problem. On a scale from 1 to 100, clients are asked to estimate the percentage of time that drinking or drug use is problematic. For example, if a client indicates that drinking is problematic 60% of the time, then the counselor would then explore with the client what is happening the other 40% of the time when drinking or drug use is non-problematic. SFT counselors also recommend that clients use graphs to chart the days of the week where exceptions are more likely or less likely to occur in order to help determine days or times of day which are more difficult for clients to enact change. Other Scaling Questions include the following:

On a scale from 1 to 10 with 10 meaning you are extremely confident that this problem can be solved and 1 meaning that you have no confidence at all, where would you put yourself? On the same scale, how realistic would you say this is? On the same scale, with 10 meaning you would do anything to solve this problem and 1 means you will probably wait and for something to happen before making changes, where would you say you are today? On the same scale how confident are you that you will be able to continue to make progress at the pace you have been at? On the same scale, with 10 meaning how you hope your life to be when you solve the problem and 1 represents how bad things were when you first called to make this appointment, where would you say you are today?

(Berg, 1992)

Another technique that SFT is something called the *Solution Lottery*. Here clients are first asked to make a list of activities or things he or she likes to do that are enjoyable or rewarding. Ideally, the activities on the list should not require a lot of preparation time or money to execute. Some of these activities might include going for a walk, listening to music, talking with a friend on the phone, going for a drive, or going shopping. Any activity can be considered reinforcing if the client is willing to engage in a less desirable behavior in order to reward themselves with the rewarding or desired behavior. The second step involves getting a paper bag or a small box and then taking several small strips of paper on which the client will write the following on each separate strip: No Reward, Immediate Reward, Reward in Four Hours, Reward in 12 Hours, Reward in 24 Hours. These strips of paper are then placed into the bag or box. The Lottery begins when the client is then asked to make a note of when exceptions occur. For example, a client notes that he did not go to the bar on his or her way home from work and had nothing to drink once he or she arrived home. The client first picks a rewarding activity from his or her list and then picks a strip of paper with the reward status. So if the strip of paper indicates No Reward, then the client does not engage in the activity. If the strip of paper indicates Immediate Reward, then the client engages in the rewarding activity immediately. You may be saying to yourself, "Why not just engage in the rewarding behavior immediately when exceptions are noted by the client?" However, the purpose of the Solution Lottery is not only to have the client engage in new behavior patterns but also to accept that rewards are not always immediate. Therefore, delaying gratification or reward can make the reward something the client can look forward to in the future, whether it be four, twelve or twenty-four hours from now (Miller & Berg, 1995).

Finally, SFT counselors also offer clients three Change Rules which are designed to help clients come up with new perspectives on change.

Rule 1: If it ain't broken, don't fix it. This rule pertains to instances where a slip or relapse takes place and the tendency of counselors to go back and pick apart the reasons for the lapse or failure. SFT counselors, on the other hand, refrain from "picking apart" the slip as it merely reinforces the client's "problem." This is not say that there's nothing to be gained by looking at antecedents to slips or relapses however, not at the expense of reinforcing the problem rather than the solution.

Rule 2: Once you know what works, DO MORE OF IT. Often there is a tendency to focus on past behaviors that didn't work. A well-known colloquial saying that's commonly heard in 12-Step meetings goes something like this, "Insanity is when you keep doing the same thing but expect a different result." (This saying is attributed to Albert Einstein!) Often, in addictions, people keep repeating the same behaviors (e.g. getting high) but somehow expect that things will end up differently (e.g. "I won't get pulled over for drinking and driving this time" or "I won't fight with my boyfriend or girlfriend this time"). Invariably, however, things turn out the same. Therefore, Rule 2 emphasizes the importance of continuing to do more of what works.

Rule 3: If it doesn't work, don't do it again. Do something different. SFT is often used with families and couples who are experiencing problems in their relationships with one another. When families enter counseling, it's often because they continue to do the same thing over and over again, continue to have the same argument or continue the same self-defeating behaviors but somehow are "expecting a different result." The purpose of Rule 3 is to try to get clients to begin to do something different with regard to drinking and drug use. By doing so, the hope is, that he or she may be closer to moving towards a solution.

Advantages and Limitations of Solution-Focused Theory

Solution-Focused Theory has many advantages. From the descriptions of theory described earlier, it is clearly a collaborative approach in which counselor and client work together to find solutions. However, collaborative approaches may be fine when clients enter treatment of their own volition and with some degree of insight into their difficulties. Solution-focused approaches may not work as well with clients who are mandated to attend treatment (e.g. court-mandated clients, DUI offender clients, intimate partner violence perpetrators, etc.). Berg (1990b) has developed a list of recommendations for negotiating goals with mandated clients.

Boxed Item 7.3 Goal Negotiation with Mandated Clients

(1) Whose idea was it that you need to come here?
(2) What makes _____ think you need to come here?
      What does _____ think is the reason you have this problem?
(3) What would _____ say minimally you need to do different?
      What do you have to do to convince_____ that you don't need to come here?
(4) When was the last time you did this? (Finding exceptions)
      What was different in your life then?
      How did you do this?
      What do you think _____ will say he/she noticed different about you then?
      What was helpful in getting you started?
(5) What is the first step you need to take to get started this time?
      How confident are you that you can do this again? (Scaling question)
      What would it take to raise your confidence level?
      What would _____ say the chance are you will do this?
(6) What do you suppose_____ would notice different about you when you do this?
(7) What difference would it make in your life then?
      What will be going on in your life that is not going on now?
(8) How will you know you've done enough?
      What difference would it make in your relationship with those closest with you?
      Who will be the first to notice you've make changes?
                                          Adapted from Berg (1990)

Boxed Item 7.4 Advantages and Limitations of Solution-Focused Theory

Advantages

- Solution-Focused Theory is simplistic and easy to grasp by both counselors and clients
- Solution-Focused Theory offers concrete, practical techniques
- Solution-Focused Therapy can be utilized in both group and individual sessions as well as in working with couples and families
- Solution-Focused Theory seeks solutions and therefore emphasizes clients' strengths and utilizes what they've done in the past that's worked while refraining from past strategies that may not have worked
- Solution-Focused Theory helps clients develop a sense of self-efficacy
- Solution-Focused counseling works collaboratively with clients in developing treatment goals

Limitations

- Solution-Focused counseling may not be an appropriate approach for all individuals with SUDs
- Solution-Focused counseling may not take into account all the other factors that influence one's SUD, such as culture, social, psychological factors, trauma or other co-occurring disorders
- Solution-Focused counseling seems to be most helpful in the early stages of counseling but is not proscriptive when it comes to how to help clients maintain change

---

Goal-setting with mandated clients becomes challenging for most addiction counselors, regardless of his or her theoretical training or approach. However, Motivational Interviewing (discussed in Chapter 9) and Solution-Focused Theory are probably the most effective in working with mandated clients in that they are both client-centered approaches. In other words, the counselor is not imposing change on the client but rather the belief is that the client possesses answers or solutions to his/her difficulties. If for nothing else, clients may agree that their goal might be to free themselves from the restrictions imposed by the mandate that they attend treatment. In order to do this, changes in behavior and attitudes will need to take place.

Not all SUD clients are appropriate candidates for SFT, which appears to be most suitable for clients who can be seen on an outpatient or intensive outpatient basis, or who are in a residential program. Similarly, clients who may need detoxification or who have medical complications, so that continued drinking or drug use poses real health dangers, would probably not be appropriate for Solution-Focused approaches, until they're stabilized medically. Another limitation to Solution-Focused Therapy is that it has a finite number of treatment techniques (i.e. the Miracle Question, Finding Exceptions and Scaling Questions). Although these treatment techniques are powerful tools that really do help clients to look at what future solutions might look like, there are only three main techniques. It should be pointed out, however, that these treatment techniques can be applied to counseling not only individuals but also to working with couples and families.

Case Example: Amanda

Amanda is a 28-year-old, single mother of a 2-year-old daughter who is seeking addiction counseling on an outpatient basis. Amanda indicates that she has been drinking and smoking cannabis since she was in high school and now finds that she's having trouble stopping. She explains that just about every weekend, she'll go out with her friends and they usually end up drinking at a local bar and then will usually go over to one of her friend's apartments where they smoke cannabis. Amanda is quick to point out that she is not foolish enough to drive, and instead will take an Uber or Lyft home. She also points out that she does not drink or get high around her 2-year-old daughter, whom she drops off at her parents when she's going out "partying" on the weekend. Amanda is worried because she feels she is "in a rut" that she can't get out of and nearly every weekend is spent getting high with her friends, no matter what time of year it is. The following is an excerpt from Amanda's session with Jennifer, who is a Solution-Focused addictions counselor.

COUNSELOR: Hello Amanda, I'm glad you could make the appointment today. Did you have any problems finding my office?

AMANDA: No, the directions you gave me were very helpful.

Jennifer then goes over some basic ground rules with Jennifer, such as confidentiality and duty to warn and she has Amanda sign an Informed Consent form.

COUNSELOR: So, tell me what brings you here today? What would you like to work on?

AMANDA: Well, like I mentioned to you on the phone when we set up today's appointment, I've been struggling with trying to stay away from drinking and smoking pot, which I do just about every weekend.

COUNSELOR: You said, "just about every weekend," does that mean there are times when you don't drink or smoke pot?

Jennifer asks this question as a means of "Exception Finding" or instances when Amanda doesn't drink or get high on weekends.

AMANDA: Yes there have been a few weekends when I didn't go out. Like the weekend of my daughter, Suzie's birthday. I didn't go out at all that weekend because we had her "kid" party on Saturday and then her relatives/adult party on Sunday.

COUNSELOR: What was that weekend like for you? Did you miss going out with your friends?

AMANDA: No, not really. I did enjoy planning Suzie's party and it was so incredible to see her get so excited opening her presents. I felt really good about hosting both parties for her.

COUNSELOR: So, you can go without drinking or drugging when you have something more important or more fun to do?

AMANDA: Yeah, I guess so ... I didn't think of it that way, but you're right. I really didn't feel like I missed anything. Every weekend when I go out partying, is just like the last one, you know "same old, same old."

COUNSELOR: With the weekend coming up, what do you have planned?

AMANDA: I'm supposed to meet up with Cathy and then we're going over to the Roadhouse (a local bar) where her boyfriend's band is playing this Friday night. She wanted everyone to go to help support his band.

COUNSELOR: How are you feeling about going out on Friday?

AMANDA: Well I work all week and there are some Fridays when I'm too tired to go out and would just like to stay home.

Jennifer asks a "Scaling Question."

COUNSELOR: On a scale from 1 to 10 with 1 being "not important at all" and 10 being Very important," how important would it be for you to go to the Roadside on Friday? Also using the same scale, how important would it be for you to stay home with Suzie on Friday?

AMANDA: I would give going out with friends about a 5 and staying home with Suzie this Friday about an 8.

COUNSELOR: So, it sounds like you're leaning more towards staying home with Suzie? What would help to make that a relaxing and fun evening?

AMANDA: Suzie loves pizza, so we would order a pizza and then watch one of her favorite movies.

Jennifer introduces the Miracle Question.

COUNSELOR: That sounds like a relaxing evening. I'm going to give you a scenario and then ask you a strange question. This requires creativity and imagination. Are you willing to give this a try?

AMANDA: Sure, why not?

COUNSELOR: Okay. You can keep your eyes open or closed whichever is more comfortable for you. I'd like you to imagine that when you go to bed tonight, that during the night a miracle takes place. The miracle is that all of the conflict that you've been having regarding drinking and smoking pot, miraculously disappears, so that when you wake up in the morning, you're no longer troubled by urges to drink or smoke.

My question is, when you wake up tomorrow, how would you know the miracle occurred during the night?

AMANDA: Wow that's a tough one. I think the first thing I'd notice is that I'm totally at peace with myself. I'd be thinking clearly, not hungover or dreading going to work. I'd look forward to doing things rather than moping around.

COUNSELOR: Anything else you'd notice?

AMANDA: I think I'd really have a different attitude. Like just feeling better about myself. I don't know, like being more at peace with myself.

This brief case illustration provides you with a glimpse into what a Solution-Focused session might look like. Amanda comes into counseling looking for a solution to her dilemma of going out partying with her friends every weekend. She describes her situation as being in a "rut" or being stuck in a pattern of behavior that she is troubled with. Solution-Focused Therapy is a perfect approach to use with Amanda because she is seeking change.

Summary

The Solution-Focused model is essentially a change model which focuses on the goals that clients want to attain once the problems he or she is experiencing are no longer impeding their progress or aspirations. This model evolved out of concerns that traditional substance use disorders model and counseling placed too much emphasis on the 3 Ds (i.e. Disease, Denial and Dysfunction). Therefore, instead of viewing the role of counselors as being able to break down client denial of having a disease which had created dysfunction or unmanageability in his or her lives, SFT focuses instead at a future point in time when the problems no longer exist. Several useful techniques have evolved out of the SFT approach such as "the miracle question," scaling questions and exception finding questions.

Recommended Reading and Resources

Berg, I.K. (1990). *Goal negotiation with mandated clients*. Milwaukee, WI: The Brief Family Therapy Center.

Berg, I.K., & Miller, S.D. (1991). The 5-Step Treatment Model. In *Working with the problem drinker: A Solution-Focused approach*. Milwaukee, WI: The Brief Family Therapy Center.

Miller, S.D., & Berg, I.K. (1995). *The Miracle Method: A radically new approach to problem drinking*. New York: W.W. Norton

Resources

Solution-Focused Brief Therapy Association: Provides an annual conference and a listing of books, videos and articles for sale. www.sfbta.org/

Denver Center for Solution-Focused Brief Therapy: Website provides information on trainings, workshops and SFT books for sale. https://denversolutions.com/Solution-focused-therapy-training-books-by-Teri_Pichot.html

Solution-Focused Brief Therapy Basics: Meet Insoo Kim Berg & Steve de Shazer: This is a helpful blog which presents the basics of SFT along with a brief video of a family therapy session. https://thefamilytherapyblog.com/2015/04/10/solution-focused-brief-therapy-basics-meet-insoo-kim-berg-and-steve-de-shazer/

Psychology Tools − Solution-Focused Brief Therapy Worksheets: This website provides several worksheets that can be used with clients, along with a listing of publications. www.psychologytools.com/professional/therapies/solution-focused-therapy/

What is Solution-Focused Therapy by Dr. Todd Grande (YouTube video): www.psychologytools.com/professional/therapies/solution-focused-therapy/

Solution-Focused Therapy Role Play with Dr. Todd Grande (YouTube video): www.youtube.com/watch?v=gcXENqOwulw

References

Berg, I.K. (1990a). *Solution-focused therapy: An interview with Insoo Kim Berg.* In J. Carlson, & J. A. Lewis, *Addiction counseling series.* Videotape series. Boston, MA: Allyn & Bacon.

Berg, I.K. (1990b). *Goal negotiation with mandated clients.* Milwaukee, WI: The Brief Family Therapy Center.

Berg, I.K. (1992, June 19–20). *Working briefly with the chemically dependent person: A Solution-Focused approach.* Workshop booklet. Ardmore, PA: Institute for Advanced Clinical Training, Inc.

Berg, I.K., & Miller, S.D. (1991). The 5-Step Treatment Model. From *Working with the problem drinker: A Solution-Focused approach.* Milwaukee, WI: The Brief Family Therapy Center.

Curran, P.J., Muthen, B.O., & Harford, T.C. (1998). The influence of changes in marital status on developmental trajectories of alcohol use in young adults. *Journal of Studies on Alcohol, 59(6),* 647–658.

Miller, S.D., & Berg, I.K. (1995). *The Miracle Method: A radically new approach to problem drinking.* New York: W.W. Norton.

Misch, D.A. (2007). "Natural Recovery" from alcohol abuse among college students. *Journal of American College Health, 55(4),* 215–218.

O'Malley, P.M. (2004). Maturing out of problematic alcohol use. *Alcohol Research & Health, 28(4),* 202–204.

Perkinson, R. (2017). *Chemical dependency counseling: A practical guide* (5th edn). Oakland, CA: Sage Publications.

Robbins, L. (1979). Addict careers. In R. Dupont, A. Goldstein, & J. O'Donnell (Eds). *Handbook on drug abuse* (p. 332). Rockville, MD: National Institute on Drug Abuse.

8 Existential Models

Margaret Smith

Learning Opportunity 8.1

Americans live in one of the most affluent countries in the world, yet we suffer from extremely high rates of substance use disorders, suicides and depression when compared to other industrialized countries. What is your opinion as to what accounts for these high rates of substance use disorders (SUDs) and mental health problems? Is America experiencing an existential crisis?

Introduction

This chapter focuses on existential therapy and its application to addiction counseling. Existential therapy is more of a philosophical approach than specific style, technique or strategy (Corey, 2017). "Rather than being a technical approach that offers a new set of rules for psychotherapy, it represents a way of thinking about human experience that can be – or perhaps should be – a part of all therapies" (Yalom & Josselson, 2014, p. 265). Existential therapy, therefore, evolved from existential philosophy in the years following World War II. It is important to take into account what was going on in the world (specifically in Europe and Scandinavian countries) at the time existentialism was being developed. Having been through two world wars, political revolutions in Russia, industrialization, there was a great deal of personal turmoil in which individuals began to question personal meaning in a meaningless world. Therapists who have contributed to existential theory include Victor Frankl, Rollo May, Abraham Maslow, Irvin Yalom and Friedrich Nietzsche.

Key Terms

existential vacuum: Frankl's term to describe a sense that life has lost all meaning.

personal responsibility: existentialists believe that people are responsible for their own conditions. They are also responsible for making meaning out of their lives.

ultimate concerns/crises: there are four ultimate concerns or existential crises that people must face: freedom, isolation, death and meaninglessness.

Existential Approach

Existential counseling is based on the belief that human beings have the need for meaning and purpose in life. They also have the capacity for freedom and choice. Further, existential counselors believe that human beings function more effectively when they take responsibility for their lives. Additionally, human beings will inevitability face limitations and challenges in their lives, and function most effectively when they face – rather than avoid or deny – these challenges (Vos, Craig, & Cooper, 2015, p. 115).

Existentialists believe that everyone experiences challenges, life crises (Johnson, Griffen-Shelley, & Sandler, 1987) or ultimate concerns (Yalom & Josselson, 2014). These challenges, ultimate concerns or crises include freedom, isolation, death, and meaninglessness. "The individual's confrontation with each of these [ultimate concerns] … constitutes the content of the existential dynamic conflict" (Yalom, 1980, p. 8).

> The life crises that all of us share are: the recognition that we are finite, that we must die; the recognition that we are free and that we cannot escape that freedom and the responsibility that it entails; the recognition that as individuals we are all inexorably alone; and the recognition that if our lives are to have meaning, it will be of our own creation.

> (Johnson, Griffin-Shelley, & Sandler, 1987, p. 17)

Further, these concerns or crises are associated with anxiety and despair which can be linked to substance use problems (Lewis, 2014). That is, some people turn to alcohol and/or drugs in order to reduce feelings of anxiety, depression and despair. However, the paradox of substance abuse is that it usually adds to feelings of isolation and despair over time. It is common as people progress deeper into SUDs that they become more isolated, lonely and disconnected from others.

The next section addresses these four crises/ultimate concerns of freedom, isolation, death and meaninglessness. The section following this discussion presents the application of this existential approach to addiction counseling. The chapter ends with a case study.

The Four Crises/Ultimate Concerns/Challenges

Freedom.

> … freedom refers to the absence of external structure – that there is a lack of structure to the universe with no inherent design. Therefore, individuals are entirely responsible for – that is, is the author of – his or her own world, life design, choices, and actions. "Freedom" in this sense, has a terrifying implication: it means that beneath us there is no ground – nothing, a void, an abyss. A key existential dynamic, then, is the clash between our confrontation with groundlessness and our wish for ground and structure.
>
> (Yalom, 1980, p. 9)

Yalom and other existentialists believe that freedom ultimately means that we are the authors of our own lives. Therefore, we must take responsibility for our own choices and perspectives "and we bear the burden for knowing that we are responsible for all of our experience" (Yalom & Josselson, 2014, pp. 266–267). Once a person realizes that s/he is "groundless" and alone in these choices, the person experiences existential anxiety (Lewis, 2014, p. 350). Failure in dealing with existential freedom may lead to compulsive behavior (Johnson et al., 1987).

Isolation. Isolation refers to the experience that we are alone in the universe (Yalom, 1980, p. 9) "Existential isolation refers to an unbridgeable gulf between oneself and any other being. It refers, too, to an isolation even more fundamental – a separation between the individual and the world" (Yalom, 1980, p. 355). Existential isolation must be separated from interpersonal isolation as it is not related to geographic or poor social skills, but to the "fundamental separation between people that underlies human existence" (Lewis, 2014, p. 351). This awareness of our fundamental isolation may lead to anxiety and powerlessness (Lewis, 2014, p. 351). Further, the "fear of existential isolation (and the defenses against it) underlies a great deal of interpersonal psychopathology" (Yalom & Josselson, 2014, p. 275).

Death. Death is the ultimate concern as we recognize our own mortality. For existentialists, a "core inner conflict is between awareness of inevitable death and the simultaneous wish to continue to live" (Yalom & Josselson, 2014, p. 276). "Death is a primordial source of anxiety and, as such, is the primary fount of psychopathology" (Yalom, 1980, p. 29). However, the acceptance of death and one's mortality can give life meaning and purpose. "Death is the condition that makes it possible for us to live life in an authentic fashion" (Yalom, 1980, p. 31). We cannot live life fully until we have grappled with death honestly (Feifel, 1969).

Meaninglessness. Frankl (1992) believed that the search for meaning is a person's primary motivation.

> The human being seems to require meaning. To live without meaning, goals, values, or ideals seems to provoke, as we have seen, considerable

distress. In severe form it may lead to the decision to end one's life. Frankl noted that in the concentration camp the individual with no sense of meaning was unlikely to survive.

(Yalom, 1980, p. 422)

Feelings of meaninglessness and emptiness are what Frankl (1992) referred to as an existential vacuum. When experiencing an existential vacuum a person feels "indifference, apathy or boredom and a sense of meaninglessness with life" (Nicholson, Higgins, Turner, James, Stickle, & Pruitt, 1994, p. 24). Consequently, this lack of meaning can lead to anxicty and psychopathology. More specifically, in relation to alcohol and other drug-related problems, Frankl (1978) stated that "addiction … is at least partially to be traced back to the feeling of meaninglessness" (p. 26). Indeed Nicholson and colleagues (1994) found that those with substance abuse problems had lower levels of meaning of life when compared to a control group of non-abusing people.

Learning Opportunity 8.2

In small groups of four, divide the ultimate concerns/crises among group members. Discuss the ultimate concerns/crises of freedom, isolation, death and meaninglessness. Then discuss how they might relate to substance use, abuse and addiction as well as how these concepts might be applied in treatment.

Application to Addiction Counseling

Existential therapists are often seen as *fellow travelers*, suggesting that "we are all in this together" without the labels of patient/therapist, client/counselor, analysand/ analyst (Yalom & Josselson, 2014, p. 269). Further, it is essential that the therapist be genuine and authentic in order to help the client make meaningful change (CSAT, 2014, p. 107). As a whole, most do not use "clever techniques, therapeutic tricks, [or use] psychological jargon" (Fernando, 2007, p. 232). Additionally, existential counselors do not diagnose or test their clients because it "dehumanizes individuals" (Lewis, 2014, p. 111).

Existential therapists address anxiety and the "factors shaping substance abuse disorders, such as lack of meaning in one's life, fear of death or failure, alienation from others, and spiritual emptiness" (CSAT, 2014, p. 106). In dealing with some of these ultimate concerns related to meaninglessness, isolation, and death, some people resort to substance use as a coping strategy. An existential therapist would work with clients to seek alternative coping strategies over using substances (CSAT, 2014).

In terms of the ultimate concerns and freedom, existential freedom is an important term when working with clients. People with addictions must become responsible for their own lives – no longer blaming others and avoiding responsibility. This realization can lead to anxiety as persons with addictions may realize that they are responsible for their success or failure in treatment (Lewis, 2014, p. 350). In this case, an existential counselor would help a client identify their avoidance of responsibility and have them take ownership of their choices and lives (Yalom & Josselson, 2014).

In terms of isolation, individuals with addictions can have difficulties with existential isolation. "Compulsive use may indeed be a response to problems in these areas [of love, intimacy, and isolation] because it leads to a powerful but temporary respite from intense isolation" (Lewis, 2014, p. 351). In this case, the existential therapist would help a client move towards authentic relationships, while recognizing their limits (Yalom & Josselson, 2014).

In terms of the ultimate concern of death, denial of death or management of death anxiety may be reasons for alcohol and other drug abuse (Lewis, 2014). Increasing awareness of one's finality can lead to a "shift in perspective and lead to personal change" (Yalom & Josselson, 2014, p. 283). Persons with addictions who recognize that they are hitting "rock bottom" or just barely survived death (e.g. alcohol- or other drug-related car accident), might see the "light" and make changes.

Lastly, in terms of meaninglessness as an ultimate concern, an existential therapist would work with clients on finding meaning. The therapist is not to tell clients what their particular meaning in life should be, but to point out that they can create meaning even in suffering. Frankl (1992) believes that we can find life's meaning in three ways: by doing a deed – that is by achieving or accomplishing something; by experiencing a value, such as a work of nature, culture or love; and by suffering – that is, by finding a proper attitude toward unalterable fate: "suffering can be a catalyst for a more fulfilling way of being – provided that people are able to see meaning and purpose in their suffering" (Hart & Singh, 2009, pp. 125–126).

Two specific types of therapies, both Logotherapy (Frankl, 1992) and Meaning, or Meaning Centered Therapy (Thompson, 2012, 2016) focus on meaning making in counseling. Meaning Therapy helps clients "move beyond abstinence and harm reduction" and move towards a "fullness of life" by finding meaning (Wong as cited in Thompson, 2016, p. 4). In Logotherapy, the "patient is actually confronted with and reoriented toward the meaning of his life" (Frankl, 1992, p. 104).

While the existential approach does not offer techniques, Frankl's Logotherapy does provide a few including dereflection, paradoxical intention and Socratic dialogue. Dereflection involves the issue of hyperreflection. Hyperreflection refers to the preoccupation with how one looks, acts and speaks to the point where s/he must "get it right" and he or she can't complete the task at hand (Logotherapy, 2012, para. 1). A technique, then to deal with this hyperreflection is to dereflect, which means taking the focus of self and directing it towards another person, or other places, things or values (Lewis, 2014, p. 359).

Paradoxical intention refers to asking for the very thing that one fears (Lewis, 2014, p. 359). "The paradox is that if one tries hard to make the symptom happen, laughs at it, and adopts a position of 'detached amusement' related to it, the symptom actually loses its power" (Lewis, 2014, p. 359).

Socractic dialogue refers to using Socratic-style questions to assess the client's irrational thoughts (Lewis, 2014, p. 359). This involves asking questions to help the client "see" his own ways of thinking.

Strengths and Limitations

One of the strengths of the existential approach, is that many clients do show up in counseling with vague concerns about meaning, death, isolation and freedom(responsibility). For example, clients may ask "Why am I going through this?" or "What is this all about?" Dealing with their existential crises may assist them with their treatment and recovery.

Limitations include the lack of techniques and strategies in this approach. It is more a philosophical than a practical approach. Further, existential therapists do not diagnose or test their clients (Gladding, 2005, p. 55), which may lead to issues with agency administrative issues and insurance companies. If interested in this approach, you may want to integrate it with other therapies.

Learning Opportunity 8.3

Would you incorporate the existential approach into your counseling work? Why or why not? If so, how might you incorporate it into your counseling work?

Case Study

Amanda is a 36-year-old African-American woman who has abused a number of substances, including cocaine, heroin, alcohol, and marijuana over the past 15 years. Amanda had two children in her early twenties, a daughter who is now 15, and a son, aged 18. Because of her substance abuse problems, they live with other relatives who agreed to raise them. Amanda has been in treatment repeatedly and has remained substance free for the last five years, with several minor relapses. She has been married for two years, to Steve, a carpenter; he is substance free and supports her attempts to stay away from substances.

Last month she was diagnosed with breast cancer and, more recently, she began to "shoot up," which led her back into treatment. Out of fear, she came to the treatment center and asked to see a counselor at the clinic one day after work. She is worried about her marriage and that her husband will be devastated by this news. She is afraid she is no longer strong enough to stay away from drugs since discovering she has cancer. She is also concerned about her children and her job. Uncertain of how she will keep on living, she is also terrified of dying.

(adapted from Sandra case study in CSAT, 2014, p. 111)

Case Conceptualization

According to the existential approach, a counselor would work with Amanda regarding her existential crises – those which include death, isolation, freedom, and meaning. In terms of her being terrified of death, an existential therapist can work with Amanda on increasing awareness of one's finality, which can lead to a "shift in perspective and lead to personal change" (Yalom & Josselson, 2014 p. 283). Additionally, the counselor could also work with Amanda on her *living* – focusing on a sense of purpose and meaning.

Amanda may be assuming that there will be issues that could lead to the separation of her and her husband over her use, and this could lead to the existential crisis of isolation. In this case, the counselor may work with Amanda on her being more authentic in her relationship with her husband.

In terms of freedom, the counselor and Amanda may need to help her identify her avoidance of responsibility and have her take ownership for her choices and life (Yalom & Josselson, 2014).

Lastly, in terms of meaning or meaninglessness, an existential therapist would work with Amanda on finding meaning and making meaning out of her suffering. She may be particularly concerned that after being sober and clean, she was diagnosed with cancer, and is attempting to make meaning out of this (adapted from Sandra case study in CSAT, 2014, p. 111).

Recommended Reading and Resources

CSAT (Center for Substance Abuse Treatment) (2014). *Brief interventions and brief therapies for substance abuse*. Rockville, MD: Substance Abuse and Mental Health Services Administration. Retrieved from www.ncbi.nlm.nih.gov/books/NBK64939/

Frankl, V. (1992). *Man's search for meaning*. Boston, MA: Beacon Press.

Frankl, V. (1978). *The unheard cry for meaning*. New York: Simon & Schuster.

Frankl, V. (1988). *The will to meaning: Foundation and application of Logotherapy*. New York: Penguin Books.

Schulenberg, S.E., Hutzell, R.R., Nassif, C., & Rogina, J.M. (2008). Logotherapy for clinical practice. *Psychotherapy: Theory, Research, Practice, Training, 45(4)*, 447–463.

Wong, P. (2012). From Logotherapy to meaning-centered counseling and therapy. In P.T.P. Wong (Ed.). *The human quest for meaning: Theories, research, and applications* (pp. 619–647). Personality and Clinical Psychology series. New York: Routledge/Taylor & Francis.

References

CSAT (Center for Substance Abuse Treatment) (1999). *Brief interventions and brief therapies for substance abuse*. Rockville, MD: Substance Abuse and Mental Health Services Administration. Retrieved from www.ncbi.nlm.nih.gov/books/NBK64939/

Corey, G. (2017). *Theory and practice of counseling and psychotherapy* (10th edn). Boston: Cengage

Feifel, H. (1969). Death-relevant variable in psychology. In R. May (Ed.). *Existential psychology* (2nd edn). New York: Random House.

Fernando, D.M. (2007). Existential theory and solution-focused strategies: Integration and application. *Journal of Mental Health Counseling, 29(3)*, 226–241.

Frankl, V. (1992). *Man's search for meaning.* Boston, MA: Beacon Press.

Frankl, V. (1978). *The unheard cry for meaning.* New York: Simon & Schuster.

Gladding, S.T. (2005). *Counseling theories: Essential concepts and applications.* Upper Saddle River, NJ: Pearson Education, Inc.

Hart, K.E., & Singh, T. (2009). An existential model of flourishing subsequent to treatment for addiction: The importance of living a meaningful and spiritual life. *Illness, Crisis, & Loss, 17(2)*, 125–147.

Johnson, R.A., Griffin-Shelley, E., & Sandler, K.R. (1987). Existential issues in psychotherapy with alcoholics. *Alcoholism Treatment Quarterly, 4(1)*, 15–25.

Lewis, T.F. (2014). *Substance abuse and addiction treatment: Practical applications of counseling theory.* New York: Pearson.

Logotherapy Group (2012). Victor Frankl's Logotherapy: Deflection: A religious perspective. Retrieved from https://meaningtherapy.wordpress.com/2012/02/01/dereflection-a-religious-perspective/

Nicholson, T., Higgins, W., Turner, P., James, S., Stickle, F., & Pruitt, T. (1994). The relation between meaning in life and the occurrence of drug abuse: A retrospective study. *Psychology of Addictive Behaviors, 8(1)*, 24–28.

Thompson, G. (2012). A meaning-centered therapy for addictions. *International Journal of Mental Health and Addiction, 10*, 428–440.

Thompson, G. (2016). Addiction treatment through the lens of meaning: Observations on a program developed in a residential facility. *International Journal of Existential Psychology and Psychotherapy, 7*, 1–13.

Vos, J., Craig, M., & Cooper, M. (2015). Existential therapies: A meta-analysis of their effects on psychological outcomes. *Journal of Counseling and Clinical Psychology, 83(1)*, 115–128.

Yalom, I.D. (1980). *Existential psychotherapy.* [Kindle version]. New York: Basic Books.

Yalom, I.D., & Josselson, R. (2014). Existential psychotherapy. In D. Wedding & R.J. Corsini (Eds). *Current psychotherapies* (10th edn). Belmont, CA: Cengage Learning.

9   The Transtheoretical Model, Stages of Change and Motivational Interviewing

Margaret Smith

Learning Opportunity 9.1

Discuss with a small group how does someone make a change regarding an unhealthy behavior? When does someone change? What are some effective counseling skills used with someone with a substance use disorder or a behavioral/process addiction?

Introduction

Think about a time when you wanted to change a behavior. This could be some undesirable behavior such as smoking, binge drinking, over-spending or overeating. When did you begin making that change? Did you actually follow through with making that change? How did you make that change? Did you have any setbacks along the way? Who were some people that helped you make a change? What were "things" that helped you change?.

This chapter focuses on the Transtheoretical Model (TTM), Stages of Change and Motivational Interviewing (MI). The TTM, the Stages of Change, and MI have had a huge impact of the profession and field of addictions: from looking at *how* (TTM) and *when* (Stages of Change) people change to *what* (MI) helps people to change.

We'll first define and explain TTM, Stages of Change and MI. Following this is a section on how one facilitates change using TTM, Stages of Change and MI. Finally, we'll provide you with a case study that illustrates the application of these models.

The Transtheoretical Model was developed in the 1970s by Prochaska, Norcross and DiClemente. Prochaska and DiClemente examined processes that led to change from a variety of theories, hence the term *Trans*theoretical (Prochaska, DiClemente, & Norcross, 1992). TTM focuses on *how* people change (e.g. change processes). Some of these processes are cognitive/experiential, while others are behavioral. They help people *move towards* behavior change or actual change of beliefs, attitudes or emotions (DiClemente, 2003).

The Stages of Change offer concerns the *when* of behavior change by tracking how clients change over time. Prochaska, DiClemente and Norcross (1992) identified five stages of change: Precontemplation, Contemplation, Preparation, Action and Maintenance. Each stage has its characteristics and change processes, along with counselor and client tasks, that can help move a client through each stage.

Finally, Motivational Interviewing is a "client-centered directive method for enhancing intrinsic motivation to change by exploring and resolving ambivalence" (Miller & Rollnick, 2002, p. 25). It moves counselors away from the more traditional confrontational approaches that were designed to "break" down denial of the harmful consequences of alcohol and drug use. For many years, this confrontational approach was utilized by many treatment programs, including therapeutic communities and Minnesota Model 28-day inpatient programs. As stated so eloquently by Abraham Maslow, "when the only tool you have is a hammer, everything looks like a nail," and for addiction counselors the "only tool" we had was heavy-duty confrontation. With the advent of MI, addiction counseling shifted to a more collaborative and empathetic style. As Rosengren (2018) points out, "motivational interviewing is more like ballroom dancing and less like wrestling" (p. 27).

Key Terms

change processes: processes of change "represent internal and external experiences and activities that enable individuals to move from stage to stage" (DiClemente, 2003, p. 32). These stages are explained in the Stages of Change.

Motivational Interviewing: Motivational Interviewing is "a skillful clinical method, a style of counseling and psychotherapy" (Miller & Rollnick, 2002, p. 35) which incorporates four general principles: (1) express empathy, (2) develop discrepancy, (3) roll with resistance, and (4) support self-efficacy.

self-efficacy: self-efficacy is the belief in one's ability to achieve or accomplish a task, activity, etc.

Stages of Change: in their research on *when* changes occur for people in changing unhealthy behaviors, Prochaska, DiClemente and Norcross (1992) identified five stages of change: Precontemplation, Contemplation, Preparation, Action, and Maintenance.

transtheoretical: transtheoretical refers to change techniques from across different theories (Prochaska, DiClemente, & Norcross, 1992). The Transtheoretical Model "emerged from an examination of 18 psychological and behavioral theories about how change occurs" (CSAT, 1999, p. 16).

The Transtheoretical Model

As stated in the introduction, TTM focuses on *how* people change. The model is the result of Prochaska's research on how people change – with and without professional help – by examining many psychological theories. In his research, he isolated the principles and processes of change from each theory, finding that among the theories there were several processes of change (Prochaska, Norcross, & DiClemente, 1994). These processes of change are techniques, methods and interventions (Prochaska, DiClemente, & Norcross, 1992). These techniques, methods and interventions are found across many psychological theories, hence the term *trans*theoretical.

Learning Opportunity 9.2

In small groups address this question: What are some activities people engage in that assist them in changing an unhealthy behavior? (How do people change?)

"Change processes are overt and covert activities that individuals engage in when they attempt to modify problem behaviors" (Norcross, Krebs, & Prochaska, 2011, p. 5). These processes of change are categorized into two types: cognitive/experiential and behavioral processes.

The cognitive/experiential processes of change include consciousness raising, emotional arousal, self-evaluation, environmental re-evaluation, and social liberation. Consciousness raising involves increasing knowledge about self and the problem. Emotional arousal involves experiencing emotions and feelings regarding one's behavior and the solutions to them. Self-evaluation involves assessing one's emotions and cognitions about oneself in regard to a problem behavior. Environmental re-evaluation refers to assessing the impact of the behavior on self and others. Lastly, social liberation refers to increasing positive alternatives available in society (DiClemente, 2003, p. 34; Norcross, Krebs, & Prochaska, 2011; Pro-change Behavior Systems, 2018; Prochaska & DiClemente, 1982; Prochaska, DiClemente, & Norcross, 1992, p. 1108; Prochaska, Norcross, Fowler, Follick, & Abrams, 1992).

Behavioral processes of change include self-liberation, stimulus generalization or control, conditioning or counterconditioning, reinforcement management, and helping relationships (DiClemente, 2003, p. 34; Norcross, Krebs, & Prochaska, 2011; Pro-change Behavior Systems, 2018; Prochaska & DiClemente, 1982; Prochaska, DiClemente, & Norcross, 1992, p. 1108). Self-liberation refers to being accountable, selecting options, and making commitments to a new behavior or behavior change. Stimulus generalization or control refers to "creating, altering or avoiding cues/stimuli that trigger or encourage a certain behavior" (DiClemente, 2003, p. 34). Counterconditioning involves substituting coping alternatives. Reinforcement management involves generating rewards for new behaviors while eliminating reinforcements for the unhealthy behavior. Lastly, helping relationships refers to pursuing and accepting support from family and friends for the new healthier behavior (DiClemente, 2003, p. 34; Norcross, Krebs, & Prochaska, 2011; Pro-change Behavior Systems, 2018; Prochaska & DiClemente, 1982; Prochaska, DiClemente, & Norcross, 1992, p. 1108).

Learning Opportunity 9.3

In small groups address the following question: In making a change regarding an unhealthy behavior, many people go through stages of change. Think of a time you changed/or tried to change an unhealthy behavior. What were the stages or steps you took to change/ or try to change the unhealthy behavior? (When does someone change?)

Stages of Change

In their research on *when* changes occur for people in changing unhealthy behaviors, Prochaska, DiClemente and Norcross (1992) identified five stages of change: Precontemplation, Contemplation, Preparation, Action, and Maintenance.

Precontemplation stage. This is when the client has no intention of changing because he or she may not perceive their alcohol or drug use as problematic. Also, the problem behavior is seen as having more positives than negatives (Connors, DiClemente, Velasquez, & Donovan, 2013). People in this stage may also be "unaware or underaware of their problems" (Prochaska, DiClemente, & Norcross, 1992, p. 1103). Oftentimes, when precontemplaters show up in therapy it is because they are coerced by family, friends and court-ordered directives (Prochaska, DiClemente, & Norcross, 1992).

People in the precontemplation stage are not engaged in any change processes, such as cognitive/experiential or behavioral processes, nor are they likely to engage in any change process at this stage (DiClemente, 2003). However, other people (family, friends, co-workers, boss) are often quite aware of the problem(s). When individuals or clients remain stuck in this stage, it may be the result of any one of the following four "R"s as described by DiClemente (2003, pp. 116–120): *reluctance* ("I really don't want to change"), *rebellion* ("No one can make me change"), *resignation* ("No matter what I do, I can't seem to change") and *rationalization* ("I'm not that bad, therefore I don't need to change because …").

Contemplation stage. Here, people are not ready to change, but are thinking about changing. They may seek information about the problem behavior as well as examine the pros and cons of said behavior. At the same time, they are ambivalent about change. They see both the risks, costs and harms of their behavior but at the same time are attached and attracted to their behavior. They want to change, but then they don't want to change (Miller & Rollnick, 2002).

Preparation stage. This stage entails readiness to change in terms of both attitude and behavior. People are making or have already made the decision to change. People are engaged in the change process (e.g. may have already tried cutting down). People in this stage are ready to develop a plan (Connors et al., 2013).

Action stage. In the Action stage, people decided they want to change, select a date, demonstrate/verbalize a commitment to change, make efforts to change the behavior or modify the environment, and are involved in behavioral change processes. In this stage, people are willing to take advice and suggestions on change strategies and activities (Connors et al., 2013).

Maintenance stage. In the Maintenance stage of change, people are continuing their change/changes. They work to prevent relapse and "consolidate the gains attained during action" (Prochaska, DiClemente, & Norcross, 1992, p. 1104). Maintenance involves sustaining change for an extended period of time and avoiding slips and relapses into old behaviors (DiClemente, 2003, p. 192).

Motivational Interviewing

Motivational Interviewing (MI) is "a skillful clinical method, a style of counseling and psychotherapy" (Miller & Rollnick, 2002, p. 35). The spirit of motivational interviewing focuses on collaboration over confrontation, evocation over education, and autonomy over authority. In referring to collaboration, the client and counselor are in a partnership relationship. The counselor focuses on creating an atmosphere that is conducive (as opposed to coercive) to change. In terms of evocation, the counselor is invested in eliciting from the client (that is, drawing out from the person), instead of imparting information (wisdom, insight, reality). Finally, there is autonomy with the decision to change being left to the client. S/ he can choose to change or not to change (Miller & Rollnick, 2002, p. 34).

Facilitating Behavior Change Using TTM, Stages of Change and MI

Now that you have an understanding of TTM, Stages of Change, and MI, let's focus on how we facilitate change using TTM, Stages of Change and MI.

The Stages of Change offer us the when of change. As previously stated, there are five states of change. Identifying what stage of change a person is in helps us to understand what change processes they may be going through as well as what helping actions "match" the stage. Each stage of change has a "task," change processes and counselor interventions.

For assessment purposes, counselors can use the Readiness to Change Questionnaire and the URICA (University of Rhode Island Change Assessment).

Precontemplation stage of change. In the Precontemplation stage of change, the task would be to discover the consequences of and concerns about the behavior (DiClemente, 2003). There needs to be an acknowledgement of the problem and awareness of the negative consequences associated with the behavior. The change processes at work here can include consciousness raising, which involves challenging views that the problem behavior is not a problem; self-evaluation, which involves shifting away from rationalizations and focusing on values and considerations that create dissonance; environmental re-evaluation, which involves recognizing the impact the behavior has on others; and social liberation, which involves the realization of shifting social norms as well as policies and laws that limit/ reduce/ eliminate unhealthy behaviors and provide alternatives (DiClemente, 2003, p. 132).

Here a counselor first needs to develop a rapport with the client (CSAT, 1999) and create interest and concern. Interventions would include Motivational Interviewing (Connors et al., 2013), personalized feedback based on assessment, as well as the examination of discrepancies between the client's and others' perceptions of the problem behavior (CSAT, 1999). Further, the counselor can use other motivational interviewing techniques and methods which include raising doubts or concerns in the client about substance-using patterns by exploring the meaning of events that brought the client to treatment or the results of previous treatments; eliciting the client's perceptions of the problem; offering factual information about the risks of substance use; providing personalized feedback about assessment findings; exploring the pros and cons of substance use; helping a significant other intervene; examining discrepancies between the client's and others' perceptions of the problem behavior; expressing concern and keeping the door open (CSAT, 1999, p. 31).

Contemplation stage of change. In this stage, the tasks are to gather and evaluate positive and negative aspects of behavior and resolve the decisional balance, tipping the scale towards change. The change processes involved here include consciousness raising, which involves discovering the negatives of behavior and positive for change; self-evaluation, which involves shifting views and values to emphasize the negatives of the behavior and the benefits of changing; environmental revaluation, which involves recognizing the impact the behavior has on others; and social liberation, which involves observing how others will support the healthier behavior (DiClemente, 2003, p. 151). Here the concept and use of decisional balance applies (DiClemente, 2003). What are the pros and cons of not changing and what are the pros and cons of changing? Tipping the balance regarding the cons of not changing and the pros of changing help here.

Strategies which are based on Motivational Interviewing techniques and methods for this stage include normalizing ambivalence. Additionally, the counselor can help the client "tip the decisional balance scales" toward change by eliciting and weighing pros and cons of substance use and change; work with clients to change extrinsic to intrinsic motivation; examine the client's personal values in relation to change; and emphasize the client's free choice, responsibility and self-efficacy for change. Further, the counselor can elicit self-motivational statements of intent and commitment (refer to MI techniques); elicit ideas regarding the client's perceived self-efficacy and expectations regarding treatment; and, finally, summarize self-motivational statements (CSAT, 1999, p. 31).

Preparation. In this stage the task is to create and strengthen commitment for action and develop an effective and acceptable change plan (DiClemente, 2003). The change processes involved in this stage are more behavioral than cognitive/experiential processes. Reinforcement, in this stage, refers to the small steps taken to make change and alternative reinforcements are seen as achievable. Counterconditioning helps identify high-risk situations and coping strategies to deal with cravings. Self-liberation involves people making choices about strategies and methods they will use and commits them to plan development. Lastly, people now seek out supports in terms of the change processes of helping relationships (DiClemente, 2003, p. 166).

The counselor's strategies in this stage, which are based on Motivational Interviewing techniques and methods, can include clarifying the client's own goals and strategies for change, and offering a menu of options for change or treatment. In this stage, the counselor could offer expertise and advice, but *only with permission*. Further, the counselor can work with the client on negotiating a plan or contract. Additionally, the counselor and client may want to think about, and lower, barriers to change. Other counselor and client tasks can include enlisting social support and exploring treatment expectancies. It is important to find out what worked with the client in the past and suggest employing similar strategies as s/he acts on change. Lastly, have the client make their decision for behavior change public (CSAT, 1999, pp. 31–32).

Action. During the action stage people begin to break the social, physiological and psychological ties that "bind them" to the behaviors associated with their addiction (DiClemente, 2003). The change processes involved in this stage include self-liberation, with the client believing they have the autonomy to change their lives. Additionally, conditioning/counterconditioning and helping relationships have a powerful role in this stage. As stated previously, conditioning/counterconditioning is making a new link between cues/stimuli and a behavior or substituting new, competing behaviors and activities in reaction to the old behavior. Helping relationships involves support from family and friends (DiClemente, 2003; Norcross, Krebs, & Prochaska, 2011; Pro-change Behavior Systems, 2018; Prochaska & DiClemente, 1982; Prochaska, DiClemente, & Norcross, 1992).

In this stage the counselor's tasks can include engaging the client in treatment and reinforcing its importance; supporting a realistic view of change through small steps; recognizing difficulties for the client in early stages of change; helping the client identify high-risk situations and develop healthy coping strategies to overcome these; assisting the client in finding new reinforcers of constructive change; and helping the client assess whether s/he has strong family and social support (CSAT, 1999, p. 32). Additionally, counselors can work with clients to develop a menu of treatment options designed to bring about change.

Maintenance. Maintenance involves the tasks of sustaining change for an extended period of time over a wide range of situations (DiClemente, 2003, p. 192). Further, it is creating a new life filled with alternative rewarding activities and coping mechanisms (DiClemente, 2003, p. 205). The change processes involved in this stage involve more of the behavioral processes: reinforcement, which refers to alternate behaviors producing rewards that reinforce recovery; counterconditioning, which refers to alternative strategies to deal with emotions, people and places that create high-risk situations that may lead to relapse; helping relationships, which replaces addictive-maintaining relationships with supportive social networks; and, finally, consciousness raising and self-evaluation, which involve recognizing and re-evaluating addictive thinking, high-risk situations and what appear to be irrelevant decisions that could lead to relapse (DiClemente, 2003, p. 205).

In this stage the counselor will want to collaborate with the client in identifying new reinforcers; supporting lifestyle changes; affirming the client's resolve and self-efficacy; helping the client practice and use new coping strategies to avoid a return to use; maintaining supportive contact (e.g. explain to the client that you are available to talk between sessions); developing a "fire escape" plan if the client resumes substance use; and reviewing long-term goals with the client (CSAT, 1999, p. 32).

Learning Opportunity 9.4

Think about an unhealthy behavior you have recently tried to change. What stages did you go through? What stage did you stop at? What were the processes of change that occurred within each stage of your change?

Motivational Interviewing

"Motivational interviewing is a skillful clinical method, not a set of techniques that can be easily learned.... It is a way of *being* with people.... It is designed to resolve motivational issues that inhibit positive behavior change" (Miller & Rollnick, 2002, p. 41). It is also a client-centered and directive method for increasing intrinsic motivation to change by exploring and resolving ambivalence (Miller & Rollnick, 2002, p. 25). As stated previously, it involves four general principles which help in facilitating change. These principles include (1) expressing empathy, (2) developing discrepancy, (3) rolling with resistance and (4) supporting self-efficacy.

In terms of expressing empathy, the MI approach emphasizes the importance of expressing empathy.

Empathy involves such therapist characteristics as warmth, respect, caring, commitment, and active interest (Miller and Rollnick, 1991). Empathy usually entails reflective listening – listening attentively to each client statement and reflecting it back in different words so that the client knows you understand the meaning. (CSAT, 1999, p. 28)

In developing discrepancy, the counselor works with the client in evaluating their present behavior in light of their goals and values. A "better way to understand this state is simply as a discrepancy between the current state of affairs and how one wants to be" (Miller & Rollnick, 2002, p. 38).

Roll with resistance focuses on avoiding arguments for change, but engaging the client in the process of problem solving. Last is the concept of self-efficacy. Self-efficacy is the belief in one's ability to achieve or accomplish a task, activity, etc. Here the counselor invests in supporting the client's self-efficacy.

In addition to these principles, MI also focuses on ambivalence, recognizing that there is an approach–avoidance conflict with addictive behaviors: while clients want to change they also do not want to change. According to Miller and Rollnick (2002), ambivalence is not seen as an obstacle to change, but "makes change possible" (p. 23). Much of the work in MI deals with ambivalence. MI involves intensifying and then resolving ambivalence by identifying the discrepancy between the actual present and the desired future (Miller & Rollnick, 2002, p. 23).

Counselors collaborate with clients and listen for and elicit change talk. Change talk falls into one of four categories: disadvantages of the status quo; advantages of change; optimism toward change; and intention to change (Miller & Rollnick, 2002, p. 24). Examples of change talk may include: "I feel terrible about how my drinking has hurt my family," "I don't know what to do, but something has got to change" and "I guess this has been affecting me more than I realize" (CSAT, 1999, p. 53).

Early methods to use in MI include: asking open-ended questions; listening reflectively; affirming, summarizing and eliciting change talk. Later methods include asking key questions; giving advice *with permission*; and negotiating a change plan (Miller & Rollnick, 2002).

Another technique of MI is to match the client's stage of change with MI methods and techniques. As explained in the Stages of Change section, counselors can use MI strategies that work best with that stage of change. These MI strategies were listed with each stage of change earlier in the chapter.

Lastly, MI is famous for its OARS, which is to be used when working with clients. The O refers to Open-ended questions. While closed questions lead to yes/no answers, open-ended questions are less restrictive and allow the client to explain. The A refers to Affirmative, which means acknowledging the client's strengths and movements towards positive change. The R refers to Reflective listening. With reflective listening the counselor listens actively and intently to the client and responds back with reflections regarding what the client stated. Here a counselor can repeat, rephrase, paraphrase or reflect back with feeling regarding what the client stated. Lastly, the S refers to Summary, which is when the counselor summarizes what has been stated.

Learning Opportunity 9.5

For this learning opportunity, each person should have a partner. Each person should pick an unhealthy behavior (smoking, binge drinking, etc.) that someone might want to change. Using Motivational Interviewing/ counseling techniques and strategies, create a counseling scenario with one person as the counselor and the other person as a client trying to change an unhealthy behavior (selected earlier). Practice using Motivational Interviewing/counseling skills for 15 minutes as the counselor. Be sure to use the following: (1) express empathy, (2) develop discrepancy, (3) roll with resistance and (4) support self-efficacy.

Strengths and Limitations

Some of the strengths of TTM, Stages of Change and MI are that there are many studies that support their usefulness and effectiveness. In integrating all three – TTM, the Stages of Change and MI – one of the great advantages is that it moves the counselor from the "old" confrontative style to a more empathetic, collaborative and client-centered approach.

In terms of Stages of Change, three of the advantages are that this approach demystifies the change process; "normalizes perceived barriers or complications towards change, such as ambivalence and relapse"; as well as promotes "patience and persistence in efforts to change. Rather than expecting or demanding instantaneous or rapid change (and being disappointed and frustrated with the results)" (Thombs & Osborn, 2019, p. 309).

In terms of limitations, there have been studies examining the stages of change that indicate that the stages are not distinct and sequential (Little & Girvin, 2002). There have been critiques that while there are short-term gains, there is limited and "disappointing" outcomes with longer term gains in the area of activity promotion (Adams & White, 2005, p. 239).

Regarding MI, MI has been applied to other health issues such as HIV/AIDS prevention, eating disorders, diet and exercise (Thombs & Osborn, 2013). There have been many studies showing the effectiveness of MI (Hettema, Steele, & Miller, 2005; Lundahl & Burke, 2009; Miller & Rose, 2009); Miller and Rollnick (2012, p. 1), however, admit that there is an "impressive number of negative trials." There have been "null findings" for several health-related conditions (eating disorders, drug abuse and dependence, smoking, etc.) and MI (Miller & Rose, 2009, p. 4). Another limitation of MI is that it appears to be best used with people in Precontemplation and Contemplation stages, who are considered to be at low risk for harm. For someone who is actively using to the point where an overdose may be imminent, a more directive approach may be required in order to encourage the individual to seek inpatient detox. MI is not a panacea and may not be appropriate with all clients. Also, another limitation is that it may be helpful (with the client's permission) to let the family or significant others know you are using this approach, otherwise, they may perceive the counselor as "agreeing" with the client's perception that he or she can continue to use alcohol/drugs non-problematically. They may perceive the counselor as a "professional enabler."

Case Study

Josie visits an outpatient substance use disorder clinic, seeking a counselor because "my wife Karen thinks I need to stop drinking but I think she is overreacting. She grew up in an alcoholic household and thinks everyone has a problem." Josie admits that Karen has threatened to leave the house and marriage if Josie doesn't "get to counseling."

Josie explains that she is a writer, and although she doesn't have a writing job at this time, she is a waitress at a local bar. She states that she loves to visit the bar when she is not working, because "the people there are real." She admits that while she did write for a local newspaper five years ago, she hasn't had a writing job since being fired. She explains that she was fired because she "didn't agree with her boss."

When addressing questions about her drinking, Josie states she does drink daily, but *only* 5–6 beers. "Beers aren't as bad as hard liquor," she states. She later admits to drinking more on the weekends, sometimes 10–12 "on a good day." When asked about if she wanted to reduce or cease use, she reports the following: "I don't think I should have to quit because someone is a sensy-bud about booze. Just because her father was an alcoholic doesn't mean I am. I mean, ya, maybe I should cut back a little – maybe we wouldn't fight so much …"

Case Conceptualization

In working with Josie, a substance use disorder counselor would first identify her stage of change. There is some indication that she is in the contemplatives stage of change because she states "I mean, ya, maybe I should cut back a little – maybe we wouldn't fight so much …"

For the contemplative stage of change, it is important to work with Josie's ambivalence. The tasks are to gather and evaluate positive and negative aspects of behavior and resolve the decisional balance, tipping the scale towards change. The change processes involved here include consciousness raising, which involves discovering the negative of behavior and positives toward change; self-evaluation, which involves shifting views and values to emphasize the negatives of the behavior and the benefits of changing; environmental revaluation, which involves recognizing the impact the behavior has on others; and social liberation, which involves observing how others will support the healthier behavior (DiClemente, 2003, p. 151).

Specifically, for this stage, a counselor will engage in the following processes of change: consciousness raising, self-evaluation, environmental revaluation and social liberation. The first (consciousness raising), might be developing a pros and cons list of drinking alcohol as well as working towards reducing or eliminating its use. The second (self-evaluation) might be to evaluate how drinking alcohol impacts her relationship as well as her previous job. The third (environmental re-evaluation) might be to explore the impact alcohol has on her wife, while the last (social liberation) might involve her attending an AA meeting.

Further, the counselor would use such MI skills as expressing empathy, developing discrepancy, rolling with resistance, and supporting self-efficacy. In this particular case, the counselor would use empathy so that Josie feels heard and understood. In developing discrepancy, the counselor may explore her commitment to the relationship and her use of alcohol, and how that use may interfere with her relationship. When Josie starts getting defensive, the counselor can "roll with resistance" instead of trying to force Josie to change. Finally, when Josie states she may have a hard time quitting, the counselor may ask Josie about other "hard things" she has been through and how she has managed – showing Josie that she has the ability to deal with hardship. This may increase her sense of self-efficacy.

Recommended Reading and Resources

Center for Alcoholism, Substance Abuse & Addictions (2017). *Motivational Interviewing and therapist manuals.* Retrieved from https://casaa.unm.edu/mimanuals.html

CSAT (Center for Substance Abuse Treatment) (1999). *Enhancing motivation for change in substance abuse treatment.* Treatment Improvement Protocol (TIP) Series No. 35. Rockville, MD: Substance Abuse and Mental Health Services Administration (download a free copy from SAMHSA).

Motivational Interviewing SAMHSA website: www.integration.samhsa.gov/clinical-practice/motivational-interviewing

Motivational Interviewing Webinars: NAADAC. Retrieved from www.naadac.org/webinars

Prochaska, J.O., DiClemente, C.C., & Norcross, J.C. (1992). In search of how people change: Application to addictive behaviors. *American Psychologist, 47(9),* 1102–1114.

Prochaska, J.O., Norcross, J.C., & DiClemente, C.C. (1994). *Changing for the good: A revolutionary six-stage program for overcoming bad habits and moving your life positively forward.* New York: HarperCollins Publishers.

You Tube offers some good examples of Motivational Interviewing: https://m.youtube.com/watch?v=cj1BDPBE6Wk; https://m.youtube.com/watch?v=67I6g1I7Zao; www.youtube.com/watch?v=NQ3w77StnOc; www.youtube.com/watch?v=DSHh6V9yNzg

References

Adams, J., & White, M. (2005). Why don't stage-based activity promotion interventions work? *Health Education Research, 20(2),* 237–243.

Connors, G.J., DiClemente, C.C., Velasquez, M.M., & Donovan, D.M. (2013). *Substance abuse treatment and stages of change: Selecting and planning interventions* (2nd ed). New York: Guilford Press.

CSAT (Center for Substance Abuse Treatment) (1999). *Enhancing motivation for change in substance abuse treatment.* Treatment Improvement Protocol (TIP) Series No. 35. Rockville, MD: Substance Abuse and Mental Health Services Administration

DiClemente, C.C. (2003). *Addiction and change: How addictions develop and addicted people recover.* New York: Guilford Press.

Hettema, J., Steele, J., Miller, W.R. (2005). Motivational interviewing. *Annual Review of Clinical Psychology, 1,* 92–111.

Little, J.H., & Girvin, H. (2002). Stages of change: A critique. *Behavior Modification, 2,* 223–273.

Lundahl, B., & Burke, B. L. (2009). The effectiveness and applicability of motivational interviewing: A practice-friendly review of our meta analyses. *Journal of Clinical Psychology, 66(11),* 1232–1245.

Miller, W.R., and Rollnick, S. (1991) *Motivational interviewing: Preparing people to change addictive behavior.* New York: Guilford Press.

Miller, W.R., & Rollnick, S. (2002). *Motivational interviewing: Preparing people for change* (2nd edn). New York: Guilford Press.

Miller, W.R., & Rollnick, S. (2012). Meeting in the middle: Motivational interviewing and self-determination theory. *International Journal of Behavioral Nutrition and Physical Activity, 9,* 1–2.

Miller, W.R., & Rose G.S. (2009). Toward a theory of motivational interviewing. *American Psychologist, 64(6),* 527–537

Norcross, J.C., Krebs, P.M., & Prochaska, J.O. (2011). Stages of change In J.C. Norcross (Ed.). *Psychotherapy relationships that work: Evidence-based responsiveness* (2nd edn, pp. 1–36). New York: Oxford University Press.

Pro-change Behavior Systems (2018). Transtheoretical Model. Retrieved from www.prochange.com/transtheoretical-model-of-behavior-change

Prochaska, J.O., & DiClemente, C.C. (1982). Transtheoretical therapy: Toward a more integrative model of change. *Psychotherapy: Theory, Research and Practice, 20,* 161–173.

Prochaska, J.O., DiClemente, C.C., & Norcross, J.C. (1992). In search of how people change: Application to addictive behaviors. *American Psychologist, 47(9),* 1102–1114.

Prochaska, J.O., Norcross, J.C., & DiClemente, C.C. (1994). *Changing for the good: A revolutionary six-stage program for overcoming bad habits and moving your life positively forward.* New York: HarperCollins.

Prochaska, J.O., Norcross, J.C., Fowler, J.L., Follick, M.J., & Abrams, D.B. (1992). Attendance and outcome in a work site weight control program: Processes and stages of change as process and predictor variables. *Addictive Behaviors, 17,* 34–45.

Rosengren, D.B. (2009). *Building motivational interviewing skills: A practitioner's workbook.* New York: Guilford Press.

Thombs, D.L., & Osborn, C.J. (2013). *Introduction to addictive behaviors* (4th edn). New York: Guilford Press.

Thombs, D.L., & Osborn, C.J. (2019). *Introduction to addictive behaviors* (5th edn). New York: Guilford Press.

10 Developmental Theories of Recovery and Personality Theory

Alan A. Cavaiola

Introduction

In this chapter we will be examining two unique theories relevant to substance use disorders. Developmental Theories are essentially *change theories* in that they examine how an individual's substance use disorder (SUD) and then their recovery develops over time (often referred to as *progression*). Personality Theory, on the other hand, examines various personality characteristics or traits and how those correlate or, in some instances, are thought to cause SUDs. As you will learn, Personality Theory has been a rather controversial area in the substance use disorder treatment profession in that counselors often recognize that there are particular *addictive personality traits* that often pre-date the onset of alcohol or substance use; others claim, however, that these traits are the *result* of years of alcohol and/or drug use, not the cause of it.

Developmental Theory

There are two ways to explore development as it pertains to substance use disorders. First, we can conceptualize development as pertaining to lifespan development (i.e. the various stages that people go through from birth to infancy to childhood, to adolescence, young adulthood, middle age and older adulthood). Second, we can also think of development from the perspective of the progression or course that one's SUD follows, from experimental alcohol or drug use to misuse/abuse and dependence. As with other diseases/disorders, SUDs also follow a particular progression or course. For example, if a person comes down with the flu, we can predict with reasonable certainty how long he or she will feel flu symptoms and it will generally take a week or so, before he or she begins to feel better. Substance use disorders also follow a course or progression. Similarly, we will explore the developmental course of recovery (i.e. those changes someone might expect to experience as they get further away from their active alcohol and/or drug use and move further into recovery). The progression of SUDs, as well as the progression or course of recovery, will greatly depend on whether the individual receives treatment and/or actively participates in a 12-Step recovery program (i.e. Alcoholics Anonymous [AA], or Narcotics Anonymous [NA] meetings) or has some other recovery support.

When exploring the concept of progression, there are two well-known individuals who have done a great deal of work in this area, E.M. Jellinek (Jellinek & Joliffe, 1940) and Terence T. Gorski (1989). Jellinek was responsible for coining the term, "the disease concept of alcoholism." Not only was he the first researcher to define alcohol use disorders (i.e. alcoholism) as a disease, he also described four stages that most alcoholics experience during the course of their active addiction. The *pre-alcoholic* or *symptomatic* stage is characterized by "relief drinking," whereby the individual finds him or herself drinking more often and drinking to manage stress and upsetting emotions. At this stage, drinking becomes more frequent and is essentially a way to cope with current problems. Drinking may appear to be done more often in social contexts. The second stage is described by Jellinek as the *prodromal* or *transitional* stage. Here, drinking evolves into a more cyclical pattern. Blackouts (i.e. the inability to recall things said or done while drinking) become more frequent. Also, at this stage the person begins to cope with problems that result from more frequent and patterned drinking. The third stage is referred to as *crucial* (or *middle* stage) in which the individual is experiencing more serious problems as a result of drinking. In order to try to manage the drinking problems, the individual may abstain for periods of time only to hastily return to drinking when life becomes too stressful. Other attempts at gaining control may included "geographical cures" (i.e. moving to another town, changing jobs or switching from vodka to scotch) as a means of trying change drinking patterns. Here the person may hide, rationalize or mask their use, which often contributes to feelings of guilt surrounding drinking behaviors. The fourth stage, referred to as the *chronic* (or *late*) stage is characterized as the time period in which the individual loses control over his or her drinking. One drink will, therefore, result in a prolonged period of intoxication or alcohol binges. Also, both mental and physical deterioration or decline is more likely to be noticed by loved ones at this particular stage. The alcoholic relies on alibis or excuses in order to rationalize their drinking. The chronic stage may last for weeks, months or years (Brande, 2018). The hope is that the alcoholic will hit bottom and ask for help. Unfortunately, many alcoholics die as a result of heavy drinking because of how drinking impacts on people physically. Interestingly, most progression charts not only provide an account of the downward spiral that many individuals with alcohol use disorders endure, but also the upward path through recovery. While Jellinek is credited with describing the aforementioned stages (i.e. prodromal, chronic, crucial), he did not emphasize what stages or process individuals go through once they "hit bottom" and begin their journey into recovery/sobriety. A British researcher by the name of Max Glatt (1975) noted deficiencies in Jellinek's progression stages, because it described only the harmful progressive nature of alcohol use disorders over time. Glatt sought to describe the changes that occur during recovery as the individual progresses in overcoming his or her alcohol use disorder. The progression chart depicted in Figure 10.1 is an approximation of the downward progression and recovery progression described by Jellinek and Glatt.

Just as Jellinek had described the downward progression of alcohol use disorders, Terence Gorski (1989) had described the "progression" or course of recovery in

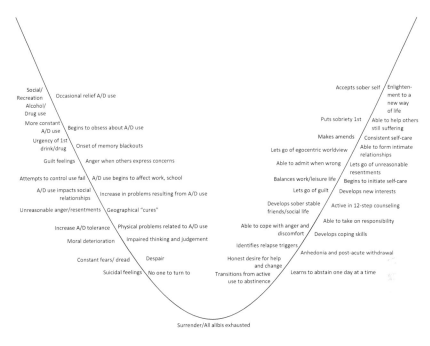

Social/
Recreation   Occasional relief A/D use
Alcohol/
Drug use
More constant
A/D use   Begins to obsess about A/D use
Urgency of 1st
drink/drug   Onset of memory blackouts
Guilt feelings   Anger when others express concerns
Attempts to control use fail   A/D use begins to affect work, school
A/D use impacts social
relationships   Increase in problems resulting from A/D use
Unreasonable anger/resentments   Geographical "cures"
Increase A/D tolerance   Physical problems related to A/D use
Moral deterioration   Impaired thinking and judgement
Constant fears/ dread   Despair
Suicidal feelings   No one to turn to

Surrender/All alibis exhausted

Accepts sober self   Enlighten-
ment to a
new way
of life
Puts sobriety 1st   Able to help others
still suffering
Makes amends   Consistent self-care
Lets go of egocentric worldview   Able to form intimate
relationships
Able to admit when wrong   Lets go of unreasonable
resentments
Balances work/leisure life   Begins to initiate self-care
Lets go of guilt   Develops new interests
Develops sober stable
friends/social life   Active in 12-step counseling
Able to cope with anger and   Able to take on responsibility
discomfort   Develops coping skills
Identifies relapse triggers
Honest desire for help   Anhedonia and post-acute withdrawal
and change
Transitions from active   Learns to abstain one day at a time
use to abstinence

Figure 10.1 Progression Chart

his classic book, *Passages through recovery*. Although similar to Glatt (1975), Gorski felt that there were distinct stages to addiction recovery. He described these stages as follows:

(1) transition
(2) stabilization (not drinking a day-at-a-time)
(3) early recovery (staying stopped)
(4) middle recovery (achieving lifestyle balance)
(5) late recovery (building depth and meaning)
(6) maintenance

In the *transition* stage, the individual is moving from active drinking and/or drug use to abstinence. Even though he or she wants to stop using and may express this goal to family and friends, it is a struggle to achieve this goal. Therefore, this stage may include a lot of "stops and starts" as the person experiences a couple of days of abstinence, then returns to active drinking for a few days, then returns to abstinence. During transition, individuals may first make attempts to control use by changing the amount and frequency of drinking or substance use, or by changing the type of alcohol/drugs used and so on. Eventually, however, the person in transition recognizes the need for total abstinence and at that point begins to put together days and then weeks of abstinence. For some, this may require that he or she enters a detoxification program in order to safely transition from active use to abstinence. This would be the case with individuals who have been using alcohol or drugs on a continual or daily basis for months or years, and who would therefore experience severe withdrawal symptoms if he or she were to stop using abruptly. Gorski (1989) indicates there are three goals that need to be accomplished during transition: (1) there is a recognition of a loss of control once alcohol or drug use begins; (2) there is a recognition that loss of control is the result of one's addiction; and (3) one must commit to a program of recovery which means asking for help.

Once the person completes detoxification, they can then move towards *stabilization*. This period takes place within the first few weeks and months of sobriety or abstinence. Here, the newly abstinent individual is learning how not to pick up a drink or drug one day at a time (as is recommended in AA/NA.) Having gone through acute withdrawal, the individual now must cope with post-acute withdrawal symptoms (e.g. irritability, anger, depression, anhedonia, etc.). Having social/family support is crucial at this stage because alcohol or drug craving is strongest during the stabilization stage; cravings usually dissipate or lessen over time, however. Also, during stabilization, individuals learn to problem-solve and cope with stress without relying on alcohol or drugs. Most importantly, as the individual experiences confidence in his or her ability to abstain, hope and motivation begins to replace the anguish and despair of active addiction.

The *early recovery* stage is thought to cover the period beyond stabilization to the first year of recovery. During this stage, the recovering person is confronting many "firsts" as he or she learns to deal with birthdays, weddings, holidays, anniversaries without drinking or using drugs. As with stabilization, having a solid support system of family/friends as well as support from an AA/NA sponsor and fellow AA/NA members is crucial to surmounting the trials and tribulations of early recovery. It is no wonder that Alcoholics Anonymous World Services estimate that only 1 in 33 make it through the first year with their sobriety intact. In addition to the aforementioned support, it's also crucial that the newly recovering individual is also participating in counseling, whether it be individual, group, couples, family counseling or a combination thereof. As Gorski (1989) points out, during stabilization, the *drinking problem* is addressed, while in early recovery the *thinking problem* must be addressed (referring to irrational thoughts, unmanageable emotions and self-defeating behaviors.) For example, it's common for individuals in early recovery to "project" negative outcomes by constantly dreading the worst possible scenario. It's also not unusual for early recovery individuals to develop substitute addictions. For example, some may turn to gambling, overeating, sex or even excessive exercise as a means to experience pleasure derived from dopamine flooding the brain. You may say to yourself, "Isn't exercise a good thing?" Exercise is certainly a healthy activity; yet it can become harmful, however, when a person exercises compulsively and excessively to the point of injury. Similarly, sex and eating are also healthy and necessary except when they become compulsive and excessive. The main goal of the early recovery stage is to put the *sober self* (rather than the *addict self*) in charge. By accomplishing this goal, the early recovery individual can begin to take control of his or her life.

Learning Opportunity 10.1 – Substitute Addictions

Can you think of other substitute addictions (sometimes referred to as process or behavioral addictions)? What would you feel is the point at which a behavior crosses the line from becoming an everyday activity to a substitute addiction? When does work become workaholism? When does shopping become overspending and so on?

In the *middle recovery* stage, the ability to achieve life balance is of the utmost importance. Therefore, being able to stay focused on one's recovery while also balancing work, love and play (or leisure activities) becomes quite a challenge. Take, for example, someone who used to play on a softball league during the spring, summer and fall as their main type of recreation or leisure activity. However, after every softball game, his or her teammates would break out cases of beer and many teammates would end up having to call a cab in order to get home without risking a DUI. In early and middle recovery, it's important to establish new activities that don't revolve around alcohol. Relapse prevention planning recommends that recovering individuals change "people, places and things" in order to help ensure sobriety. Changing a leisure activity is an example of changing "things" that may result in a return to drinking or drug use. It's not unusual for individuals in middle recovery to try and "make up for lost time." Here, the individual realizes how many years they wasted drinking or using drugs and there's often an internal pressure to regain one's life or career once sober. Yet this attitude can often result in added pressure or stress, which, for some, may be a relapse trigger. Of paramount importance during this stage is that individuals learn self-care, which can include going for regular medical and dental check-ups, proper nutrition, sleep and exercise.

Learning Opportunity 10.2 – Leisure Activities

Imagine that you are no longer drinking or using any mood-altering drugs or engaging in some other type of process/compulsive behavior. What would you do with your leisure time? In small groups, come up with a list of leisure activities you might do that don't involve alcohol, drugs, process or behavioral addictions. Share your list with others in your class or in your chat room.

With *late recovery* the emphasis is on building depth and meaning in one's recovery. With the difficult days of struggling with not picking up a drink or drug one day at a time behind him or her, there's now an opportunity to focus on other issues. For example, strengthening relationships that may have been damaged due to years of active substance use or strengthening one's role as a parent or grandparent can become very fulfilling ventures. Individuals in late recovery often find ways to free themselves of past family dysfunction or family problems and let go of rigid behavioral patterns. Some find satisfaction on working on building a new career or business, or going back to school to complete a degree or certification that was abandoned due to active alcohol or drug use. The possibilities for personal, spiritual and intellectual growth are exponential during late recovery. While AA/NA (as well as other self-help support groups), provide a solid base for reinforcing recovery, usually in later recovery, the role of the recovering person in the program changes as they begin to sponsor others or goes out on speaking commitments to other AA/NA groups or provides other types of service. These are activities that are stressed in the 12th Step of AA: "Having had a spiritual awakening as the result of these steps, we tried to carry this message to alcoholics, and to practice these principles in all our daily affairs." Carrying the message to others still suffering is an important aspect of late recovery.

In the *maintenance* stage, the emphasis is on maintenance activities that help to consolidate the progress made and to help insure its continuation into the future. As an analogy, you have to maintain your car (with oil changes, tire rotations, etc.) in order to keep it running. The same holds true with recovery. Developmental psychologist, Erik Erikson (1963) said that, in later life, people struggle with something he refers to as Generativity versus Stagnation (see Table 10.1). Generativity is about continued growth and one's ability to give back to others, whether it's the younger generation or those less fortunate. However, those who face stagnation are usually "stuck" in their development and are not really giving to others nor are they connected to others in a meaningful way. This is why it's important to *maintain* one's recovery by taking a very active approach, one that involves connection with others as well as activities that help promote one's growth.

Table 10.1 Erikson's Psychosocial Developmental Stages www.StudyLib.net

Stage	Age	Primary Crisis	Positive Resolution of Crisis
1	First year	Trust vs. Mistrust	Infant develops sense of security
2	Second year	Autonomy vs. Shame/doubt	Child develops independence
3	3 to 5 years	Initiative vs. Guilt	Child is able to restrain impulses, yet can also be spontaneous
4	6 years to puberty	Industry vs. Inferiority	Child develops self-confidence
5	Adolescence	Identity vs. Role confusion	Teen develops self-esteem and sense of self
6	Young adulthood	Intimacy vs. Isolation	Young adult is able to form close relationships
7	Middle adulthood	Generativity vs. Stagnation	Adult is able to promote the well-being of others
8	Late adulthood	Integrity vs. Despair	Sense of satisfaction with a life well-lived, free of regret/despair

Source: Figure derived from Erikson, E.H. (1963). *Childhood and Society* (2nd Ed.). New York: W.W. Norton.

Finally, author Earnie Larsen (2009) has written extensively on what he refers to as "Stage 2 Recovery." In Stage 1 recovery the substance-abusing individual learns how to abstain from alcohol or drugs "a day at a time," while in Stage 2 recovery the goal is rebuild one's life now that alcohol and drug abstinence has been achieved. Through many years of clinical experience, Larsen finds that individuals in Stage 2 recovery must address their own co-dependency or self-defeating personality traits which he refers to as "people-pleasers," "tap dancers," "caretakers," "workaholics," "perfectionists" and "martyrs." He finds that by avoiding addressing these dysfunctional roles, individuals tend to get "stuck" in their development as recovering persons. Larsen also emphasizes the importance of building solid intimate relationships and positive social relationships. Similar to Gorski's stages or progression of recovery, Larsen also hypothesizes that there is a progression to one's recovery, the longer the individual puts more sober or clean time together and works at improving his or her life in recovery.

Learning Opportunity 10.3 – Continued Growth

Imagine you were given limitless funds and your benefactor says to you, "I will pay all your expenses so long as you engage in activities that allow you to grow as a person and/or will benefit others. What would you do? Are there things you've wanted to learn (e.g. learning a new language or a musical instrument)? Come up with a list and share it in small groups or your chat room.

Gorski's stages are really about continued growth. Think for a second why that's important in recovery. Now consider the following: for decades alcohol and drug counselors have recognized that whenever a person's SUD began, often his or her emotional maturity or growth either stopped or was greatly impeded. So, if you were to be counseling a person who began drinking or using drugs when they were 13 years old, and continued to use up until age 35 when he or she entered treatment, in many respects that person may be functioning more like a 13-year-old than a mature 35-year-old. This is not an empirically based finding but rather one that is often seen clinically by counselors. This is also one of the reasons why counseling, along with 12-Step program involvement, is so important. Both emphasize the importance of growth and maturity.

Case Example: Vinnie

Vinnie is currently 28 years old, divorced and lives at home with his parents. He completed a residential program for SUD about two months ago and is currently participating in an intensive outpatient program. He also attends AA and NA meetings about four times a week. Vinnie had begun using alcohol and cannabis when he was a sophomore in high school. He indicates that he began to use more regularly in his junior and senior year but managed to keep his grades up and stay out of trouble. Upon graduation, Vinnie went off to college; however, he pledged a fraternity in the second half of his freshman year and his grades plummeted. By the second semester of his sophomore year, he had stopped going to classes and was eventually academically dismissed. When Vinnie returned home, he was able to land a job with his uncle, working as car salesman. It was there that Vinnie met his wife-to-be, Joann and they married when Vinnie was 22 years old. Unfortunately, Vinnie's drinking and cannabis use became more frequent and more problematic. He received a DUI and was also arrested for assault after getting into a fight in a bar. There were nights where Vinnie would not come home, which infuriated Joann, who eventually gave him an ultimatum that either he stop drinking or she would seek a divorce. Vinnie stopped drinking for a few weeks but then eventually relapsed. Joann felt that she wasn't "married to an adult but to a teenager." She felt that she had to handle the responsibilities of paying all the bills, cleaning the house and food shopping. Most months Vinnie wouldn't even contribute financially to the household bills. Instead, he would spend money on cannabis, drinking with his friends and sports gambling. When Joann filed for divorce, Vinnie moved back in with his parents, blaming Joann for "not understanding him."

Case Conceptualization

Vinnie provides an example where early alcohol and drug use in teen years interferes with normal adult development. Joann's frustration that she felt she was "married to a teenager" was probably an accurate reflection of Vinnie's being irresponsible. Interestingly, there have been a few follow-up studies of long-term cannabis users which found that these individuals often do not complete education beyond high school, they have difficulty in establishing a career path and instead jump from job to job and also have difficulty establishing long-term intimate relationships (see Green, Doherty, & Ensminger, 2017; Brook, Zhang, Leukefeld, & Brook, 2016; Juon, Fothergill, Green, Doherty, & Ensminger, 2011; Washburn & Capaldi, 2015). These findings certainly apply to Vinnie, as he appears to be functioning more like an adolescent than an adult. Also, he is unable to take responsibility for the failure of his marriage and instead places blame on his wife, which is also common for individuals struggling with SUDs.

Advantages and Limitations of Developmental Models

The developmental models described above are extremely helpful to addictions counselors in being able to assess where their client may be in terms of the downward progression so common to many of the substance use disorders. The course or progression of active SUDs are truly a downward spiral in which individuals tend to get worse over time in a progressive manner. Yet the developmental models are also helpful in describing what recovery would look like in someone who is truly focusing consciously on his or her recovery. The disadvantage, however, is that with human growth and development, people do tend to progress at different rates cognitively and emotionally (see Boxed Item 10.1).

Boxed Item 10.1 Advantages and Limitations of Developmental Theory

Advantages

- Developmental theory describes both the downward progression as well as the progression of recovery
- Developmental theory helps to explain how and why SUDs impact on cognitive-emotional development which can persist into recovery
- Developmental theory helps to explain expected challenges that an individual faces as he or she progresses from early to middle to later recovery

Limitations

- SUDs do not impact all individuals in the same way.
- higher functioning individuals with SUDs may not experience the same progression as someone who has suffered many or extreme losses
- although there are expected changes that may occur in recovery, not everyone will develop cognitively or emotionally in the same way or at the same pace

Personality Theory

Before we explore ways in which Personality Theory is linked to substance use disorders let's first define what is meant by personality. According to Watson, Clark and Harkness (1994, p. 18), personality is defined as "internal organized and characteristic of an individual over time and situations … [and has] motivational and adaptive significance." Roberts, Caspi and Moffitt (2001, p. 670) offer the following definition, "individual differences in the tendency to behave, think and feel in certain consistent ways." According to Littlefield and Sher (2016, p. 351) "personality can be thought of as coherent individual differences in thought, behavior and affect that demonstrate both stability and change across time."

Learning Opportunity 10.4 – Defining Personality and Personality Traits

Given the various definitions of "personality" listed above, what would you add to these definitions? Also, in small groups (or chat rooms) come up with as many personality traits as you can. After you've made your lists of personality traits, circle those traits you feel would be more common among people with substance use disorders.

Some of the early writing on Personality Theory and substance use disorders, which began as early as the 1960s, arose out of two somewhat conflicting views of substance use disorders. First, many counselors working in residential and out-patient programs with individuals impacted by SUDs began to notice similar personality characteristics or traits among the men and women they were treating. Traits such as low frustration tolerance (i.e. becoming easily frustrated), being very demanding of others, quick to anger, immaturity and tendencies to quickly develop addictions to other substances (e.g. caffeine, nicotine) and/or non-substance or process addictions (e.g. spending, eating, sex, gambling) were commonly noted. This resulted in many counselors hypothesizing that substance use disorders came about as the result of an *addictive personality*, that is, a set of personality traits that would predispose one to become addicted to alcohol and/or drugs (Nakken, 1988). Even during the early days of Alcoholics Anonymous there was a recognition that alcoholics tended to share particular personality traits which in Steps 4, 5 and 6 (of AA's 12 Steps) are referred to as "defects of character." Although Alcoholics Anonymous made no claims regarding whether these "character defects" were precursors or antecedents to alcoholism. Instead, AA founders would have viewed these personality defects as being the result of years of heavy, problematic drinking.

The second approach examined personality traits as having etiological significance in the development of substance use disorders and came out of empirical research studies (e.g. Sher, Bartholow, & Wood, 2000; Caspi et al., 1997; Galen, Henderson, & Whitman, 1997; Sher, Trull, Bartholow, & Vieth, 1999). Although there were some similarities between the types of personality traits noted by those working in substance use disorder treatment programs, there were also other traits which appeared to correlate consistently with SUDs. This second perspective originated as an attempt to describe key personality differences among individuals with SUDs, which turned out to be a very diverse or heterogeneous population. Many researchers concluded that there needed to be some way to describe some of these differences. So while the *addictive personality* movement really helped to describe similarities among alcoholics and addicts noted by counselors, this second perspective attempted to describe differences among this rather diverse population, which became the goal of several researchers. An early example, was Jellinek's attempts to classify various types of alcoholics, whom he labeled using Greek alphabet letters. *Alphas* were essentially functional alcoholics who drank heavily, had few physical/medical problems and managed to maintain their occupational and family lives. *Betas* were also individuals who drank heavily and were somewhat functional, however, these individuals experienced some physical or medical problems as a result of their drinking. *Gammas* are what most people think of when they think of individuals with alcohol use disorders (i.e. alcoholics). These are individuals who experience a loss of control whenever he or she drinks and can be considered both psychologically and physically addicted to alcohol. Finally, *Epsilons* are what is referred to as "periodic" or "binge" alcoholics. These are individuals who may go weeks or months without drinking however, once they pick up a drink, it then results in a binge which also may last days or weeks, followed by periods of abstinence which may also last for days, weeks or months.

Other researchers also attempted to come up with "types" or "classifications" for individuals with SUDS. For example, Bohman (Bohman, Sigvardson, & Cloninger 1981) hypothesized there were two distinct types of individuals who develop alcohol use disorders. Type 1 includes individuals who are considered to be functional alcoholics. These were men and women who tended to be more established in their jobs, careers and families, and who also tended to be more cautious. Type 2 alcoholics, on the other hand, were usually young men who were characterized as being impulsive risk-takers, who often had histories of criminality and other acting-out behaviors. Babor et al. (1992) also concluded that there were two types of alcoholics. Type A was associated with higher rates of anxiety and depression (i.e. internalizing pathology) while Type Bs tended to have higher rates of antisocial behavior and other substance use patterns (externalizing pathology.) These typologies were developed because of the recognition that individuals with SUDs were a very diverse or heterogeneous population composed of individuals from all socioeconomic strata, races, ethnic groups and educational levels (Hesselbrock & Hesselbrock, 2006; Jackson et al., 2014).

At first glance, it would appear that Personality Theory would fall under causal models of substance use disorders, as it was speculated that certain personality traits pre-dated the onset of SUDs and therefore caused various types of addiction (including process addictions such as gambling, sexual addictions, internet gaming addictions, etc.). However, other researchers concluded that the so-called "addictive personality" traits were not the cause of addiction but rather were the result of the years of heavy and/or consistent alcohol or drug use. Most researchers and addiction professionals conclude that there is no such entity as an "addictive personality" (Troncone, 2014), yet there are studies and anecdotal accounts which conclude that there are personality traits which appear to be common among those with alcohol, substance and some process addictions like gambling and sexual addictions. Similarly, there is a phenomena noted in the addictions treatment profession referred to as "cross-addiction" or "addiction transfer" (Hazelden, 2019), which occurs when an individual has two or more addictions. Whether addictive personality causes one to become addicted or whether certain personality traits develop as a result of years of alcohol or substance abuse is a classic "chicken and egg" dilemma.

There is a third possible explanation, which is that certain personality traits and SUDs co-occur or correlate with one another, however they do not cause one another. We will explore this notion of correlation when we explore co-occurring disorders later in this chapter.

Key Terms

externalizing pathology: often associated with acting out behavior such as impulsivity, risk-taking and antisocial behaviors (e.g. crime, delinquency).★

internalizing pathology: often associated with individuals who experience anxiety and depression. Internalizing pathology can be further divided into the "distress cluster" (which includes major depressive disorder, dysthymic disorder, generalized anxiety disorder and PTSD) and the "fearful cluster" (which includes panic disorder, agoraphobia, social phobia and specific phobias).★

co-morbidity and co-occurring disorders: when two distinct mental health and/or substance use disorders coexist with one another, such as when a person manifests both an alcohol use disorder and bipolar disorder at the same time.

sensation-seeking: refers to individuals who seek out excitement and sometimes high-risk activities such as skydiving.

low harm-avoidance: often coincides with high sensation-seeking, whereby individuals do not behave cautiously but rather engage in risky behavior regardless of possible harmful consequences.

low frustration tolerance: the inability to manage everyday frustrations or annoyances. Individuals with low frustration tolerance often over-react to minor irritations or annoyances.

low self-esteem: lack of self-confidence or self-efficacy. This often occurs with individuals who tend to hold negative perceptions about themselves

progression: the course or stages of a disease or disorder. SUDs are considered to have a progression which occurs over months or years

developmental stages: human development is said to progress through various stages which may correspond to one's age. For example, childhood and adolescence are considered to be examples of stages in the human growth process that are characterized by various changes physically, cognitively, and intellectually and emotionally.

developmental milestones: during the course of the various developmental stages that are particular milestones that individuals experience. For example, the onset of speech occurs around 6 months, walking around 1 year. Developmental psychologist Erik Erikson proposed particular milestones or tasks which are thought to occur throughout human development. For adolescents, the ability to form an identity or sense of self is a key milestone. For young adults, the ability to form intimate relationships is a key milestone

impulsivity: often unplanned, rapid reactions without consideration of the possible negative or harmful consequences or outcomes. For example, stealing something from a store.

★ Adapted from Kotov, Gamez, Schmidt, & Watson (2010)

What exactly are the personality traits which are thought to correlate with substance use disorders? There are several personality traits models which have attempted to answer this question. For example, the Big Five and Big Three models both attempt to describe essential personality traits in the general population. The Big Five model evolved from attempts to describe essential personality traits using everyday language descriptions (Goldberg, 1993; John &

Srivastava, 1999; McCrae et al., 2000). The five factors were: (1) Extraversion, (2) Agreeableness, (3) Conscientiousness, (4) Neuroticism and (5) Openness. The Big Three dimensions (Clark, Watson, & Mineka, 1994; Clark & Watson, 1999; Markon, Krueger, & Watson, 2005) include (1) negative emotionality, (2) positive emotionality and (3) disinhibition. In a large meta-analysis study, Kotov et al. (2010) found individuals with SUDs had higher rates of disinhibition, low disagreeableness and low conscientiousness. The authors of this study conclude that their research may have important implications for prevention efforts in terms of identifying particular personality types that may be at higher risk for developing SUDs.

Another personality theory model (similar to the Big Five and Big Three) which has been used to describe individuals with SUDs is referred to by the acronym UPPS-P (which stands for *urgency, pre-meditation, perseverance, sensation-seeking* and *positive urgency*. *Urgency* is similar to impulsivity, whereby a person may experience an obsessive-like need to act on an impulse when in a negative mood state (such as feeling angry, irritable or depressed), whereas *positive urgency* describes impulsive behavior that occurs during positive mood states (Smith et al., 2007). *Pre-meditation* refers to instances where individuals consider or weigh out the consequences of their decisions and/or actions, while *perseverance* describes one's ability to stick to a plan in order to achieve certain goals. In research utilizing the UPPS-P model with a people with different types of SUDS (Moraleda-Barreno, Diaz-Batanero, Perez-Moreno, Gomez-Bukedo, & Lozano, 2018), relationships were found between the severity of heroin and cocaine dependence and particular impulsive personality traits, while weaker relationships were found for alcohol and cannabis users. The *sensation-seeking* trait is described throughout this section of the chapter.

Belcher, Volkow, Moeller and Ferre (2014) found that greater impulsivity and sensation-seeking were risk or vulnerability factors for SUDs while positive emotionality and extraversion (PEM/E) constituted resilience or protective factors. The authors described PEM/E as "a state of positive affect, strong motivation, desire, wanting, as well as feelings of being excited, enthusiastic, active and optimistic (Belcher et al., 2014, p. 211).

Other personality research has examined particular sub-populations. For example, Wieczorek and Nochajski (2005) and Jonah (1997) found that many DUI offenders scored high on sensation-seeking trait scales and those who are high sensation-seekers often have multiple drunk driving offenses. It was hypothesized that because these sensation-seekers would become bored at one drinking location, they were more likely to drive to find another, more exciting drinking location. Ball, Jaffe, Crouse-Artus, Rounsaville and O'Malley (2000) found, in a group of DUI offenders they studied, that there were more Type B alcoholics who also exhibited more psychiatric distress and lower abstinence self-efficacy (i.e. confidence in their ability to abstain) than the Type A alcoholics. Several other studies have also concluded that high novelty-seeking is highly correlated with impulsivity and high sensation-seeking, which are predictive of substance use disorders in general (Battaglia, Przybeck, Bellodi, & Cloninger, 1996; Cloninger, Sigvardsson,

Przybeck, & Svrakic, 1995; Galen et al., 1997; Sher, Wood, Crews, & Vandiver, 1995; Zuckerman & Cloninger, 1996).

Another area of Personality Theory research has linked personality traits with people's response to treatment and treatment outcome. For example, Blonigen, Bui, Britt, Thomas and Timko (2016) studied a group of veterans who were being treated for SUDs and found that those with higher levels of externalizing (acting-out) psychopathology had poorer treatment outcomes compared to veterans with more internalizing (anxiety-depression) psychopathology. Similarly, other research found that lower levels of psychiatric distress, higher levels of social support, better coping styles and higher levels of abstinence self-efficacy (i.e. confidence in one's ability to remain sober) were also found to be correlated with better treatment outcomes (Ilgen, McKellar, & Tiet, 2005; Long, Williams, Midgley, & Hollin, 2000: Moggi, Ouimette, Moos, & Finney, 1999.)

Finally, as alluded to earlier, there are also correlations between particular personality traits with both substance use disorders and mental health disorders. Before we explore some of these correlations, it's important to remember that correlations do *not* imply causality. In other words, we are not claiming that SUDs are caused by mental health/psychiatric disorders; yet the two disorders may coexist or co-occur with one another. One example, is the apparent correlation between SUDs and antisocial personality disorder (APD). The personality traits that often correlate with *both* disorders are average levels of extraversion, low conscientiousness, low agreeableness and characteristic externalizing psychopathology (Ruiz, Pincus, & Schinka, 2008; Malouff, Thorsteinsson, & Schutte, 2005). With regard to the tendencies towards externalizing pathology, we are also not saying that all individuals with SUDs can also be diagnosed with antisocial personality disorder, but rather the two can often correlate with one another. It's important to keep in mind that alcohol and substance abuse often result in disinhibited behavior, therefore, it's not unusual to see similar types of acting out in both groups of individuals.

Correlations have also been noted between bipolar disorder and SUDs as well as attention deficit hyperactivity disorder (ADHD) and SUDs. In terms of personality traits which were common to both the mental health and substance use disorders, Bizzarri et al. (2007) found that bipolar disorder and SUD were both linked by sensation-seeking traits and substance sensitivity (i.e. those who experience more profound mood changes or strong sensations as a result of ingesting particular substances or medications). There are several hypotheses as to why individuals with bipolar disorder are more likely to abuse substances and/or develop SUDs. For example, substance abuse may be an attempt to self-medicate; or it could represent a symptom of bipolar disorder; or both SUD and bipolar might share a common risk factor (such as high sensation-seeking; Strakowski & DelBello, 2000). Sensation-seeking has also been found to be a personality correlate of adult cocaine abusers who had been diagnosed with childhood ADHD (Ballon, Brunault, & Cortese, 2015).

In a group of university students who self-reported non-prescription stimulant use (e.g. Ritalin, Adderall, Concerta) primarily for appetite/weight-control motives or recreational purposes had higher levels of impulsivity and perfectionism and lower distress (or frustration) tolerance (Thiel, Kilwein, DeYoung, & Looby, 2019). A prior study hypothesized correlations between nonmedical prescription stimulant use and high sensation-seeking traits (Yomogida, Mendez, Figueroa, & Bavarian, 2018).

Case Example: Billy

From the time he was a young toddler, his parents described Billy as an extremely active (almost hyperactive) child. His mother recalls that even when Billy was about a year old and was learning to walk, "he went from walking to running." His mother would often find Billy climbing up on kitchen counters and bouncing up and down on his bed. Billy's younger brother was quieter and would be satisfied reading books or watching TV, but Billy had to constantly be "on the move." Billy's father thought it would be helpful to channel Billy's energy by playing sports and, fortunately, Billy was a good athlete. Part of his athletic ability came from his having no fear when it came to taking risks, such as diving for a baseball or football. Billy had several sports injuries as a child. He also reports that he would become "obsessed" with collecting things. When Billy started collecting baseball cards it wasn't enough that he had 60 cards, he had to have hundreds. He felt that no matter how many cards he had, "it was never enough." As Billy approached adolescence, he remained a high sensation-seeker. During the summer, Billy gained a reputation as the kid who would jump off the neighborhood bridge into the water or the kid who would go out in the ocean in rough waves.

Billy was about 13 years old when a friend of his stole some of his father's cigarettes and asked Billy if he was interested in smoking them with him. It didn't take long for Billy to begin smoking on a regular basis. When this same friend stole some vodka from his parent's liquor cabinet, Billy was the first to gulp down about a third of the bottle. At age 15 Billy tried smoking pot for the first time and soon thereafter tried psilocybin mushrooms and ecstasy. When Billy was introduced to methamphetamines (crystal meth), it was like he found the "love of his life." He described cocaine in the same way. When Billy ended up in rehab at age 18 after being arrested for drug distribution (i.e. dealing), he told the intake counselor that the reason that he loved crystal meth and coke so much was that it helped heighten his sensations and made everything "super-incredible."

Case Conceptualization

Without a doubt, Billy falls into the category of a "high sensation-seeker." It is not unusual for high sensation-seekers to exhibit the types of impulsivity and risk-taking behaviors that Billy engages in. Readers may also note the similarity between high sensation-seeking traits and attention-deficit hyperactivity disorder (ADHD). Also, his baseball card collection was similar to a process addiction in that he became obsessed with wanting more cards. Indeed, many hyperactive children do engage in impulsive, high-risk type sensation-seeking. However, not all sensation-seekers have ADHD although there are correlations between ADHD and SUDs (Adams, 2008; Weiss, 1993; Young, 2007.)

Advantages and Limitations of Personality Theory

Although the research reviewed in this chapter does appear to suggest that there are common personality traits and types among individuals with substance use disorders, there are some caveats to some of this research and how it was conducted (see Boxed Item 10.2). For example, much of the research which attempted to look for the elusive "addictive personality" was based on retrospective studies, which examined individuals who were already impacted by SUDs. Therefore, were the addictive personality traits discovered really the result of years of substance use? More recently, there has been some interesting prospective research that has uncovered some common personality traits that were predictive of one's propensity or likelihood of developing a SUD later in life (e.g. as adolescents or young adults).

Boxed Item 10.2 Advantages and Limitations of Personality Theory

Advantages

- research indicates that there are several common personality traits among individuals who manifest SUDs, such as impulsivity or high sensation-seeking behaviors
- it is possible for many recovering individuals to change some of these "character defects" as a result of counseling, 12-Step and other self-help types of programs
- some personality traits noted in individuals with SUDs may overlap with other mental health disorders, such as personality disorders, mood disorders or anxiety disorders
- many counselors note similar types of personality traits (and as a result similar types of interpersonal struggles) among clients they treat

Limitations

- some of the "addictive personality" research was done with adult individuals with SUDs which could have resulted in personality traits that developed as a result of years of substance use rather than being true precursors or antecedents to substance use
- not all individuals with SUDs will manifest the same types of personality traits

Summary

This chapter covers both Developmental Models of Addiction and Personality Theory. Developmental Models examine both the course or progression of substance use disorders as well as how these disorders impact on normal human development (e.g. how substances interfere with the attainment of developmental milestones) through the lifespan.

Personality Theories examine whether there are particular personality traits that may serve as precursors or antecedents to SUDs and how particular traits appear to correlate with SUDs (not cause them). Impulsivity, high sensation-seeking and other traits are examined as correlates of SUDs.

Recommended Reading and Resources

Galen, L.W., Henderson, M.J., & Whitman, R.D. (1997). The utility of novelty-seeking, harm avoidance, and expectancy in the prediction of drinking. *Addictive Behaviors, 22,* 93–106.

Glatt, M.M. (1975). Today's enjoyment – tomorrow's dependency: The road to rock bottom and the way back. *British Journal of Addiction, 70(Supp. 1, Apr.),* 25–34.

Gorski, T.T. (1989). *Passages through recovery: An action plan for preventing relapse.* Center City, MN: Hazelden.

Nakken, C. (1988). *The addictive personality: Understanding compulsion in our lives.* Center City, MN: Hazelden Foundation.

Sher, K.J., Bartholow, B.D., & Wood, M.D. (2000). Personality and substance use disorders: A perspective study. *Journal of Consulting & Clinical Psychology, 68(5),* 818–829.

Sher, K.J., Trull, T.J., Bartholow, B.D., & Vieth, A. (1999). Personality and alcoholism: Issues, methods, and etiological processes. In K. Leonard & H. Blaine (Eds). *Psychological theories of drinking and alcoholism* (2nd edn, pp. 54–105). New York: Guilford Press.

Wieczorek, W.F., & Nochajski, T.H. (2005). Characteristics of persistent drinking drivers: Comparisons of first, second and multiple offenders. In D.A. Hennessy & D.L. Wiesenthal (Eds). *Contemporary issues in road user behavior and traffic safety* (pp. 153–166). Hauppauge, NY: Nova Science Publishers.

Resources

Roadmap to Recovery (website-video): This Substance Abuse & Mental Health Services Administration website provides a look at the recovery progression as far as maintenance. Retrieved from www.youtube.com/watch?v=dkAY8m-uJI0

Earnie Larsen: The Starfish Story (website – YouTube video): This website provides a number of videos created by author, Earnie Larsen. Retrieved from www.youtube.com/watch?v=BIxvOo077Jo&list=PL4vdI3lR5b1gFZN1xcLvW8mkMYZ2wkPKU

Alcohol & Drug Addiction Recovery: Dr. David Streem (YouTube video): This video presents some basic information regarding addiction and progression. Retrieved from www.youtube.com/watch?v=J11rcoORHBU

References

Adams, A. (2008). ADHD grown up: A guide to adolescent and adult ADHD. *Journal of Family Therapy, 30(1),* 113–115.

Babor, T.F., Hofmann, M., DelBoca, F.K., Hesselbrock, V., Meyer, R.E., Dolinsky, Z.S., & Rounsaville, B. (1992). Types of alcoholics, I. Evidence for an empirically derived typology based on indicators of vulnerability and severity. *Archives of General Psychiatry, 49,* 599–608. http://dx.doi.org/10.1001/archpsyc.1992.01820080007002

Ball, S.A., Jaffe, A.J., Crouse-Artus, M.S., Rounsaville, B.J., & O'Malley, S.S. (2000). Multidimensional subtypes and treatment outcomes in first-time DWI offenders. *Addictive Behaviors, 25,* 167–181. http://dx.doi.org/10.1016/S0306-4603(99)00053-2

Ballon, N., Brunault, P., & Cortese, S. (2015). Sensation seeking and cocaine dependence in adults with reported childhood ADHD. *Journal of Attention Disorders, 19(4),* 335–342. http://dx.doi.org/10.1177/1087054714543651

Battaglia, M., Przybeck, T.R., Bellodi, L., & Cloninger, C.R. (1996). Temperament dimensions explain the comorbidity of psychiatric disorders. *Comprehensive Psychiatry, 37,* 292–298

Belcher, A.M., Volkow, N.D., Moeller, F.G., & Ferre, S. (2014). Personality traits and vulnerability or resilience to substance use disorders. *Trends in Cognitive Science, 18(4),* 211–217. http://dx.doi.org/10.1016/.tics.2014.01.010

Bizzarri, J.V., Sbrana, A., Rucci, P., Ravani, L., Massei, G.J., Gonnelli, C., Spagnolli, S. et al. (2007). The spectrum of substance abuse in bipolar disorder: Reasons for use, sensation-seeking and substance sensitivity. *Bipolar Disorders, 9,* 213–220.

Blonigen, D.M., Bui, L., Britt, J.Y., Thomas, K.M., & Timko, C. (2016). Internalizing and externalizing personality subtypes predict differences in functioning and outcomes among veterans in residential substance use disorder treatment. *Psychological Assessment, 28(10),* 1186–1197.

Bohman, M., Sigvardsson, S., & Cloninger, C. R. (1981) Maternal inheritance of alcohol abuse: Cross-fostering analysis of adopted women. *Archives of General Psychiatry, 38,* 965–969.

Brande, L. (2018, Dec. 7) *Alcoholism and the stages of recovery.* Retrieved from www.recovery. org/alcohol-treatment/stages/

Brook, J.S., Zhang, C., Leukefeld, C.G., & Brook, D.W. (2016). Marijuana use from adolescence to adulthood: Developmental trajectories and their outcomes. *Social Psychiatry – Psychiatric Epidemiology, 1,* 1405–1415.

Caspi, A., Begg, D., Dickson, N., Harrington, H., Langley, J., Moffitt, T.E., & Silva, P.A. (1997). Personality differences predict health-risk behaviors in young adulthood: Evidence from a longitudinal study. *Journal of Personality & Social Psychology, 73,* 1052–1063.

Clark, L.A., & Watson, D. (1999). Temperament: A new paradigm for trait psychology. In L.A. Pervin & O.P. John (Eds). *Handbook of personality: Theory and research* (2nd edn, pp. 399–423). New York: Guilford Press.

Clark, L.A., Watson, D., & Mineka, S. (1994). Temperament, personality, and the mood and anxiety disorders. *Journal of Abnormal Psychology, 103,* 103–116. http://dx.doi.org/10.1037/0021-843X.103.1/103

Cloninger, C.R., Sigvardsson, S., Przybeck, T., & Svrakic, D. M. (1995). Personality antecedents of alcoholism in a national area probability sample. *European Archives of Psychiatry and Clinical Neuroscience, 245,* 239–244.

Erikson, E.H. (1963). *Childhood and society* (2nd edn). New York: Norton

Galen, L.W., Henderson, M.J., & Whitman, R.D. (1997). The utility of novelty-seeking, harm avoidance, and expectancy in the prediction of drinking. *Addictive Behaviors, 22,* 93–106.

Glatt, M.M. (1975). Today's enjoyment – tomorrow's dependency: The road to rock bottom and the way back. *British Journal of Addiction, 70(Supp. 1, Apr.),* 25–34.

Goldberg, L.R. (1993). The structure of phenotypic personality traits. *American Psychologist, 48,* 26–34.

Gorski, T.T. (1989). *Passages through recovery: An action plan for preventing relapse.* Center City, MN: Hazelden.

Green, K.M., Doherty, E.E., & Ensminger, M.E. (2017). Long-term consequences of adolescent cannabis use: Examining intermediary processes. *American Journal of Drug and Alcohol Abuse, 43(5),* 567–575. https://doi.org.10.1080/00952990.2016.1258706

Hazelden (2019, January 17). *What is cross-addiction?* Center City, MN: Hazelden Publishing. www.hazeldenbettyford.org/articles/what-is-cross-addiction

Hesselbrock, V.M., & Hesselbrock, M. . (2006). Are there empirically supported and clinically useful subtypes of alcohol dependence? *Addiction, 101(Suppl. 1),* 97–103.

Ilgen, M., McKellar, J., & Tiet, Q. (2005). Abstinence self-efficacy and abstinence 1 year after substance use disorder treatment. *Journal of Consulting and Clinical Psychology, 73,* 1175–1180. http://dx.doi.org/10.1037/0022-006X.73.6.1175

Jackson, K.M., Bucholz, K.K., Wood, P.K., Steinly, D., Grant, J.D., & Sher, K.J. (2014). Towards the characterization and validation of alcohol use disorder subtypes: Integrating consumption and symptom data. *Psychological Medicine, 44,* 143–159. http://dx.doi.org/10.S0033291713000573

Jellinek, E.M., & Joliffe, N. (1940). Effects of alcohol on the individual: Review of the literature of 1939. *Quarterly Journal of Studies on Alcohol, 1,* 110–181.

John, O.P., & Srivastava, S. (1999). The Big Five trait taxonomy: History, measurement, and theoretical perspectives. In L.A. Pervin & O.P. John (Eds). *Handbook of personality: Theory and research* (2nd edn, pp. 102–138). New York: Guilford Press.

Jonah, B. (1997). Sensation-seeking and risky driving: A review and synthesis of the literature. *Accident Analysis & Prevention, 29(5),* 651–666.

Juon, H.S., Fothergill, K.E., Green, K.M., Doherty, E.E., & Ensminger, M.E. (2011). Antecedents and consequences of marijuana use trajectories over the life course in an African American population. *Journal of Alcohol & Drug Dependence, 118,* 216–223.

Kotov, R., Gamez, W., Schmidt, F., & Watson, D. (2010). Linking "big" personality traits to anxiety, depressive and substance use disorders: A meta-analysis. *Psychological Bulletin, 136(5),* 768–821.

Larsen, E. (2009). *Stage 2 recovery: Life beyond addiction.* New York: Harper One.

Littlefield, A.K., & Sher, K.J. (2016). Personality and substance use disorders. In K.J. Sher (Ed.). *The Oxford handbook of substance use and substance use disorders Vol. 1* (pp. 351–374). Oxford: Oxford University Press.

Long, C.G., Williams, M., Midgley, M., & Hollin, C.R. (2000). Within program factors as predictors of drinking outcomes following cognitive-behavioral treatment. *Addictive Behaviors, 25,* 573–578. http://dx.doi.org/10.1016/S0306-4603(99)00018-0

Malouff, J.M., Thorsteinsson, E.B., & Schutte, N.S. (2005). The relationship between the five-factor model of personality and symptoms of clinical disorders. A meta-analysis. *Journal of Psychopathology and Behavioral Assessment, 27,* 101–114. http://doi:10.1007/s10862-005-5384-y

Markon, K.E., Krueger, R.F., & Watson, D. (2005). Delineating the structure of normal and abnormal personality: An integrative hierarchical approach. *Journal of Personality & Social Psychology, 88,* 139–157.

McCrae, R.R., Costa, P.T. Jr, Ostendorf, F., Angleitner, A., Hrebickova, M., Avia, M.S., & Smith, P.B. (2000). Nature over nurture: Temperament, personality and life-span development. *Journal of Personality & Social Psychology, 78,* 173–186. doi.10.1037/0022-3514.78.1.173

Moggi, F., Ouimette, P.C., Moos, R.H., & Finney, J.W. (1999). Dual diagnosis patients in substance abuse treatment: Relationship of general coping and substance-specific coping to 1-year outcome. *Addiction, 94,* 1805–1816.

Moraleda-Barreno, E., Diaz-Batanero, C., Perez-Moreno, P.J., Gomez-Bujedo, J., & Lozano, O.M. (2018). Relations between facets and personality domains with impulsivity: New evidence using the DSM-5 Section III framework in patients with substance use disorders. *Personality Disorders: Theory, Research and Treatment, 9(5),* 490–495.

Nakken, C. (1988). *The addictive personality: Understanding compulsion in our lives.* Center City, MN: Hazelden Foundation.

Roberts, B.W., Capsi, A., & Moffitt, T.E. (2001). The kids are alright: Growth and stability in personality development from adolescence to adulthood. *Journal of Personality and Social Psychology, 81,* 582–893.

Ruiz, M.A., Pincus, A.L., & Schinka, J.A. (2008). Externalizing pathology and the five-factor model: A meta-analysis of personality traits associated with antisocial personality disorder, substance use disorder and their co-occurrence. *Journal of Personality Disorders, 22,* 365–388. http://doi:10.1521/pedi.2008.22.4.365

Sher, K.J., Trull, T.J., Bartholow, B.D., & Vieth, A. (1999). Personality and alcoholism: Issues, methods, and etiological processes. In K. Leonard & H. Blaine (Eds). *Psychological theories of drinking and alcoholism* (2nd edn, pp. 54–105). New York: Guilford Press.

Sher, K.J., Bartholow, B.D., & Wood, M.D. (2000). Personality and substance use disorders: A perspective study. *Journal of Consulting & Clinical Psychology, 68(5),* 818–829.

Sher, K.J., Wood, M.D., Crews, T.M., & Vandiver, P.A. (1995). The Tridimensional Personality Questionnaire: Reliability and validity studies and derivation of a short form. *Psychological Assessment, 7,* 195–208.

Smith, G.T., Fischer, S., Cyders, M.A., Annus, A.M., Spillane, N.S., & McCarthy, D. M. (2007). On the validity and utility of discriminating among impulsivity-like traits. *Assessment, 14,* 155–170. http://dx.doi.org/10.1177/1073191106295527

Strakowski, S.M., & Del Bello, M.P. (2000). The co-occurrence of bipolar and substance use disorders. *Clinical Psychology Review, 20,* 191–206.

Thiel, A.M., Kilwein, T.M., De Young, K.P., & Looby, A. (2019). Differentiating motives for nonmedical prescription stimulant use by personality characteristics. *Addictive Behaviors, 88,* 187–193.

Troncone, J. (2014, Oct. 10). Cross addiction and what it means. *Psychology Today Blog: Where addiction meets your brain.*

Washburn, I.J., & Capaldi, D.M. (2015). Heterogeneity in men's marijuana use in the 20s: Adolescent antecedents and consequences in the 30s. *Developmental Psychopathology, 27,* 279–291.

Watson, D., Clark, L.A., & Harkness, A.R. (1994). Structures of personality and their relevance to psychopathology. *Journal of Abnormal Psychology, 103,* 18–31.

Weiss, G. (1993). *Hyperactive children grown up: ADHD in children, adolescents and adults* (2nd edn). New York: Guilford Press.

Wieczorek, W.F., & Nochajski, T.H. (2005). Characteristics of persistent drinking drivers: Comparisons of first, second and multiple offenders. In D.A. Hennessy & D.L. Wiesenthal (Eds). *Contemporary issues in road user behavior and traffic safety*. Hauppauge, NY: Nova Science Publishers, p. 153–166.

Yomogida, K., Mendez, J., Figueroa, W., & Bavarian, N. (2018). Correlates of recreation versus Academic-motivated misuse of prescription stimulants. *Journal of Drug Issues, 48(3)*, 472–484. https://doi.org/10.1177/0022042618774825.

Young, J.L. (2007). *ADHD grown up: A guide to adolescent and adult ADHD*. New York: Norton.

Zuckerman M., & Cloninger, C.R. (1996). Relationships between Cloninger's, Zuckerman's, and Eysenck's dimensions of personality. *Personality and Individual Differences, 21*, 283–285.

11 Relapse Prevention

Margaret Smith

Introduction

Have you ever tried to stop engaging in an unhealthy behavior (e.g. smoking, nail biting, overeating)? Have you ever returned to the unhealthy behavior after you stopped? What are some reasons for returning to that unhealthy behavior? Did you have thoughts, actions, and/or emotions that led you back to the unhealthy behavior? What could you have done – or could do differently in the future – related to staying stopped? These questions all relate to relapse and relapse prevention.

While not an etiological theory of addiction, relapse prevention falls under models of change and is a major aspect working with clients who have addictions. Relapse prevention should be an integral part of every client's treatment plan and/or program.

Key Terms

abstinence violation effect (AVE): abstinence violation effect refers to the negative cognitive and affective responses experienced by an individual after a return to substance use following a period of abstinence from substances (Collins & Witkiewitz, 2013).

high-risk situation (HRS): a HRS is any experience, emotion, setting, thought or context that presents an increased risk for a person to engage in some transgressive behavior (Witkiewitz & Marlatt, 2007, p. 5).

lapse: "an initial set-back or the first instance of a previously changed behavior" (Witkiewitz & Marlatt, 2007, p. 3). Sometimes referred to as a "slip."

relapse (Gorki and colleagues): relapse is a "process that occurs within the patient and manifests itself in a progressive pattern of behavior that reactivates the symptoms of a disease or creates related debilitating conditions in a person that has previously experienced remission from an illness" (Gorski & Miller, 1982, pp. 21–22).

relapse (Marlatt and colleagues): relapse is a "setback that occurs during the
   behavior change process, such that progress toward the initiation or
   maintenance of a behavior change goal (e.g. abstinence from drug use)
   is interrupted by a reversion to the target behavior" and is a "dynamic,
   ongoing process" (Hendershot, Witkiewitz, George, & Marlatt, 2011, p. 2).
relapse prevention: is an "intervention strategy for reducing the likelihood and
   severity of relapse following the cessation or reduction of problematic
   behaviors" (Hendershot et al., 2011, p. 1).

Relapse Prevention

As stated, relapse, and relapse prevention, are major aspects of working with people
who have addictions. Clients may show up to an outpatient counseling session
reporting a risk for relapse ("I'm having cravings and thoughts about using") or
have relapsed ("I shot up yesterday"). Addressing the potential for, or an actual,
relapse is therefore vital in establishing lasting recovery. But what is a relapse?
According to Marlatt and George (1984) "relapse refers to a breakdown or failure
in a person's attempt to change or modify any target behavior" (p. 261).

There is stigma related to relapse and addiction, with many people associating
relapse only with addiction. However, there is a variety of disorders where relapses
occur. When compared with other chronic medical conditions, McLellan, Lewis,
O'Brien, and Kleber (2000) found that rates of relapse in drug dependence (40–
60%) were comparable to relapse rates in type 1 diabetes (30–50%) and hypertension or asthma (50–70%). Weight loss is another area where relapses commonly
occur. After dieting and exercising for weeks or months, it's not unusual for individuals to return to eating high calorie foods and/or sweets.

What then is relapse prevention? It is an "intervention strategy for reducing the
likelihood and severity of relapse following the cessation or reduction of problematic behaviors" (Hendershot et al., 2011, p. 1). As you will see, relapse prevention
planning or interventions are best accomplished when based on the individual needs
of the client. Since each client is unique, so too, will be his or her relapse triggers.

Learning Opportunity 11.1

Think of a time you stopped engaging in an unhealthy behavior. Did you
"relapse" back to this unhealthy behavior? If so, what were some of the
"things" that led you back to this unhealthy behavior? If you did not, why
do you think you did not relapse? What were some "things" you did to
prevent a relapse? After you address these questions, break into groups and
discuss with your peers.

There are two dominant names who – along with their colleagues – focused
their work on relapse and relapse prevention: Terence T. Gorski and G. Alan

Marlatt. Gorski and his CENAPS (Center for Applied Sciences) model use such terminology as "relapse dynamic," "relapse warning signs" and "relapse prevention planning." Marlatt and his colleagues use such terminology as "lapse," "high-risk situations," "relapse precipitants," "coping strategies," "cognitive behavioral model" and eventually included meditation and medications in relapse prevention planning.

Gorski's Relapse Model

Gorski wrote that addiction is like any other disease, where relapse is a "process that occurs within the patient and manifests itself in a progressive pattern of behavior that reactivates the symptoms of a disease or creates related debilitating conditions in a person that has previously experienced remission from an illness" (Gorski & Miller, 1982, pp. 21–22). Gorski's conceptualization of relapse is similar to what we will discuss in relation to Marlatt, in that he believes that relapse is a process where there are "objective and predictable warning signs of relapse that are present long before the patient starts [using]" (Gorski & Miller, 1982, p. 54). Interrupting these warning signs is the key to preventing relapse.

Gorski and Miller (1982, pp. 57–66) list 37 warning signs of relapse which include the following: apprehensive of well-being, denial, adamant commitment to sobriety, compulsive attempts to impose sobriety on others, defensiveness, compulsive behavior, impulsive behavior, tendencies toward loneliness, tunnel vision, minor depression, loss of constructive planning, plans begin to fail, idle daydreaming and wishful thinking, feeling that nothing can be solved, immature wish to be happy, periods of confusion, irritation with friends, easily angered, irregular eating habits, listlessness, irregular sleeping habits, progressive loss of daily structure, periods of deep depression, irregular attendance at treatment meetings, development of an "I don't care" attitude, open rejection of help, dissatisfaction with life, feelings of powerlessness and helplessness, self-pity, thoughts of social drinking, conscious lying, complete loss of self-confidence, unreasonable resentments, discontinuing all treatment, overwhelming loneliness, frustration, anger and tension, start of controlled drinking, and loss of control. As stated, interrupting these warning signs is the key to preventing relapse. It's often said that relapses occur months before a person actually picks up a drink or uses drugs and it's usually the aforementioned warning signs that clues in counselors and significant others that a relapse may be in process.

Application of Gorski's model to counseling follows this next section on Marlatt and Colleague's approach to relapse prevention.

Learning Opportunity 11.2

In reference to Learning Opportunity 11.1, and after reading Gorski and Miller's 37 warning signs, identify warning signs that led to your relapse. If you did not relapse, did you notice any warning signs of a potential relapse and what did you do to avoid this relapse? Break into groups and share your answers with your peers.

Boxed Item 11.1 Gorski's 37 Warning Signs of Relapse

- apprehensive of well-being
- denial
- adamant commitment to sobriety
- compulsive attempts to impose sobriety on others
- defensiveness
- compulsive behavior, impulsive behavior
- tendencies toward loneliness
- tunnel vision
- minor depression
- loss of constructive planning
- plans begin to fail
- idle daydreaming and wishful thinking
- feeling that nothing can be solved
- immature wish to be happy
- periods of confusion
- irritation with friends
- easily angered
- irregular eating habits
- listlessness
- irregular sleeping habits
- progressive loss of daily structure
- periods of deep depression
- irregular attendance at treatment meetings
- development of an "I don't care" attitude
- open rejection of help
- dissatisfaction with life
- feelings of powerlessness and helplessness
- self-pity
- thoughts of social drinking
- conscious lying
- complete loss of self-confidence
- unreasonable resentments
- discontinuing all treatment
- overwhelming loneliness
- frustration
- anger and tension
- start of controlled drinking, loss of control

(Gorski & Miller, 1982, pp. 57–66)

Marlatt's Relapse Model

Marlatt and colleagues' model of relapse prevention is based on the cognitive behavioral and social learning theories. Just as addictions can be thought of as learned maladaptive behaviors, so too clients, can be taught strategies for avoiding relapse (Lewis, 2014). While Marlatt and colleagues would agree with Gorski on the conceptualization of relapse as a process, Marlatt articulates a difference between a lapse and a relapse. A lapse is "an initial set-back or the first instance of a previously changed behavior" (Witkiewitz & Marlatt, 2007, p. 3). A relapse is a "setback that occurs during the behavior change process, such that progress toward the initiation or maintenance of a behavior change goal (e.g. abstinence from drug use) is interrupted by a reversion to the target behavior" and is a "dynamic, ongoing process" (Hendershot et al., 2011, p. 2).

Articulating relapse in cognitive behavioral terms, Marlatt and colleagues wrote about identifying high-risk situations (HRS). An HRS is "any experience, emotion, setting, thought or context that presents an increased risk for a person to engage in some transgressive behavior" (Witkiewitz & Marlatt, 2007, p. 5). Further, Marlatt and colleagues also present the idea of *apparently irrelevant decisions*, which refers to the notion that "individuals make decisions that initiate the lapse process well before they realize the process was triggered" (Witkiewitz & Marlatt, 2007, p. 11).

Marlatt and colleagues also identified outcome expectancies as a variable leading to relapse. Outcome expectancies involve the anticipation of the effects of using. These expectancies can be physical, psychological, or behavioral effects. Positive outcome expectancies regarding these three areas might include "I am going to feel more relaxed after I drink." The psychological may be that "I'm going to be much happier after I drink" and the behavioral may be "I'm going to be more social with other people after I drink." These positive outcome expectancies are associated with relapse, while negative outcome expectancies (e.g. "my driving drunk will lead to another DUI") lead to better treatment outcomes (Marlatt & Donovan, 2005, p. 10).

Additionally, Marlatt and colleagues identified relapse precipitants such as negative emotional states, positive emotional states, coping, self-efficacy, abstinence violation effect, craving, and interpersonal precipitants. We will now explore these precipitants in greater detail.

Negative emotional states may include anxiety, depression, boredom, frustration and anger. Positive emotional states would include celebrations such as weddings, graduations, birthdays and anniversaries; they could also include positive memories that one may experience when passing a favorite bar. These fond memories of good times drinking with friends could lead to relapse. These emotional states can be intrapersonal perceptions of certain situations (e.g. feeling that one has been wronged or betrayed) or by interpersonal conflicts (e.g. feeling angry after a verbal altercation with one's boss, spouse or partner) (Larimer, Palmer, & Marlatt, 1999, p. 153).

Coping includes the implementation of coping strategies and skills in response to high-risk situations or future anticipated HRSs. Marlatt and Donovan (2005, p. 12) state that the most critical predictor of relapse is a person's ability to use cognitive and/or behavioral coping strategies in relation to high-risk situations (HRSs). Increasing the number of strategies used decreased the probability of a relapse and active, over avoidant, strategies worked best (Moser & Annis, 1996).

A client's self-efficacy refers to his/her personal belief that s/he has the ability to successfully abstain from substance use. A lack of self-efficacy is linked to increased risk of relapse. There are studies cited that indicate that increased levels of self-efficacy decrease the likelihood of a relapse, while decreased levels of self-efficacy are linked to relapses (Witkiewitz & Marlatt, 2004, 2007).

Cravings, described as cognitive experience focused on desire to use and urges, the behavioral intention or impulse to use, are also related to relapse (Marlatt & Donovan, 2005).

Lastly, relapse has been linked to interpersonal precipitants including either support for abstinence or use (support for abstinence decreases likelihood of relapse, while support to use increases the likelihood) (Witkiewitz & Marlatt, 2007, p. 9).

Learning Opportunity 11.3

After reading Marlatt and colleagues' HRSs and relapse precipitants, identify HRSs regarding the relapse event or identify how you avoided a relapse. Break into groups and share your answers with your peers.

Application of Relapse Prevention to Addiction Counseling

Gorski's Application to Addiction Counseling

According to Gorski and Miller (1986), relapse prevention planning should include: (1) stabilization, (2) assessment, (3) patient education, (4) warning sign identification, (5) review of the recovery program, (6) inventory training interruption of the relapse dynamic, (7) involvement of significant others, and (8) follow-up and reinforcement.

Let's go into a little more detail on Gorski and Miller's relapse prevention planning. (1) Stabilization includes regaining control over thoughts, feelings, memory, judgement and behavior after relapsing. There is the plan not to drink within the next 24 hours (Gorski & Miller, 1982, p. 93). Here is where counseling and help may be useful if a client is unable to get control over aspects of their life. (2) Assessment is learning what led up to the relapse. (3) Education involves learning about relapse and relapse warning signs – educating oneself about the process of relapse and how to prevent it. (4) Identification means looking at specific relapse warning signs that contributed to the relapse. (5) Warning sign prevention follows identification, where a client needs to prepare for specific problems (warning signs) before they occur. (6) Inventory training involves conducting a twice daily inventory of warning signs so that the client can correct problems before they get out of control. This step involves reviewing the current recovery plan to make certain that there are coping strategies for the relapse warning signs. (7) Involvement of others includes decreasing isolation and including significant others in the recovery and relapse prevention process. (8) Lastly, there is follow-up and reinforcement, which refers to revising the relapse prevention plan at regular intervals (Gorski & Miller, 1986, pp. 159–170).

Marlatt's Application to Addiction Counseling

Marlatt and colleagues focus on a variety of strategies to deal with, or decrease the likelihood of, relapse. First, Marlatt and colleagues believe that the essentials for relapse prevention work include the identification and discussion of HRSs and *apparently irrelevant decisions* for lapse and relapse. First, in terms of HRSs, Larimer et al. (1999) recommend identifying high-risk situations with clients through the use of past lapses or relapses, relapse dreams or fantasies. Further, they recommend that those who have not initiated abstinence yet may want to self-monitor their drinking behavior for people, places and things that may increase the likelihood of relapse. Once these HRSs have been identified, Larimer et al. (1999) suggest two intervention strategies: teaching the client to recognize the warning signs of "imminent danger" and apply an effective coping strategy or avoid the situation altogether. Another strategy incorporates assessing the client's current strategies and increasing them.

Another important area to address is *apparently irrelevant decisions.* These are seemingly insignificant decisions that eventually led to a lapse or relapse. For example, a person decides to go food shopping and passes by the street where s/he once used. This may seem like an apparently irrelevant decision, but can lead to a lapse or relapse. It is important that apparently irrelevant decisions are identified and the client and counselor develop strategies for coping with them.

One of the main goals of relapse prevention is to develop effective cognitive and behavioral coping strategies for cravings, urges, emotions and risky situations (Witkiewitz & Marlatt, 2007, pp. 11–12). Coping strategies may include cognitive or behavioral strategies. Some cognitive strategies include, but are not limited to, cognitive restructuring (of negative thinking), challenging beliefs, problem solving, anger/emotion management, reminding self of successes, and mindfulness meditation. Behavioral coping strategies can include but are not limited to avoidance of HRSs, engaging in pleasurable (healthy) behaviors (e.g. bike riding, socializing with sober friends), seeking supportive environments (e.g. 12-Step or other self-help meetings), relaxation techniques (e.g. deep breathing, muscle relaxation), self-care techniques and strategies (e.g. good sleep and diet), and exercise.

Marlatt and Witkiewitz (2007) identify the period following a lapse as a dangerous time. Therefore, clients should attend to this time period with the following strategies: "stop (using), look and listen to what is happening; keep calm; renew commitment to abstinence with focusing on past successes; review the situation leading up to the lapse; make an immediate plan for recovery; and deal with the abstinence violation" (p. 12).

Larimer et al. (1999) write of other specific intervention strategies to help decrease the likelihood of relapse. These include identifying and coping with high-risk situations, enhancing self-efficacy, eliminating myths and placebo effects, lapse management, cognitive restructuring, global self-control strategies, developing positive addiction(s), stimulus-control techniques, urge-management and relapse road maps.

Enhancing self-efficacy is another way to reduce the likelihood of a lapse or relapse. Here Larimer et al. (1999) state that the collaborative relationship between client and therapist is pivotal. Another method for enhancing self-efficacy is to break down goals set by the client into smaller, more manageable goals. "Because an increase in self-efficacy is closely tied to achieving preset goals, successful mastery of these individual smaller tasks is the best strategy to enhance feelings of self-mastery" (Larimer et al., 1999, p. 156). A third strategy regarding self-efficacy is to provide feedback on the client's small successes, as well as bigger ones.

Eliminating myths and placebo effects refers to responding to the misperceptions and mistaken positive beliefs and expectancies about a drug's (usually) physiological effects (Larimer et al., 1999). Counselors can work with their clients on correcting misperceptions, dispelling myths, cognitive restructuring (explained later) and reducing positive expectancies.

Lapse management focuses on halting the relapse and dealing with abstinence violation effect to prevent an "uncontrollable relapse" (Larimer et al., 1999, p. 156). Lapse management may include developing a written contract with the client in preparation for a lapse.

Cognitive restructuring involves the reframing of a lapse from a "failure to an error," or a mistake and lesson to be learned. This strategy also includes countering drinking or drugging thinking, as well as challenging thinking errors or negative thoughts (Douaihy, Stowell, Park & Daley, 2007; Larimer et al., 1999). When clients disclose a lapse to their counselor, it also becomes an opportunity to talk about what may have been missing in that person's recovery program; for example, was this individual isolating from others, were they ignoring emotional distress or physical pain, had their lives become unbalanced by putting too much emphasis on their work or careers and so on?

Global lifestyle self-control strategies incorporate lifestyle changes that increase life balance and coping strategies. Here it is important to "modify individual lifestyle factors and covert antecedents that can increase exposure or reduce resistance to high-risk situations" (Larimer et al., 1999, p. 157).

Developing "positive addictions" may include meditation, exercise or yoga that in turn effect lifestyle balance (Larimer et al., 1999). It should be noted, however, that some addiction professionals, prefer not to use the term "positive addiction." The addiction in "positive addiction" is associated with, among many issues, dysfunction, loss, impaired control, as well as interpersonal and emotional problems. Therefore, it is not positive by any means.

Stimulus-control techniques are those strategies that involve deconditioning of urges and cravings related to events, people, places and things that were related to past and current drug use (Larimer et al., 1999, p. 158). For example, deconditioning might be removing all drug paraphernalia and drug-using friends from the client's life so that they do not "trigger" cravings or urges.

Urge-management techniques include those strategies that involve the client's learning methods to handle urges and cravings. This technique involves reframing the urge or cravings not as a reason to drink but as an "emotional or physiological response to an external stimulus in his or her environment" (Larimer et al., 1999, p. 158). Clients can also engage in systematic relaxation, visual imagery, behavioral alternatives (such as listening to music, calling a friend or sponsor, going for a walk, etc.), and cognitive strategies (Douaihy et al., 2007). Here the goal is to divert one's attention away from the craving by engaging in other activities. Like the old AA/ NA saying, "move a muscle, change a thought." Craving management may also include "thinking the drink (or drug) through to what will happen after the initial euphoria wears off and most substance users begin to feel emotional distress, withdrawal, guilt and physically sick (e.g. hungover).

Lastly, specific relapse prevention strategies include developing a relapse road map. This involves "mapping out" HRSs and possible outcomes and planning ahead for these situations by identifying coping strategies (Larimer et al., 1999).

Within Marlatt's model, Douaihy et al. (2007) offer clinical steps in helping to reduce relapse risk among clients. They offer the following steps:

> 1) Help clients understand relapse as a process and event, and learn to identify early warning signs; 2) Help clients identify their high-risk situations and develop cognitive and behavioral coping responses; 3) Help clients enhance communication skills, interpersonal relationships and social networks; 4) Help clients manage negative emotional states; 5) Help clients identify and manage cravings and "cues" that precede cravings; 6) Help clients identify and challenge cognitive distortions; and 7) consider the use of medications.
>
> (Douaihy et al., 2007, pp. 50–55)

In addition to a consideration for the use of medications (e.g. Antabuse, Nicotine Replacement Therapy, buprenorphine, methadone), Marlatt and Witkiewitz (2005) also suggest meditation.

Much of Marlatt and colleagues' work as been supported by research (Lewis, 2014; Marlatt & Donovan, 2005).

Utilizing Relapse Prevention

In working with either the Gorski and colleagues' and/or Marlatt and colleague's models, it is important that relapses are not treated as failures but as lessons to be learned. This approach can make all the difference in how the client (and the counselor) work with relapse-related issues.

In "doing" relapse prevention, many substance use disorder (SUD) counseling offices and treatment organizations offer workbooks and handouts regarding relapse prevention work. Oftentimes these handouts and workbooks have checklists of warning signs and HRSs. Clients can check these off, recognizing their vulnerability to a lapse or relapse. Additionally, these handouts usually have an area identifying coping strategies (or providing space for the client to identify them). Working within the relapse prevention model, counselors should collaborate with clients on identifying and increasing both cognitive and behavioral coping strategies (as listed earlier).

Additionally, with the advances in pharmacological agents, counselors may also refer their clients for an evaluation for medication to help reduce the risk of relapse. As stated previously, a variety of medications are available. Lastly, many counseling offices and treatment centers offer relapse prevention groups.

Learning Opportunity 11.4

With two or three other peers from your class, design a relapse prevention plan for an unhealthy behavior of yours based on the material from Gorski and colleagues as well as Marlatt and colleagues' work.

Strengths and Limitations

Strengths of the relapse prevention approach include the following: relapse prevention can be a stand-alone intervention or used throughout counseling sessions; it can be used in individual and group work; Marlatt and colleagues' approach is supported by research; and relapse prevention work is accessible in terms of language and application for clients (Lewis, 2014, p. 177). Further relapse prevention can be applied to other conditions, such as eating disorders and obesity, gambling disorders, and sexually risky behaviors (Marlatt & Donovan, 2005).

There are also limitations to relapse prevention: it is more of an educational and cognitive/behavioral approach and therefore less favorable for those who are invested in process approaches; "Relapse prevention strategies work at the level of cognition and behavior but may do little to address fundamental disorders of personality that may be significantly contribute to substance use" (Lewis, 2014, p. 177). Another limitation can include the challenge "for counselors to walk the line between preparing a client for potential relapse without inadvertently giving permission to use" (Lassiter and Culbreth, 2018, p. 376).

Case Study

Maureen, a 48-year-old woman, was referred to an alcohol and other drug outpatient department for counseling following a DUI conviction. At the time of her arrest, she was tested and had both opiates and alcohol in her system. She was then mandated to counseling after completing a DUI screening program. Maureen admits that she does have a problem because she has been in treatment before and learned "all that stuff about the disease." She states that she is now "ready to quit" but is anxious about her ability to remain sober and clean. "I've tried this [abstinence] before and I just can't make it stick." Given Maureen's goals, she is a prime candidate for relapse prevention counseling.

Case Conceptualization

In relation to relapse prevention planning with Maureen, the counselor would begin by educating her regarding warning sign and HRS identification; and regarding management of HRSs and urges. The counselor would enhance her self-efficacy; review Maureen's recovery program; carry out an interpersonal and social relationship evaluation, and look at the impact of these relationships on her recovery; and put in place plans to re-evaluate the relapse prevention plan on a regular basis. Lastly, there may be recommendations for medication and meditation.

More specifically, in terms of patient education, the counselor may educate Maureen on the disease of addiction and relapse, and/or addiction as a maladaptive behavior (Marlatt, 2005). The counselor may explore warning signs with Maureen by providing a checklist of warning signs. Maureen could go through the checklist and identify which warning signs put her at risk.

Further, Maureen and the counselor may explore high-risk situations to avoid occasions such as parties with heavy use of alcohol and spending evenings at the bar with friends. Additionally, the counselor would explore any cravings or urges that Maureen may be experiencing.

To increase Maureen's level of self-efficacy, the counselor can explore past instances where she utilized successful strategies in order to maintain sobriety. With urges, the counselor can assist Maureen in recognizing that her urge is not necessarily an "desire" to drink, but more a conditioned reaction to external stimuli that physiologically trigger her. She can then plan in advance for those reactions and how to cope with them.

In order to help reduce the likelihood of a relapse, Maureen and the counselor would evaluate and (over time) re-evaluate her recovery program to see if there is anything missing or needed to help her maintain her sobriety. Further, the counselor and Maureen would explore who supports as well as who challenges her recovery so that Maureen can make healthier choices about who she "hangs out with." This may include a recommendation to attend AA.

The counselor may also refer Maureen for an evaluation for medication (particularly if there are repeated lapses) as well as recommending meditation.

Lastly, the counselor may develop a relapse road map with Maureen to "map out" high-risk situations and related choices and consequences. This map will include ways to cope with these HRSs.

Recommended Reading and Resources

Coping Skills handouts: available at https://depts.washington.edu/hcsats/PDF/TF-%20CBT/pages/cognitive_coping.html

Gorski, T.T., & Miller, M. (1982). *Counseling for relapse prevention*. Independence, MO: Herald House-Independence Press.

Gorski, T.T., & Miller, M. (1986). *Staying sober: A guide for relapse prevention*. Independence, MO: Herald House-Independence Press.

Gorski, T.T. (2000). The CENAPS Model of Relapse Prevention Therapy (CMRPT). In National Institute of Drug Abuse. *Approaches to drug abuse counseling* (pp. 23–38). Washington, DC: National Institute of Drug Abuse.

Marlatt, G.A., & Donovan, D.M. (2005). *Relapse prevention: Maintenance strategies in the treatment of addictive behaviors* (2nd edn). New York: Guilford Press

National Institute of Alcohol Abuse and Alcoholism: https://pubs.niaaa.nih.gov/publications/aa06.htm

National Institute of Drug Abuse: www.drugabuse.gov/publications/drugs-brains-behavior-science-addiction/treatment-recovery

Witkiewitz, K., & Marlatt, G.A. (Eds). (2007). *Therapist's guide to evidence-based relapse prevention*. Boston, MA: Elsevier.

References

Collins, S., & Witkiewitz, K. (2013). Abstinence violation effect. *Encyclopedia of behavioral medicine* (pp. 8–9). New York: Springer.

Douaihy, A., Stowell, K.R., Park, T.W., & Daley, D.C. (2007) Relapse prevention: Clinical strategies for substance use disorders. In K. Witkiewitz & G.A. Marlatt (Eds). *Therapist's guide to evidence-based relapse prevention*. Boston, MA: Elsevier.

Gorski, T.T., & Miller, M. (1982). *Counseling for relapse prevention*. Independence, MO: Herald House-Independence Press.

Gorski, T.T., & Miller, M. (1986). *Staying sober: A guide for relapse prevention*. Independence, MO: Herald House-Independence Press.

Hendershot, C.S., Witkiewitz, K., George, W.H., & Marlatt, G.A. (2011). Relapse prevention for addictive behaviors. *Substance Abuse Treatment, Prevention and Policy, 6,* 1–17.

Larimer, M.E., Palmer, R.S., & Marlatt, G.A. (1999). Relapse prevention: An overview of Marlatt's Cognitive Behavioral Model. *Alcohol Research & Health, 23(2),* 151–160.

Lassiter, P.S., & Culbreth, J.R. (2018). *Theory and practice of addiction counseling*. Thousand Oaks, CA: Sage Publications.

Lewis, T.F. (2014). *Substance abuse and addiction treatment: Practical application of counseling theory*. Upper Saddle River, NJ: Pearson.

Marlatt, G.A., & Donovan, D.M. (2005). *Relapse prevention: Maintenance strategies in the treatment of addictive behaviors* (2nd edn). New York: Guilford Press.

Marlatt, G.A., & George, W.H. (1984). Relapse prevention: Introduction and overview of the model. *British Journal of Addiction, 79,* 261–273.

McLellan, T.A., Lewis, D.C., O'Brien, C.P., & Kleber, H.D. (2000). Drug dependence, a chronic medical illness: Implications for treatment, insurance, and outcomes evaluation. *Journal of the American Medical Association, 284,* 1689–1695

Moser, A.E., & Annis, H.M. (1996). The role of coping in relapse crisis outcome: A prospective study of treated alcoholics. *Addiction, 91(8),* 1101–1114.

Witkiewitz, K., & Marlatt, G.A. (2004). Relapse prevention for alcohol and drug problems: That was zen, this is tao. *American Psychologist, 59(4),* 224–235.

Witkiewitz, K., & Marlatt, G.A. (2005). Relapse prevention or alcohol and drug problems. In G.A. Marlatt & D.M. Donovan (Eds). *Relapse prevention: Maintenance strategies in the treatment of addictive behaviors* (2nd edn). New York: Guilford Press

Witkiewitz, K., & Marlatt, G.A. (Eds). (2007). *Therapist's guide to evidence-based relapse prevention*. Boston, MA: Elsevier.

12 The Diathesis–Stress Model

Margaret Smith

Introduction

For those of you who may have taken an Introductory Psychology course, one of the questions that has plagued psychologists and psychiatrists is whether mental health problems come about as the result of natural predispositions (or biological causes) *or* nurture (or environmental stressors). For decades, there have been long-held beliefs that mental illness results from either premorbid dispositions (nature) that clearly differentiate those who develop psychiatric illness from those who don't versus those who believe that stress is the major factor in determining whether someone will develop mental disorders (Monroe & Simons, 1991). The "nature–nurture" debate has stumped researchers, who tend to line up on one side of the debate or the other. The Nature vs Nurture question was first raised by Sir Francis Galton in 1874 when he was investigating the influences of genetics on various human traits or characteristics. Later, research which began in the 1960s (Meehl, 1962; Bleuler, 1963; Rosenthal, 1963) began to explore whether mental health disorders (more specifically schizophrenia and depression) might be the result of *both* nature and nurture (e.g. Mednick et al., 1998; Bebbington, 1987; Beck, 1987; Robins & Block, 1988). In other words, isn't it possible for individuals to be influenced by both natural causes like having a biological predisposition (such as genetic influences) for an alcohol use disorder *and* environmental factors such as living in a poor section of town where drugs are readily available or going off to a college that is known for being a "party school"? In these examples, it's entirely possible for someone to be influenced by both factors. Let's consider another scenario, whereby a person has genetic influences (e.g. their father, paternal grandfather and paternal great grandfathers all had alcohol use disorders; however, the son decides to join a monastery or a religious order where drinking is strictly forbidden. In this latter case, it's possible that, despite having genetic predispositions, for alcoholism, this individual might not ever experience drinking problems if they live in an environment that doesn't condone drinking.

Learning Opportunity 12.1

Discuss the following questions in small groups: What are some factors that may contribute to addiction based on the "nature" part of the nature vs nurture debate? What may contribute to addiction based on the "nurture" part of the debate?

Key Terms

diathesis: diathesis refers to a vulnerability which is a predispostional factor, or set of factors, that lead to a disordered/diseased state.

stress: life events (major or minor) that disrupt those mechanisms that maintain the stability of individuals' physiology, emotion, or cognition (Ingram & Luxton, 2005, p. 33). Another definition to include is stress refers to environmental events (e.g. death of a significant other, work or parental role stress, neighborhood disorganization) that impact the mental health and daily functioning of people) (Windle, 2010, p. 127).

risk and protective factors: those factors that increase the likelihood or mitigate the risk of development of a psychiatric or substance use problem(s).

Terminology

The diathesis in the diathesis-stress model involves a vulnerability which is a predispostional factor, or set of factors, that lead to a disordered/diseased state. While historically the term has referred to biological or genetic factors, the term now includes psychological factors (e.g. cognitive and interpersonal variables) (Ingram & Luxton, 2005, p. 34). A more comprehensive list includes genetic make-up, cognitions, personality, family history of psychological disorders, brain abnormalities (e.g. birth complications, learning difficulties, traumatic brain injury) or neurological problems (Goforth, Pham, & Carlson, 2011)

The "stress" in the diathesis-stress model refers to "undesirable" significant life events, the accumulation of minor events or hassles and/or socioeconomic factors (low socioeconomic status and so on) "that disrupt those mechanisms that maintain stability of the individual's physiology, emotion and cognition" (Ingram & Luxton, 2005, p. 33). Another definition includes stress as environmental events (e.g. death of a significant other, work or parental role stress, neighborhood disorganization) that impact the mental health and daily functioning of people (Windle, 2010, p. 127). Stressors can be both acute (car accident) or chronic (ongoing childhood sexual abuse); minor (daily hassles) or major (death of wife/husband/partner) events; and external (hurricane) or internal (appraisal of an event) (Monroe &

Simons, 1991). In Chapter 6 on sociocultural models, we also presented several examples of environmental stressors.

The interaction of the diathesis (vulnerability) and stress results in psychopathology such as mood disorders, anxiety disorders and substance use disorders. Additive models of diathesis-stress focus "the combined effects of the stress and the loading of the diathesis" in terms of the development of a disorder (Ingram & Luxton, 2005, p. 36). In some cases, a person may be less vulnerable but have more stressors, triggering a psychiatric or substance use disorder. In other cases, the person may be more vulnerable biologically and require less stressors to trigger the psychiatric or substance use disorder. In addition to biological and environmental influences there are also psychological factors that need to be taken into account. These include risk factors such as impulsivity, high sensation-seeking, low self-esteem and low frustration tolerance. These psychological risk factors were explored in Chapter 10. This brings us to an anonymous quote which helps to summarize the essence of the diathesis-stress model:

> If Biology loads the gun, Psychology points the gun, but Environment pulls the trigger.

Think about what this quote means. Biological factors, such as genetic vulnerability, may predispose one to substance use disorders; psychological factors also play a role in terms of influencing one towards curiosity about drug use or experimentation, perhaps even for self-medication purposes; however, environmental factors or stressors (e.g. peer influence or drug availability) may be the deciding factor in "pulling the trigger" towards eventual alcohol or drug use.

There are three sub-models with the diathesis-stress model which help to further explain the balance between biological predispositions and environmental stressors. The ipsative model of diathesis-stress hypothesizes that there can be an inverse relationship between factors, suggesting that the "degree of effect of diathesis or stress can be offset or compensated by the other in the summation of [what] is needed for psychopathology" (Ingram & Luxton, 2005, p. 37). Mega-stress models of diathesis-stress view psychopathology as the "combination of significant life stress *and* heightened vulnerability" (Ingram & Luxton, 2005, p. 37). Substantial levels of both vulnerability and stress are required for a disorder to develop.

Lastly, dynamic models of diathesis-stress view the relationship between diathesis and stress as changing over time. This changing dynamic is referred to as kindling. "Kindling suggests that repeated instances of a disorder cause neuronal changes that result in more sensitivity to stress. With heightened sensitivity, less stress becomes necessary to activate the requisite processes that lead to psychopathology" (Ingram & Luxton, 2005, p. 37). Consequently, with kindling there is more of a vulnerability that has developed over time that requires less stress to "activate" psychopathology.

Learning Opportunity 12.2

In small groups discuss the following questions: What do you think are some risk factors that would contribute to the problem of addiction among young people? What do you think are some protective factors that could contribute to the problem of addiction among young people?

Risk and Protective Factors

The diathesis-stress model also offers a framework for examining risk and protective factors related to substance use disorders. Let's just clarify the difference between risk and diathesis/vulnerability: "risk suggests only an increased probability of the occurrence of a disorder; it does not specify what causes the disorder" (Ingram & Luxton, 2005, p. 35). Risk acts in "concert with vulnerability" (Rutter as cited in Ingram & Luxton, 2005, p. 35). Vulnerability, on the other hand, refers to causal and predispositional factors that lead to a disordered/diseased state.

Risk factors for young people are those traits, qualities, experiences or contexts that may increase the likelihood that someone develops a substance use disorder. The National Institute of Drug Abuse (NIDA) (2018) lists the following risk factors for substance use disorders: aggressive behavior in childhood, lack of parental supervision, poor social skills, drug experimentation, availability of drugs at school, and community poverty.

Protective factors for young people are those traits, qualities, experiences or context that mitigate against one developing a substance use disorder. According to NIDA (2018), protective factors for substance use disorders (SUDs) include good self-control, parental monitoring and support, positive relationships, good grades, school anti-drug policies and neighborhood resources.

> A diathesis-stress model for AUD posits that individuals have a premorbid liability (diathesis) for AUD that is increased by risk factors.... and decreased by protective factors.... If the cumulative diathesis-stress level surpasses a certain threshold, the individual has an increased risk of developing AUD.
>
> (Schepis, Rao, Yadav, & Adinoff, 2011, p. 595)

Learning Opportunity 12.3

Make four columns. For the first column, write the heading diathesis. For the second column, write stress. For the third column, write risk factors and, finally, for the fourth column, write protective factors. Based on your reading, develop your own diathesis, stress, risk and protective factors chart by filling in items for each column. For example, what are some genetic/

biological cognitive vulnerabilities for the diathesis column? What are some stressors for the stress column? What are some risk and protective factors for those columns?

Application to Addiction Counseling

From our clinical experience, it's unusual for some people to enter treatment with awareness and insight into how his or her alcohol or drug use has impacted their lives and created unmanageability. More often, individuals perceive alcohol or substance use to be a solution to their problems, not the cause. This is one of the reasons why treatment programs begin with a biopsychosocial assessment in order to get a more complete picture of this person's life and how substance use may have impacted him or her. Essentially, the biopsychosocial assessment examines biological risk factors, psychological risk factors and social/environmental risk factors.

Many intake forms require information pertaining to vulnerabilities, risk and protective factors. For example, an intake form may ask about family history psychiatric and addiction issues (diathesis/liability). Many forms also ask about risk and protective factors, including but not limited to childhood experiences, parental relationships, social relationships, and educational experiences. Lastly, there may be questions pertaining to current stressors or events that led to counseling.

The diathesis–stress model is applicable to addiction counseling because it helps us understand the diathesis (liability/predisposition), risk and protective factors along with stressors that contribute to the problem of substance use (as well as other) disorders. Sharing this understanding with clients may help them frame their substance use disorder in a way that may reduce stigma and self-blame, recognizing that biology (e.g. genetics, physiological dispositions), psychology (e.g. cognitive processes) and environmental stressors (e.g. trauma, crises, daily stressors) play a role in their SUD(s).

Lastly, if young people are involved in prevention work, prevention specialists can assist them in reducing some of the risk factors that contribute to substance use disorders and increasing some of the protective factors. For example, a prevention specialist might work with parents on issues related to aggressive behavior in childhood, increasing parental monitoring and supervision. Further, they may develop school programs to focus on poor social skills and refusing drugs at school. Lastly, a prevention specialist might work on policies with the community regarding poverty and community resources.

Strengths and Limitations

The strength of the diathesis–stress model is that it involves a predisposition or vulnerability to substance use disorders that incorporates risk and protective factors along with the environmental stressors that may "pull the trigger", thus leading to a substance use disorder. The model offers a way of describing who will, and who will not, develop a disorder based on his/her diathesis/vulnerability and stress (Ingram & Luxton, 2005, p. 36). Also, having a biological predisposition does not necessarily doom one to developing a particular disorder. For example, a person may be biologically predisposed to heart disease such as high blood pressure or heart attacks, but does that mean this individual will die of a heart attack at a young age? As mentioned earlier, this may be where prevention comes into play. What if this biologically predisposed individual exercises, eats a low-fat diet, watches their weight, gets regular cardiac check-ups and tests, or perhaps even takes medication to prevent high blood pressure – these actions will certainly help to reduce this person's chances of having a stroke or heart attack. The same holds true with substance use disorders.

According to Tiegel (2017), one of the issues with the diathesis-stress model is how we operationally define the constructs of diathesis and stress. In reading research and related materials on the topic of diathesis/stress, one must pay attention how it is defined and applied. Additionally, the diathesis-stress model has been applied to schizophrenia and depression, with little literature and research related to substance use disorders.

Case Study

Andrea is a 17-year-old woman who is the only child of Barbara and Sam. Both parents have never experienced problems with alcohol or other drugs, but there is a grandparent with an untreated alcohol use disorder. Further, her aunt suffers from a major depressive disorder (MDD), but is currently taking medication that has reduced the MDD symptoms.

Andrea and her parents live in an upper-class neighborhood where there is an active youth center, a community pool and walking trails. While her parents are strict about who she "hangs out with" and what she is "up to," Andrea states that she has had happy life until recently, when a male classmate at her school started harassing her after she said no to his offering her some pot and wanting to "hook up." After her refusal, he has started referring to her as a "wimp" and a "slut," and sometimes comes up and pushes her from behind. He also encouraged his friends to taunt Andrea. Andrea also admits that her schoolwork has suffered and she is experiencing anxiety related to her grades. Lastly, she has learned that her parents have been experiencing problems and are thinking of a separation. Andrea has become very weepy and has problems sleeping and eating. She also reports feeling sad most of the time.

Andrea was invited over to a friend's house when the friend's parents were out shopping. The two tried some of the liquor in the liquor cabinet. Andrea felt such relief that it seemed to make her feel better. Now at night she sneaks downstairs and goes into her parent's liquor cabinet and drinks some of the alcohol. Her parents finally noticed that the liquor levels were lower and asked Andrea about this observation. She started crying and confessed to drinking but only because it really helped her feel better. She also admitted that she was being harassed by a fellow student. Because of the amount of alcohol missing from the liquor cabinet, the parents bring Andrea in for a "little" assessment.

Cases Conceptualization

What are some of the biological, psychological and social factors that one should consider when working with Andrea?

Using the diathesis-stress model, what may lead Andrea to be vulnerable to a substance use disorder? What are some of Andrea's protective factors? What are some of her risk factors? What are some stressor(s) that may contribute? In examining Andrea's story at this time, she may be vulnerable to a substance use disorder in terms of genetics (untreated alcohol use disorder and MDD in family); some of the protective factors could include her upper-class neighborhood and parental involvement. She would need to be evaluated for some risk factors, such as drug experimentation and drug availability at school. Additionally, the harassment (a stressor) from the male student, along with the related academic and familial stress, could have triggered the problem.

In terms of an assessment, Andrea's genetic predisposition/vulnerability to depression and addiction (e.g. extended family with mental health and substance use disorders) needs to be considered along with stressors (harassment from fellow student; academic and family problems). Further assessing for risk factors, such as drug experimentation and drug availability at school, is important. Lastly, a counselor should evaluate what protective factors are present to help mitigate the problems. That is, Andrea has a safe neighborhood in which she can be active, as well as involved parents who may help in supporting her and preventing further problems.

References

Bebbington, P. (1987). Misery and beyond: The pursuit of disease theories of depression. *International Journal of Social Psychiatry, 33,* 13–20.

Beck, A.T. (1987). Cognitive models of depression. *Journal of Cognitive Psychotherapy, 1,* 5–38.

Bleuler, M. (1963). Conception of schizophrenia within the last fifty years and today. *Proceedings of the Royal Society of Medicine, 56,* 945–952.

Goforth, A.N., Pham, A.V., & Carlson, J.S. (2011). Diathesis-stress model. In S. Goldstein & J.A. Naglieri (Eds). *Encyclopedia of child behavior and development.* Boston, MA: Springer.

Ingram, R.E., & Luxton, D.D. (2005). Vulnerability-stress models. In B.L. Hankin & J.R.Z. Abela (Eds). *Development of psychopathology: A vulnerability-stress perspective* (pp. 32–46). Thousand Oaks, CA: Sage Publications.

Mednick, S.A., Watson, J.B., Huttunen, M., Cannon, T.D., Katila, H., Machon, R., Mednick, B. et al. (1998). A two-hit working model of the etiology of schizophrenia. In M.F. Lenzenweger & R.H. Dworkin (Eds). *Origins and development of schizophrenia: Advances in experimental psychopathology* (pp. 557–589). Washington, DC: American Psychological Association.

Meehl, P.E. (1962). Schizotaxia, schizotypy, schizophrenia. *American Psychologist, 17,* 827–838.

Monroe, S.M., & Simons, A.D. (1991). Diathesis-stress theories in the context of life-stress research: Implications for the depressive disorders. *Psychological Bulletin, 110,* 406–425.

National Institute of Drug Abuse (2018). *Drugs, brains, and behavior: The science of addiction.* Washington, DC: US Department of Health and Human Services.

Robins, C.J., & Block, P. (1988). Personal vulnerability, life events, and depressive symptoms: A test of a specific interactional model. *Journal of Personality and Social Psychology, 54,* 847–852.

Schepis, T.S., Rao, H., Yadav, H., & Adinoff, B. (2011). The limbic–hypothalamic–pituitary–adrenal axis and the development of alcohol use disorders in youth. *Alcoholism: Clinical and Experimental Research, 35(4),* 595–605.

Tiegel, I.M. (2017). Diathesis-stress models for understanding physiological and psychological effects of stress. In S. Wadhwa (Ed.). *Stress in the modern world: Understanding science and society* (pp. 35–44). Santa Barbara, CA: Greenwood Press/ABC-CLIO.

Windle, M. (2010). A multilevel developmental contextual approach to substance use and addiction. *BioSocieties, 5,* 124–136.

Index

Printed in the United States
by Baker & Taylor Publisher Services